CW01425732

"Taking his stand ahead of two impossible alternatives—fossilized Traditionalism and deconstructive Modernism—Gerhard Cardinal Müller brings to the confusions of twenty-first-century Church life a penetrating vision of what it means to be a Catholic Christian, while displaying deep and broad learning, human sensitivity, and, above all, the charity too often lacking in intra-Catholic debates today."

GEORGE WEIGEL
Ethics and Public Policy Center

"Part exposition of the Catholic faith, part historical and theological analysis of the Church's mark of catholicity, and part diagnosis of the post-Enlightenment situation facing the Church, *True and False Reform* is a profound summation of Gerhard Müller's Catholic vision. Grounded in Scripture and apostolic Tradition, the book functions as a mini-summa, combining reflections on God, Christ, the Church, faith and salvation, sin and grace, the sacraments, the moral life, and so on with existential meditations on prayer, death, and the meaning of life. Why be a Catholic, and what does it mean to be Catholic? If you seek answers to such questions, this book is for you."

MATTHEW LEVERING
University of St. Mary of the Lake, Mundelein Seminary

"*True and False Reform* provides solid orientation for tempestuous times: of global political, social, and ecclesial upheaval, crisis, division, and confusion. In a disciplined and systematic manner, Cardinal Müller reminds us that we can only master these challenges by way of a confident and joyful recommitment to follow Our Lord. The cross is the unmistakable sign of Christian discipleship. Leading through lofty philosophical heights and profound theological thoughts, he shows us with a priestly heart how Our Lord renews his ever-self-same Church and how we may participate in this renewal. Most timely and needed!"

FR. EMERY DE GAÁL
University of St. Mary of the Lake, Mundelein Seminary

"Gerhard Cardinal Müller has given us a beautiful exposition and defense of the Church's teaching on what it means to be Catholic. The Catholic Church is a gift from God to mankind. Her teaching is no mere human attempt to communicate what Christ once taught. Catholic doctrine is Christ's saving revelation faithfully handed down to us by the Church under the guidance of the Holy Spirit. Christ teaches us through the doctrines proclaimed by the Church. Cardinal Müller sets forth various historical and current efforts to reshape and change that teaching, exposing them for what they are: attempts to usurp God's truth with human errors. The power of this divinely revealed truth resists all attempts to cast it aside. Cardinal Müller has done a great service to the Church in these times of doctrinal trouble and confusion."

Fr. Gerald E. Murray
Holy Family Church, New York

TRUE AND FALSE
REFORM

TRUE AND FALSE REFORM

What It Means to Be Catholic

GERHARD CARDINAL MÜLLER

Translated by Susan Johnson

EMMAUS
ACADEMIC

Steubenville, Ohio
www.emmausacademic.com

In grateful recognition of the Collegium Institute for Catholic Thought & Culture

EMMAUS
A C A D E M I C

Steubenville, Ohio
A Division of The St. Paul Center for Biblical Theology
Editor-in-Chief: Scott Hahn
1468 Parkview Circle
Steubenville, Ohio 43952

The original German edition *Was ist katholisch?* was published in 2021 by Verlag Herder.

The English edition was translated from the German by Susan Johnson.

© Gerhard Cardinal Müller
All rights reserved. Published 2023.
Printed in the United States of America.

Library of Congress Cataloging-in-Publication Data applied for.
ISBNs 978-1-64585-277-3 hardcover / 978-1-64585-278-0 paperback / 978-1-64585-279-7 ebook

All Bible quotations (except in quoting other sources) are from the New Revised Standard Version, Anglicized Catholic Edition (NRSVACE) © 1989, 1993, 1995 the Division of Christian Education of the National Council of the Churches of Christ in the United States of America. English Standard Version Anglicized (ESV) The Holy Bible © 2001 by Crossway Bibles, a division of Good News Publishers.

Cover design by Allison Merrick and Emma Nagle
Layout by Emma Nagle
Cover art: *Pentecost* by Juan Bautista Maíno, 17th century

Note from the Translator on "non-inclusive" language: The word "man" with masculine pronouns is used throughout for "Mensch" but is to be understood inclusively as male and female individuals or humanity as a whole. This is done solely in order to avoid clumsy formulations or plurals where the individual is meant. Most Vatican documents and translations of older works also contain this usage.

To my Catholic family
In eternal gratitude

TABLE OF CONTENTS

ὅπου ᾖ Χριστός Ἰησοῦς,
ἐκεῖ ἡ καθολικὴ ἐκκλησία

Wherever Jesus Christ is, there is the Catholic Church.
St. Ignatius of Antioch († ca. AD 110)
Epistula ad Smyrnaeos 8.2

Christianus mihi nomen est, catholicus vero cognomen.

Christian is my name, but Catholic my surname.
St. Pacian of Barcelona († AD 390)
Epistula 1.7

Catholicus non est, qui a Romana ecclesia
in fidei doctrina discordat.

He is not a Catholic who disagrees with the Roman Church
in doctrines concerning the faith.
Epigraph on the monument to Cardinal
Stanislaus Hosius († 1579) in S. Maria Trastevere

ACKNOWLEDGEMENTS

The English translation of the text was made possible by the sponsorship of the Collegium Institute for Catholic Thought and Culture. Collegium Institute is a Catholic intellectual apostolate in University City, Philadelphia, Pennsylvania. Its Catholic vision is twofold: (1) it promotes appreciation for the Catholic intellectual tradition and draws secular higher learning into conversation with it; (2) it cultivates reflection on the catholic, or universal, questions that animate every human life. For more information about its programs, projects, and publications on University City campuses and online, see collegiuminstitute.org.

The Neumann Forum also provided financial support for this project.

NOW IS THE TIME TO ASK THE MEANING OF "CATHOLIC"

Catholic Christians are making use of their freedom of conscience and religion, rooted as it is in the spiritual and moral nature of man, when they confess "Jesus Christ, the Son of God" (Mark 1:1); and "truly the Saviour of the world" (John 4:42).[1] The Fathers of the Second Vatican Council explained the self-understanding of the Catholic Church as follows:

> God Himself has made known to mankind the way in which men are to serve Him, and thus be saved in Christ and come to blessedness. We believe that this one true religion subsists in the Catholic and Apostolic Church, to which the Lord Jesus committed the duty of spreading it abroad among all men. Thus He spoke to the Apostles: "Go, therefore, and make disciples of all nations, baptizing them in the name of the Father and of the Son and of the Holy Spirit, teaching them to observe all things whatsoever I have enjoined upon you" (Matt 28:19–20). On their part, all men are bound to seek the truth, especially in what concerns God and His Church, and to embrace the truth they come to know, and to hold fast to it.[2]

---

[1]   Second Vatican Council, *Dignitatis Humanae* (1965), §2.
[2]   Vatican II, *Dignitatis Humanae*, §1.

The Church's profession of her builder and foundation is based on Jesus's promise to the first among the apostles and his successor, the Bishop of Rome:

> "[Y]ou are Peter, and on this rock I will build *my* church, and the gates of Hades will not prevail against it. I will give you the keys of the kingdom of heaven, and whatever you bind on earth will be bound in heaven, and whatever you loose on earth will be loosed in heaven." (Matt 16:18–19, emphasis added)

The Church as the sign and instrument of God's universal salvific will in Jesus Christ is both the subject and the object of the Catholic faith. Both the Apostles' Creed, upon which we build our lives at Baptism, and the Great Niceno-Constantinopolitan Symbol contain the statement "*Credo ecclesiam catholicam*" (I believe in the Catholic Church).

For this reason, the Catholic Church does not see herself in any way as being something political that is immanent in the world, or as a man-made organization for the amelioration of living conditions on earth, but rather as the "universal sacrament of salvation" instituted by God.[3] The Church that we profess in faith is a truth of the self-revelation of the Triune God in the history of salvation. Her inner being and essence can only be known in the light of supernatural faith. Her temporal impact on world history, nations, and cultures must be measured primarily against their mission to serve the eternal salvation of mankind and not vice versa.

To the basic existential questions "What is man? What is the meaning of pain, evil, and death?" the Catholic Church has but one answer, which is the same both for societies that believe in progress and for nations that are filled with doom and gloom: "Christ, who died and was raised up for all, can through His Spirit offer man the light and strength to measure up to his supreme destiny."[4]

But can this hope-filled faith in God, as the origin and goal of all creation, stand up to the brutal realities of a human history in which quite different powers call the tune? People prefer to bend their knees to false gods and worship them under a variety of names, such as fame and power, wealth and luxury, instead of saying what Jesus said when he was tempted: "Away with you, Satan! for it is written, 'Worship the Lord your God, and serve only him'" (Matt 4:10).

A genuine ranking is reflected more in the Church's calendar of saints than in the Forbes list of billionaires. But, as the saying goes, "Money makes the world go round." To this Sacred Scripture retorts, "The love of money is a

---

3   Second Vatican Council, *Lumen Gentium* (1964), §48.
4   Second Vatican Council, *Gaudium et Spes* (1965), §10.

root of all kinds of evil, and in their eagerness to be rich some have wandered away from the faith and pierced themselves with many pains" (1 Tim 6:10). But the pursuit of profit is merely the force propelling the "will to power," in which nihilism manifests its inescapable futility. The hour will come when God says to the rich man, vaunting his lack of worries after he has made a fabulous profit, "You fool! This very night your life is being demanded of you. And the things you have prepared, whose will they be?" (Luke 12:20). And Jesus concludes the parable with the statement: "So it is with those who store up treasures for themselves but are not rich towards God" (Luke 12:21).

To many people, it seems that the law which governs world history is the "struggle for existence," swinging endlessly back and forth between power and the spirit, a struggle in which, in the end, power seems to triumph over the spirit and death over life.

"Only now is the mountain in labor with humanity's future. God died: Now *we* want the overman [superman] to live."[5] Nietzsche's followers mindlessly parrot back their deranged prophet's jingle from the rooftops of posthumanism. If, as he thought, Christianity had tried in vain to master the "beast of prey," man,[6] how would it then be possible for such a monstrosity on his way "from worm to man" via the ape to finally make the leap to the "superman" who wants to be "the meaning of the earth"?[7]

Faced with this de-ranged (*ver-rückt*) image of man, which struggles between the images of animal and angel, the Christian prefers, after all, to remain grounded and enjoy his God-given unity of body and the freedom of his spirit. He stands with both feet on the ground of the earth that God assigned to him as his house with a beautiful garden (cf. Gen 2:8). When we walk upright, our head is always up so that we can perceive the world and, through thinking, understand it empirically and scientifically in its immanent causes, and metaphysically in its transcendent ontological and cognitive principles. With our ears we can *hear* the word of God, and with our eyes we can *see* God's saving deeds; and we have even "touched with our hands" the word of life (1 John 1:1). "[M]y eyes have seen your salvation, which you have prepared in the presence of all peoples, a light for revelation to the Gentiles and for glory

5   Friedrich Nietzsche, *Also sprach Zarathustra IV. Vom höheren Menschen: Sämtliche Werke 4* (München: 1980), 357; Eng.: "On the Higher Man," in part 4 of *Thus Spoke Zarathustra: A Book for All and None*, ed. Adrian del Caro and Robert B. Pippin, Cambridge Texts in the History of Philosophy (Cambridge, MA: Cambridge University Press, 2006), 232.

6   Friedrich Nietzsche, *Der Antichrist 22: Sämtliche Werke 6*, 189; Eng.: *The Antichrist*, trans. H. L. Mencken (New York: Alfred A. Knopf, 1918), 122, https://www.gutenberg.org/files/19322/19322-h/19322-h.htm#THE_ANTICHRIST.

7   Friedrich Nietzsche, *Also sprach Zarathustra I: Sämtliche Werke 4*, 14; Eng.: *Thus Spoke Zarathustra*, I, 14.

to your people Israel" (Luke 2:30–32). With these words, Simeon praised God at Jesus's Presentation in the temple, when he had taken the child in his arms and recognized in him the promised Messiah of Israel.

At creation, "the LORD God formed man from the dust of the ground, and breathed into his nostrils the breath of life; and the man became a living being" (Gen 2:7). In the beginning, there was not the hermaphrodite of an anarchically brutish, instinct-driven being that set out on idealistic flights of fancy but rather man "crowned . . . with glory and honour" (Ps 8:6). Subject to the social and historical conditions under which he lives in the world, man is master of himself in thought and action and, as a person, the bearer of his unity of spirit and body.

The law of the kingdom of God is the spirit of love, which is God himself and through which we worship him (1 John 4:8, 16). "God is spirit, and those who worship him must worship in spirit and truth" (John 4:24). But the Spirit is truth (cf. 1 John 4:6). Only those who know the truth will be made free by it (cf. John 8:32). Truth came into the world through Jesus Christ (cf. John 1:17). He redeems worldly power from its contradiction of human freedom and transforms it into a constructive potentiality by giving "to all who received him . . . power to become children of God, who were born, not of blood or of the will of the flesh or of the will of man, but of God" (John 1:12–13).

While the "law of the strongest" may apply in sub-spiritual nature to ensure survival at all costs, it is the infinitely lavish grace with which God breathes life into his creation (cf. Gen 1:2; 2:7) that unfolds the true dynamic of human history and awakens the sole hope that is never disappointed: "For God so loved the world that he gave his only Son, so that everyone who believes in him may not perish but may have eternal life" (John 3:16).

Christ's kingdom does not come from the power and possibilities of this world, and its nature is not that of state, military, economic, or ideological "power of people over people." It was not with even greater imperial power and brute force that Jesus outdid Pilate, who as a governor of the Roman Empire had brazenly challenged the kingdom of God; rather, it was by confidently revealing the liberating power of God over lies and death: "You say that I am a king. For this I was born, and for this I came into the world, to testify to the truth. Everyone who belongs to the truth listens to my voice" (John 18:37).

All who listen to his voice belong to the community of his disciples, the "church of the living God, the pillar and bulwark of the truth" (1 Tim 3:15; cf. Matt 16:18).

The members who are part of the one, holy, catholic and apostolic Church form a *communio* of faith in the Triune God. Continuing Christ's *missio*, they bear witness to the Gospel of the truth of God, "who desires everyone to be saved and to come to the knowledge of the truth" (1 Tim 2:4).

From the very beginning, the name of Jesus Christ faced everyone with the need to make a decision about the whole of their existence. "[F]or there is no other name under heaven given among mortals by which we must be saved" (Acts 4:12). The positive or negative reaction reflects on the messengers and witnesses of the Gospel.

It is not because Christians champion this or that political option or scientific position that they are viewed with suspicion, ridiculed, and subjected to bloody persecution. The reason they give offense is that Jesus is the cornerstone and rock on which the house of life is built, or which leads people to stumble and fall (1 Pet 2:7–8; cf. Acts 4:11). And this is why Jesus said to the disciples shortly before his Passion, "You will be hated by all *because of my name*" (Luke 21:17, emphasis added). And to this day, the Christians are the most oppressed and opposed religious community. As was already the case in the Great Fire of Rome (AD 64) at the time of the Emperor Nero, the Christians seem to have remained the object of mob hatred, or to stand convicted to this day "for their hate and enmity to human kind [odio humani generis convicti]."[8] Like the prophet of doom of postmodern nihilism, Friedrich Nietzsche condemned the Church as "the greatest of all imaginable corruptions" in human history: "I call Christianity the one great curse, the one great intrinsic depravity, the one great instinct of revenge, for which no means are venomous enough, or secret, subterranean and small enough—I call it the one immortal blemish upon the human race."[9] And he would feel himself to be corroborated by the leaders of the New World Order.

In the most populous country on earth, Christians are threatened with a ruthless Sinicization of their identity as disciples of Jesus.[10] Fanatical Hindus suspect them of betraying Indian culture. In most countries dominated by Islam, they are regarded—and treated—as second-class citizens. The power and money elites in Canada, the USA, Australia, and most countries of the European Union employ sophisticated methods to implement the agenda of a cultural de-Christianization. Catholics prepared to conform—right into the ranks of their pastors—to jump on the bandwagon of secularization in the vague hope that it would carry the Church into a new future. In Hans Urs von Balthasar's book *Cordula oder der Ernstfall* (The Moment of Christian Witness), the commissar of the Socialist International and One World

---

[8] Tacitus, *Annals* 15.44.

[9] Friedrich Nietzsche, *Der Antichrist*. Fluch auf das Christenthum 62: *Sämtliche Werke 6*, 253; Eng.: *The Antichrist*, 181, https://www.gutenberg.org/files/19322/19322-h/19322-h.htm#THE_ANTICHRIST.

[10] See Clive Hamilton and Mareike Ohlberg, *Hidden Hand: Exposing How the Chinese Communist Party Is Reshaping the World* (Melbourne: Oneworld, 2020).

ideologies is willing to engage in dialogue with those secularized Christians whose faith has been diluted into seeing the Church as just another organization for making the world happy. But in the end, he himself draws the conclusion about their adaptation to a world without God: "You've liquidated yourselves and spared us the trouble of persecuting you."[11]

What a brilliant mathematician and Christian thinker stated about the structural de-Christianization of Europe that began at the beginning of the seventeenth century is still relevant today:

> Men despise religion; they hate it, and fear it is true. To remedy this, we must begin by showing that religion is not contrary to reason; that it is venerable, to inspire respect for it; then we must make it lovable, to make good men hope it is true; finally, we must prove it is true. Venerable, because it has perfect knowledge of man; lovable, because it promises the true good.[12]

What Blaise Pascal (1623–1662) meant here by religion is the Catholic faith. Then as now, the message of the faith is controversial. Some reject any truth based on God's revelation in Jesus Christ, because they consider specifically the Catholic faith to be an assault on tolerance.

Thomas Hobbes (1588–1679), one of the leading English empiricists, grounded religion not in God's revelation or in the spiritual and moral nature of man but instead in the laws of the state, concluding that the state therefore had the right to prohibit the teachings of individual religious communities that were incompatible with the common good of the citizens.[13] A pluralistic society, so the contemporary totalitarian and uniform thinking of political correctness concludes, must perceive a truth with universal validity to be intolerable, and definitively reject it as intellectually dishonest and no longer possible to get across to people. Deviant thinking is punished with social ostracism and even with the means of criminal justice.[14]

---

[11] Hans Urs von Balthasar, *Cordula oder der Ernstfall* (Einsiedeln, 1966), 112; Eng.: *The Moment of Christian Witness* (San Francisco: Ignatius Press, 1994).

[12] Blaise Pascal, *Pensées*, frag. 187: Oeuvres complètes, ed. J. Chevalier (Paris, 1954), 1089–1990; Eng.: *Pascal's Pensées*, intro. T. S. Eliot (New York: Dutton, 1958), online at https://www.gutenberg.org/files/18269/18269-h/18269-h.htm#SECTION_II.

[13] Thomas Hobbes, *Elementa Philosophica de Cive*, 6, 11 (London: 1647). Republished in *Philosophische Bibliothek* 158 (Hamburg: Gmeiner, 1977), 136; Eng.: http://www.public-library.uk/ebooks/27/57.pdf.

[14] Cf. Alfredo Mantovano, ed., *Omofobi per Legge? Colpevoli per non aver commesso il fatto* (Siena, 2020).

John Locke (1632–1704), the groundbreaking theorist of English liberalism, in his *A Letter concerning Toleration* (1685–1686), specifically excluded Catholics from general religious toleration. Totally at variance with the Catholic self-understanding, he reinterpreted religious obedience to the pope, constraining it into conflict of allegiance between one's own head of state and a foreign "prince."[15] Even today, the Communist Party leadership in the "Middle Kingdom" sees the relationship of Chinese Catholics to the pope as a relationship to a foreign "head of state." Unfortunately, Vatican diplomacy has not succeeded in explaining to them the fundamental difference between politics and religion, power and truth.

Jean-Jacques Rousseau (1712–1778), an important trailblazer for the French Revolution, failed to notice that, in rightly rejecting all coercion *in belief*, he was handing over freedom *to believe* to, of all things, a totalitarian state with his words, "But whoever dares to say: *Outside the Church is no salvation*, ought to be driven from the State, unless the State is the Church, and the prince the pontiff."[16]

The same author, in the *Contrat social* (1762), rejected the religious dogmas of the Church as the height of intolerance, but at the same time demanded the death penalty for rejecting the civil profession of faith. For anyone who does not believe the dogmas of social conscience as the supreme sovereign "has committed the worst of all crimes, that of lying before the law."[17] This was then used by the Jacobins to justify the Reign of Terror (1792–1794), to which at least 200,000 people fell victim, and also their right to force people to think along their lines or have their heads cut off. Fascists[18] and Stalinists venerated them by outdoing them in their hostility to the Church and their crimes against humanity.[19]

---

[15] John Locke, *Ein Brief über Toleranz* (= PhB 289) (Hamburg, 1975), 92–93; Eng.: *A Letter concerning Toleration and Other Writings*, ed. Mark Goldie (Indianapolis: Liberty Fund, 2010), online at http://files.libertyfund.org/files/2375/Locke_1560_EBk_v6.0.pdf.

[16] Jean-Jacques Rousseau, *Contrat social*, 4, 8; Eng.: *The Social Contract and Discourses* (London: J. M. Dent, 1920), https://www.gutenberg.org/files/46333/46333-h/46333-h.htm.

[17] Rousseau, *Contrat social*, 1, 8.

[18] Markus von Hänsel-Hohenhausen, *Hitler und die Aufklärung: Der philosophische Ort des Dritte Reiches. Beitrag zur Theorie der modernen Despotien und zum Mythos der politischen Religion* (Frankfurt a. M., 2013).

[19] Arthur Koestler, *Sonnenfinsternis. Roman* (1940) (Vienna, 1983); Eng.: *Darkness at Noon*, first published in 1940; Jörg Baberowski, *Verbrannte Erde: Stalins Herrschaft der Gewalt* (Munich: Verlag C.H.Beck, 2012).

When, therefore, in the first phase of the detachment of the West[20] from its Christian Tradition,[21] the new infidels blustered about Christianity, Pascal sighed, "Let them at least learn what is the religion they attack, before attacking it."[22]

And he was right. For since then, too, the criticism of religion has reveled more in refuting self-fabricated caricatures than in penetrating to the very heart of Christianity: love of God above all else (Deut 6:5) and love of neighbor in the same measure as of love of oneself (Matt 22:34–40) as the image and likeness of God (Gen 1:27).

In the Catholic Tübingen School[23] and among important thinkers of the twentieth century, theology has provided intellectually viable answers to the challenge of Enlightenment philosophy and the criticism of Christianity.[24] The contributions of Catholic social teaching to solving problems that arose with the Industrial Revolution are just as remarkable as the reflections on the ethical management of the opportunities and risks of modern medicine, economics, and ecology.[25] Not to be forgotten is the commitment, even to the point of martyrdom, of priests, religious, and lay people for the freedom of the Church, human rights, social justice, constitutional democracy, and peace in the world.[26]

It remains a permanent task of modern Christianity to maintain the balance between the identity of the faith and its relevance for modern humanity, between the necessary fidelity to Tradition and essential innovation, between the "worldliness and Christianness of the Church."[27] For orientation towards God and responsibility for the world form an indissoluble relational unity in the religion of Christ, the God-man. This then raises the question, "What is Catholic?" beyond the ideological extremes, which occur in a number of

---

[20] Peter Brown, *The Rise of Western Christendom: Triumph and Diversity, AD 200–1000*, 10th anniversary rev. ed. (Oxford: John Wiley, 2013).

[21] Karl Löwith, *Von Hegel zu Nietzsche. Der revolutionäre Bruch im Denken des 19. Jahrhunderts*: Löwith, *Sämtliche Schriften* (Stuttgart, 1988), 1–490.

[22] Pascal, *Pensées*, frag. 194: " Qu'ils apprennent au moins quelle est la religion qu'ils combattent avant que de la combattre."

[23] Joseph Rupert Geiselmann, *Die katholische Tübinger Schule. Ihre theologische Eigenart* (Freiburg, 1964).

[24] Heinrich Fries and Georg Kretschmar, *Klassiker der Theologie II* (Munich, 1983).

[25] See Pope Francis, *Laudato Si'* (2015).

[26] Gustavo Gutièrrez and Gerhard L. Müller, *An der Seite der Armen. Theologie der Befreiung* (Augsburg, 2004); Eng.: *On the Side of the Poor: The Theology of Liberation* (New York: Orbis, 2015).

[27] Dietrich Bonhoeffer, lecture: „*Das Wesen der Kirche*" (1932); Eng.: "The Nature of the Church," *Dietrich Bonhoeffer Works* II (Munich, 1994), 239–303, at 298–301.

variations. On the one hand, there is "Traditionalism," which clings to forms shaped by a certain time, and on the other hand, "Modernism," which dissolves the substance. On a higher level of reflection, this can also be formulated using the classical pair of opposites: classical fideism stands against rationalism. Both positions were rejected by the First Vatican Council (1870) as incompatible with the Catholic faith, because nature is dynamically ordered towards grace and does not work against it dialectically.[28] So while faith cannot be derived from human reason, where it is freely accepted in the light of God's Word and grace, its "divine logic"[29] is evident to the believer's reason and gives it joy at knowing the truth.[30] This is why Paul, despite all his sufferings and trials as an apostle, could say, "I *know* the one in whom I have put my trust" (2 Tim 1:12, emphasis added). Christian worship in accordance with the Logos is "reasonable worship [*rationabile obsequium*]" (Rom 12:1).

At the turn of the twentieth century, the distinguished Würzburg theologian Hermann Schell (1850–1905) already published reform monographs bearing the significant titles *Der Katholicismus als Princip des Fortschritts* (Catholicism as a Principle of Progress [1897]) and *Die neue Zeit und der alte Glaube* (The New Times and the Old Faith [1898]).[31]

One can also mention the Church historian Albert Ehrhard (1862–1940), who as a "reform-minded" Catholic, not a "modernist," wrote a book entitled *Der Katholizismus und das zwanzigste Jahrhundert im Lichte der kirchlichen Entwicklung der Neuzeit* (Catholicism and the Twentieth Century in the Light of Ecclesiastical Development in the Modern Age).[32]

Karl Adam (1876–1966) also attempted to present a positive overview in his book *Das Wesen des Katholizismus* (The Spirit of Catholicism [1924]).[33]

---

28 Cf. on this Eberhard Mechels, *Analogie bei Erich Przywara und Karl Barth. Das Verhältnis von Offenbarungstheologie und Metaphysik*, Neukirchen-Vluyn 1974; Jan Bentz, *Das Sein und die Geschichte des Seins bei Gustav Siewert* (Aachen, 2019).

29 Henri Bouillard, *Logik des Glaubens* (= QD 29) (Freiburg, 1966).

30 First Vatican Council, *Dei Filius* (1870) [DH 3000–3045].

31 Paul-Werner Scheele, *Hermann Schell im Dialog. Beiträge zum Werk und zur Wirkung von Hermann Schell* (Würzburg, 2006).

32 Albert Ehrhard, *Der Katholizismus und das zwanzigste Jahrhundert im Lichte der kirchlichen Entwicklung der Neuzeit* (Stuttgart, 1902); Ehrhard, *Liberaler Katholizismus? Ein Wort an meine Kritiker* (Stuttgart, 1902).

33 Karl Adam, *Das Wesen des Katholizismus*, Düsseldorf, 1957; Eng.: *The Spirit of Catholicism* (New York: Sheed and Ward, 1929).

From Cardinal Henri de Lubac (1896–1991) comes the patristic-infused work *Catholicisme: Les aspects sociaux du dogme*,[34] which, along with his other writings on the Eucharist and the Church, had a strong influence on Vatican II.

In the period of post-conciliar new departures and discontinuities, the brilliant Hans Urs von Balthasar (1905–1988) published the clear-sighted booklet *Katholisch: Aspekte des Mysteriums* (Catholic: Aspects of the Mystery),[35] in which he elaborated on the profile of the Catholic faith, its styles of thought, and its attitudes to life: the *incarnatus est* and the sacramentality and apostolicity of the Church as a communion of saints. With his famous *Einführung in das Christentum* (Introduction to Christianity [1968]), Joseph Ratzinger, later Pope Benedict XVI (r. 2005–2013), provided a groundbreaking orientation for what is meant by "Catholic" in the modern world and in the wake of the 1968 cultural revolution.[36]

Of particular note is the presentation of the entire "world of the Catholic Faith"[37] that we owe to Cardinal Leo Scheffczyk (1920–2005).

The causes and consequences of an inner dissolution of catholicity and the chances of overcoming the crisis from the depths of the Catholic faith are analyzed by the Bonn dogmatist Karl-Heinz Menke in his fundamental work—*Sakramentalität: Wesen und Wunde des Katholizismus* (Sacramentality: The Essence and Wound of Catholicism).[38]

In view of the need to maintain and constantly readjust the balance of substance and relevance of the Catholic, the following reflections are not intended as a catechism[39] or a textbook of Catholic dogmatics[40] but rather as a navigation aid amid all the confusions and crises, tensions and divisions, disappointments, and hopes in the Church of today and tomorrow. What it

---

34 Henri de Lubac, *Glauben aus der Liebe. „Catholicisme"* (Einsiedeln, 1970); Eng.: *Catholicism: Christ and the Common Destiny of Man* (San Francisco: Ignatius Press, 1988); orig. transl. 1950.

35 (Einsiedeln, 1975).

36 Joseph Ratzinger, *Einführung in das Christentum*, Joseph Ratzinger Gesammelte Schriften 4, ed. Gerhard Ludwig Müller (Freiburg, 2014), 31–342.

37 Leo Scheffczyk, *Katholische Glaubenswelt. Wahrheit und Gestalt* (Paderborn, 2008); Karl-Heinz Menke, *Sakramentalität. Wesen und Wunde des Katholizismus* (Regensburg, 2012); Max Seckler, *Die schiefen Wände des Lehrhauses. Katholizität als Herausforderung* (Freiburg, 1988).

38 (Regensburg, 2012).

39 *Catechismo della Chiesa Cattolica. Testo integrale*, Milan, 2017; VELKD, Evangelischer Erwachsenenkatechismus (Gütersloh, 2001).

40 Gerhard Kardinal Müller, *Katholische Dogmatik: Für Studium und Praxis der Theologie* (Freiburg, 2016); Eng.: *Catholic Dogmatics for the Study and Practice of Theology* (New York: Herder and Herder, 2017); Mauro Gagliardi, *La Verità è sintetica. Teologia dogmatica cattolica* (Siena, 2017).

means to be Catholic is not only something contained in doctrine but also a state of mind and a way of life.

The question "What is Catholic?" will be addressed in five topic areas:

I.   Being Catholic in the contemporary spiritual situation.
II. Catholic life with God in his Church.
III. The origin and profile of the concept of "catholic."
IV. "Catholic": the attribute of the one Church of Christ that links all Christian communions.
V.   Quo vadis, ecclesia catholica?

It is not inconstant human beings who reform the Church with their visions and utopias, resolutions, and decisions, or who enable the Church to connect—to whatever train and in whatever direction—by filling key positions and with their group-dynamic power games. Christ alone is the future of every human being and the goal of our pilgrimage to the "new Jerusalem." The holy city comes down out of heaven from God, and human beings will never create "a new heaven and a new earth" (Rev 21:1–2).

Citing St. Augustine, Vatican II described the journey of the pilgrim Church in world history to its consummation beyond time as follows:

> The Church, "like a stranger in a foreign land, presses forward amid the persecutions of the world and the consolations of God," announcing the Cross and death of the Lord until he comes (cf. 1 Cor 11:26). By the power of the Risen Lord she is given strength that she might, in patience and in love, overcome her sorrows and her challenges, both within herself and from without, and that she might reveal to the world, faithfully though darkly, the mystery of its Lord until, in the end, it will be manifested in full light.[41]

---

[41] Vatican II, *Lumen Gentium*, §8 (DS 4121), quoting Augustine, *De civitate Dei* 18.51.2 (PL 41:614).

Chapter 1

BEING CATHOLIC IN THE CONTEMPORARY SPIRITUAL SITUATION

Pandemic crises of meaning and the saving serum

Among the almost eight billion inhabitants of the earth in 2021, 18 percent belong to the Catholic faith. Spiritually related to Catholics are the Christians of other churches and ecclesial communities in their belief in Jesus Christ, the Son of God and Savior of the world.[1] This community, with its worldwide presence and global activity, is made up of—according to the *2018 Papal Yearbook*[2]—1.3 billion people who recognize in the Bishop of Rome and successor to the apostle Peter the highest representative of its unity,[3] and which calls itself *the Catholic Church*.

It is a community which worships "the Father in spirit and truth" (John 4:23) and through which the gracious and merciful God prepares in time and history the coming of his eternal kingdom.

A uniquely close relationship exists between Christians and Jews, because they are inwardly connected in their faith in the same one true God who chose Israel as his people and made a covenant with them. Jews and Christians are one in their belief in the transcendent God who has power over history and helps the oppressed and the poor to their rights. They share a belief in the messianic-eschatological promise of a perfection of the world in God's future, which rules out any cyclical-mythical and materialistic-nihilistic view of history,

---

[1]   Second Vatican Council, *Unitatis Redintegratio* (1964), §§13–24.

[2]   Secreteria Status, *Annuarium Statisticum Ecclesiae* (Città del Vaticano, 2018).

[3]   See Second Vatican Council, *Lumen Gentium* (1964), §§18, 23.

or any utilitarian ethics of "the greatest happiness of the greatest number." For God is the origin and goal of creation and of every individual human being in and after history—and not of something abstract called "humanity."[4] The Church has included the entire Psalter and other Old Testament hymns in her treasury of prayers, and she prays with confidence to God the Father through his Son and our brother Jesus Christ in the Holy Spirit, through whom "God's love has been poured into our hearts" (Rom 5:5).[5]

In prayer and liturgy, it becomes evident that faith is not a theory about God, but that, when people pray, they can pour out to God—even shout out—their whole existence with all its ups and downs, joys and sufferings; they do this with thanks, praise, requests, complaints, and rejoicing, ultimately certain that their Creator and Redeemer hears them and listens to them. On the Cross, Jesus cried out to his Father with a loud voice, "My God, my God, why have you forsaken me?" (Mark 15:34; Ps 22:2). He expressed his abandonment in the words of the Psalm, whose prayer continues, "For he did not despise or abhor the affliction of the afflicted.... For dominion belongs to the Lord, and he rules over the nations.... [F]uture generations will be told about the Lord, and proclaim his deliverance to a people yet unborn" (Ps 22:24, 28, 30–31).

Catholic Christians feel a deep bond with everyone in this world who believes in the one personal God (Rom 1:20),[6] or who has a mystical reverence for life, or who at least seeks the truth and feels a responsibility that goes beyond his or her own interests (Acts 14:15; 17:23).[7] It is possible and necessary, despite all their differences in matters of faith, for all people to work together for the common good in the individual states and in world society—in the "search for a better world" beyond war and hatred and without the misery of poverty and all the glaring injustices.[8]

With regard to non-believers, the Catholic takes the view that an atheism pursued without contradictions is impossible,[9] because

---

[4]   Second Vatican Council, *Nostra Aetate* (1965), §4.

[5]   Georg Langgärtner, *Jesus Christus ist der Herr: Gebete, Hymnen, Meditationen aus Liturgien des Ostens und des Westens* (Munich, 1978).

[6]   See the joint declaration of Pope Francis and the Grand Imam of Al-Azhar, Ahmed el-Tayeb, "A Document on Human Fraternity for World Peace and Living Together" (2019); cf. Gerhard Cardinal Müller, *Das Abu Dhabi Dokument: Eine katholische Lesehilfe: Communio* 49 (2020): 293–311.

[7]   Vatican II, *Nostra Aetate*, §3.

[8]   Second Vatican Council, *Gaudium et Spes*, §§21, 36, 43.

[9]   Joseph Ratzinger and Paolo Flores d'Arcais, *Gibt es Gott? Wahrheit, Glaube, Atheismus* (Berlin, 2006).

every man remains to himself an unsolved puzzle, however obscurely he may perceive it. For on certain occasions no one can entirely escape the kind of self-questioning mentioned earlier, especially when life's major events take place. To this questioning, only God fully and most certainly provides an answer as he summons man to higher knowledge and humbler probing.[10]

However, Catholics are not prepared to compromise on the denial and disregard of the dignity of the human person in his or her inalienable rights: prenatal infanticide; euthanasia of the sick, the elderly, and those who are tired of life; racism; enslavement and human trafficking; inhumane penal systems; individual and state crimes against humanity; warmongering and genocide. So they also oppose any restriction of freedom of conscience and religion in totalitarian ideologies, in surveillance states gagged by single-party rule, and in the face of propaganda hostile to families and children.

For instead of confining themselves to ensuring the infrastructure of social life (i.e., "temporal welfare"), the ideological representatives of the totalitarian state define man as a robot or as a biological bundle of instincts and treat the "masses of the common people" as human material. However, each individual human being is always an end and meaning in himself. Never and under no circumstances may anyone be degraded to a resource for scientific or economic ends and deprived of the dignity of personhood. This is why the Catholic faith is completely incompatible with any totalitarian ideology.

Despite the ecumenical, inter-religious, and interdisciplinary academic dialogue and the culture of reconciliation and tolerance associated with it, anti-Catholicism has continued: beginning among the anti-religious circles of the eighteenth-century Enlightenment, it survived in the culture wars of the nineteenth century and in the totalitarian political systems of the twentieth century.[11] Today, in neo-atheism, with its "hatred of all things Catholic," it has returned with a vengeance in the international abortion and gender lobbies, in agenda journalism, and in anti-Catholic "Christian sects" that remain stuck in sixteenth-century hate speech, making a mockery of Jesus's prayer for the unity of his disciples (John 17:21).

The late anti-theist Christopher Hitchens (1949–2011)—may his soul nonetheless be commended to God—aggressively entitled one of his books *God Is Not Great,*[12] while his kindred spirit Richard Dawkins (1941–), in his

[10] Vatican II, *Gaudium et Spes,* §21.

[11] Vatican II, *Gaudium et Spes,* §21.

[12] Originally published in 2007 in the United Kingdom as *God Is Not Great: The Case against Religion,* and in the United States instead with the bitter subtitle *How Religion Poisons*

book *The God Delusion*,[13] tries to attribute faith to a genetic defect or a brain malfunction. Based on an ideologically truncated Darwinism, he offers an inner-worldly doctrine of salvation entitled *Outgrowing God: A Beginner's Guide*.[14] He is seconded by the French private philosopher Michel Onfray with his titles *Traité d'athéologie: Physique de la métaphysique*,[15] translated into English more explicitly as *Atheist Manifesto: The Case against Christianity, Judaism, and Islam*; and *La puissance d'exister: Manifeste hédoniste* (A Hedonist Manifesto: The Power to Exist).[16] In both cases, the German translation of the title is even more provocative: *Wir brauchen keinen Gott: Warum man jetzt Atheist sein muss* (We Don't Need a God: Why We Have to Be Atheists Today) and *Die Freude am Sein: Wie man ohne Gott glücklich wird* (The Joy of Being: How to Be Happy without God).

It was the perennial issue of the "end of Christianity" that led Friedrich Nietzsche (1844–1900) to the concept of the "death of God," whom he sent packing in his work *The Anti-Christ*.[17] Quivering with fury, he demands the transvaluation of all Christian values into their opposite. He issues a "Law against Christianity" which contains, among other things, the provision: "The 'holy' history should be called by the name it deserves, the *accursed* history; the words 'God,' 'savior,' 'redeemer,' 'saint,' should be used as terms of abuse, to signify criminals."[18] And he signs it: "The Anti-Christ."

What is shocking from a Christian point of view is not just such blindness to the symbolic and transcendental dimension of existence but even more so the intellectual nosedive which gave wings to an anticlericalism that was prepared to resort to literary and political violence until it finally mistook its crash landing for a "earthing" of man without God in the groundless (*das Bodenlose*):

> That the eighteenth century witnessed the birth of a race of men, thereafter perpetuated, whose sole spiritual nourishment was

---

Everything; it was republished in 2017 with no subtitle.

[13] Richard Dawkins, *The God Delusion* (London: Black Swan, 2006).

[14] Richard Dawkins, *Outgrowing God: A Beginner's Guide* (London: Penguin Audio, 2019).

[15] Michel Onfray, *Traité d'athéologie: Physique de la métaphysique* (Paris, 2005); *Atheist Manifesto: The Case against Christianity, Judaism, and Islam* (New York: Arcade, 2007).

[16] Michel Onfray, *La puissance d'exister: Manifeste hédoniste* (Paris, 2006); Eng.: *A Hedonist Manifesto: The Power to Exist* (New York: Columbia University Press, 2015).

[17] Nietzsche, *Der Antichrist: Fluch auf das Christenthum*, Kritische Studienausgabe 6 (Munich, 1980), 167–253; Eng.: *The Anti-Christ*, in: *The Anti-Christ, Ecce Homo, Twilight of the Idols, and Other Writings*, ed. Aaron Ridley and Judith Norman, trans. Judith Norman (New York: Cambridge University Press, 2005), http://krishnamurti.abundanthope.org/index_htm_files/The-Anti-Christ-Ecce-Homo-Twilight-Of-The-Idols-And-Other-Writings-by-Nietzsche.pdf.

[18] Nietzsche, *The Anti-Christ*, 254.

anti-clericalism, who made anti-clericalism the sole item on their program, and who deemed that that would suffice to remodel governments, to perfect societies, and lead the way to happiness—for this, many men are responsible—and not all of them belong to the Encyclopaedist camp—but none of them to the same degree as Voltaire.[19]

As if anticipating the Western world of today, the Marquis René Louis d'Argenson (1694–1757), a great friend of Voltaire's, as early as 1753 offered a perceptive description of the effect of anti-clerical propaganda:

> The hatred of priests has risen high. The clergy are hardly allowed to show themselves in the streets if they do not want to be hissed at. Since our nation is far more enlightened in our century than it was in Luther's time, it will also go further and shake off all priests, revelations, and mysteries. . . . One no longer dares to stand up for the clergy in good company; anyone who nevertheless does so is ridiculed and taken for a friend of the Inquisition. . . . The Jesuit College is emptying. . . . At the masked balls in Paris, there are more costumes of bishops, abbés, monks, and nuns appearing than ever.[20]

Friedrich Nietzsche wanted to mark the hundredth anniversary of Voltaire's death on May 30, 1878, with a monument to the "greatest liberator of the spirit"[21] and an even more radical critique of Christianity. The only mystery that remains unsolved is why the "free thinkers" inspired by their two idols, both now dead as dodos, should reject any historical-critical querying of the consistency of their criticism of the Bible and the Church as some sort of blasphemy. What Christian who has existentially embraced the Gospel of Christ, be he a scholar or the simple pilgrim on the road of life, could recognize in the distorted image fabricated by Voltaire and Nietzsche the faith on which he builds his life? Only those who regard hatred as the superior cognitive faculty to love believe (!) this. Love may cause temporary blindness, but hate makes the heart forever foolish.

---

[19] Paul Hazard, *La Pensée Européenne au XVIIIe siècle de Montesquieu à Lessing,* 1946; Eng.: *European Thought in the Eighteenth Century: From Montesquieu to Lessing* (New Haven, CT: Yale University Press, 1954), 415.

[20] Translated from the German text quoted from Georg Siegmund, *Der Kampf um Gott. Zugleich eine Geschichte des Atheismus* (Buxheim, 1976), 172.

[21] Friedrich Nietzsche, *Menschliches, Allzumenschliches. Ein Buch für freie Geister* (1878): *Sämtliche Werke 2* (Munich, 1980), 10.

A differentiated historical view will appreciate the merits of Voltaire's fight against superstition and religious fanaticism,[22] and against the brutal methods of the administration of justice in his day, which he opposed in his *Traité sur la Tolérance* (Treatise on Tolerance) (1763), written on the occasion of the affair of Jean Calas (1698–1762), who was innocently convicted and horribly tortured to death. But this is not a feature of the "Enlightenment" alone. Opposition to witch-hunts and inhuman torture as a method of interrogation and execution,[23] or to fanatical anti-Judaism, had already been expressed on Christian and humanitarian grounds by the Jesuits Adam Tanner (1572–1632), Friedrich Spee von Langenfeld (1591–1635), and also Richard Simon (1638–1712), the first proponent of the historical-critical interpretation of the Bible.[24] The absolutism of Kings Louis XIV and Louis XV in France, which was the politically and culturally dominant nation at the time, and the politics of the *parlements* (courts), which were friendly towards the Jansenists, were rarely of any benefit to the popes and the Church and were mostly a source of very serious harm (Gallicanism as a state doctrine in 1682; the ban on the Jesuits in France in 1764; the Jansenist controversy).[25]

The Church is not committed to any specific model of the state or form of government, which, being present over the centuries and in the many different forms of society, is something she is anyway unable to choose for herself. However, where it is possible, she must in principle advocate a state based on human rights and support what is under the concrete circumstances the relatively best form of government.[26]

However, the dignity and freedom that are not dependent on the arbitrariness of the rulers is the experience that has distinguished Christians both philosophically and in the history of religion ever since the liberation of Israel from slavery under Pharaoh, and the saving of the righteous from all tribulation with the coming into the world of the kingdom of God in Jesus Christ. Jesus reveals himself through the miracles of the kingdom of God that has come near as the redeeming grace which heals body and soul and reconciles estranged humanity with God. This is why salvation already takes place in this life and

---

[22]   Ronald A. Knox, *Enthusiasm: A Chapter in the History of Religion with Special Reference to the Seventeenth and Eighteenth Centuries* (Oxford: Oxford University Press, 1950).

[23]   Georg Schwaiger, ed., *Teufelsglaube und Hexenprozesse* (Munich, 1987).

[24]   Sascha Müller, *Richard Simon (1638–1712). Exeget, Theologe, Philosoph und Historiker. Eine Biographie* (Würzburg, 2005), 31–32 (in Simon's *Defense of the Jews of Metz*).

[25]   Ludwig von Pastor, *Geschichte der Päpste im Zeitalter des fürstlichen Absolutismus*; von Pastor, *Geschichte der Päpste seit dem Ausgang des Mittelalters XIV-XVI* (Freiburg, 1961 [in many editions]).

[26]   Vatican II, *Gaudium et Spes*, §§69, 75; *Dignitatis Humanae* (1964), §§3, 6.

not spiritually in a Platonic heaven of ideas and only later in a religiously imagined afterlife. Anyone who takes God's Incarnation seriously cannot confuse Christianity with a religion of the hereafter. Those who have died in Christ are also united with us in the new life that will be revealed in all its fullness at the end. They are not dozing in a semi-conscious state in the shadowy realm of Hades, and in no way rely on vegetating in the forgetful memory of their descendants. "And as for the resurrection of the dead, have you not read what was said to you by God, 'I am the God of Abraham, the God of Isaac, and the God of Jacob'? He is God not of the dead, but of the living" (Matt 22:31–32).

Everything is crammed into the short span of life from birth to death. The psalmist states quite realistically: "The days of our life are seventy years, or perhaps eighty, if we are strong; even then their span is only toil and trouble; they are soon gone, and we fly away" (Ps 90:10). For the sake of human dignity, it must remain on the agenda of current spiritual life to have "faith in God in the Secular Age."[27]

In view of the ideological splitting up of many formerly Christian societies since the French Revolution into Girondists and Jacobins, "rightists" and "leftists," "conservatives" and "liberals"—whether in a moderate or a radical form—it is the task of the Catholic Church to bring people together on the basis of recognizing human dignity and the natural moral law as the foundation of all humanity. For apart from working for the "closely knit union" of human beings with God, the Church of Christ is also a "sign and instrument . . . of the unity of the whole human race"—a *sacramentum mundi.*[28]

The Church is in Christ "the universal sacrament of salvation."[29] She strives after the one goal: the coming of the kingdom of God and to bring about the salvation of all humanity.[30] It is not humanism without God that creates the future but only the new humanism through "the goodness and loving-kindness of God our Saviour" (Tit 3:4) that offers the saving vaccine from the pandemic chaos of alienation from God and man's self-abolition:

> For the grace of God has appeared, bringing salvation to all, training us to renounce impiety and worldly passions, and in the present age to live lives that are self-controlled, upright, and godly, while we wait for the blessed hope and the manifestation of the glory of our great

---

[27]   Gerhard Kardinal Müller, *Der Glaube an Gott im säkularen Zeitalter* (Freiburg i.Br., 2020).

[28]   Vatican II, *Lumen Gentium*, §1.

[29]   Vatican II, *Lumen Gentium*, §48; *Gaudium et Spes*, §45.

[30]   Vatican II, *Lumen Gentium*, §48.

God and Savior, Jesus Christ. He it is who gave himself for us that he might redeem us from all iniquity and purify for himself a people of his own who are zealous for good deeds. (Tit 2:11–14)

The respect that Catholics have for the consciousness of truth (*Wahrheitsgewissen*) of those who belong to other Christian communions, other religions, and other worldviews is something they can also expect and demand for themselves. Without self-doubt, inferiority complexes, and fear of the pressure to conform to a post-Christian or even anti-Catholic environment, Catholics stand up for their faith, even on points where they differ from other Christian communions, doing so in particular when these points cannot be readily understood on the basis of the teachings of other Christian communions: the nature and sevenfold number of the sacraments,[31] the sacrificial character of the Mass[32] and the Real Presence at the Eucharist,[33] the hierarchical constitution of the Church,[34] the infallibility of the pope and the ecumenical councils in matters of faith and morals,[35] the evangelical counsels of poverty, chastity, and obedience (the monastic life in *vita activa* and *contemplativa*),[36] the indissolubility

---

[31] Robert Hotz, *Sakramente, im Wechselspiel zwischen Ost und West* (Gütersloh, 1979); Alexandre Ganoczy, *Einführung in die katholische Sakramentenlehre*, 1979; Gunther Wenz, *Einführung in die evangelische Sakramentenlehre* (Darmstadt, 1989); Paul McPartlan, *The Eucharist Makes the Church: Henri de Lubac and John Zizioulas in Dialogue* (Edinburgh: T and T Clark, 1993; new ed., Fairfax, VA: Eastern Christian Publications, 2006) ; Louis-Marie Chauvet, *Symbol und Sakrament. Eine sakramentale Relecture der christlichen Existenz* (Regensburg, 2015); Joseph Ratzinger, *Theologie der Liturgie. Die sakramentale Begründung christlicher Existenz* (= JRGS 11) (Freiburg, 2008).

[32] Carl Wislöff, *Abendmahl und Messe. Die Kritik Luthers am Messopfer* (Berlin, 1969); Ulrich Beyer, *Abendmahl und Messe. Sinn und Recht der 80. Frage des Heidelberger Katechismus.* Neukirchen-Vluyn, 1963; Karl Lehmann and Edmund Schlink, *Das Opfer Christi und seine Gegenwart in der Kirche. Klärungen zum Opfercharakter des Herrenmahls* (= Dialog der Kirchen 3) (Freiburg, 1983); Gerhard Kardinal Müller, *Das Geheimnis der Eucharistie - das Opfer der Kirche: Eucharistie*, ed. G. Augustin (Mainz, 2020), 123–65.

[33] Hans Bernhard Meyer, *Eucharistie. Geschichte, Theologie, Pastoral* (Regensburg, 1989); Martin Stuflesser, *Eucharistie. Liturgische Feier und theologische Erschließung* (Regensburg, 2013); Lawrence Feingold, *The Eucharist: Mystery of Presence, Sacrifice, and Communion* (Steubenville, OH: Emmaus Academic, 2018).

[34] Joseph Ratzinger, *Kirche – Zeichen unter den Völkern* (= JRGS 8) (Freiburg, 2010).

[35] Gerhard Kardinal Müller, *Der Papst. Sendung und Auftrag* (Freiburg, 2017); Eng.: *The Pope: His Mission and His Task* (Washington, DC: The Catholic University of America Press, 2021); Müller, *Römische Begegnungen* (Freiburg, 2019); Eng.: *Roman Encounters* (Irondale, AL: EWTN, 2019).

[36] Louis Bouyer, *Vom Geist des Mönchtums* (Salzburg, 1958) = *Le Sens de la vie monastique* (Paris, 1950); Karl Suso Frank, *Grundzüge der Geschichte des christlichen Mönchtums* (Darmstadt, 1983).

of sacramental marriage,[37] priestly celibacy,[38] the veneration of Mary and the saints,[39] and a sexual ethic determined by the dignity of the human person.[40]

The realistic view of God's revelation and saving will, which embraces the whole human being, implies a realistic epistemology and insight into the identity of truth and reality. It excludes a priori any nihilism in metaphysics that studies "being qua being"[41] and any relativism in ethics that determines the "good to which all aspire."[42]

Christ's kingdom is not of this world; nor is it of the nature of political rule with police and judicial enforcement or of imperial power to subjugate. The Church does not have military, techno-scientific, financial, and economic power, or instruments of control and surveillance at her disposal. And if they were offered to her, she would have to reject the proposal in the interests of religious freedom and the dignity of the human person. Quite the opposite, the Church rejects the thought control imposed by a digital dictatorship of opinion (*Meinungsdiktatur*) that pursues a policy of total "mainstreaming." She does not behave in a self-important manner like the philanthropists and potentates of this world, who set up multi-billion "foundations" and use them to impose their ideas and programs of how to make the world happy on the poor of this world, trying to gain their compliance through the luxury and glitter of their wealth.

God's truth does not coerce but liberates.

It is one of the major tenets of Catholic doctrine that man's response to God in faith must be free: no one therefore is to be forced to

---

[37]   Angelo Scola, *Das hochzeitliche Geheimnis*, 2006. George Augustin and Rainer Kirchdörfer, eds., *Familie. Auskaufmodell oder Garant der Zukunft?* (Freiburg, 2014); José Granados, ed., *Amoris laetitia. Accompagnare, discernere, integrare* (Siena, 2016); Rocco Buttiglione, *Risposte amichevole ai critici di Amoris laetitia. Saggio introduttivo di Cardinal Gerhard Ludwig Müller*, Milan, 2017; George Augustin and Ingo Proft, eds., *Zum Gelingen von Ehe und Familie. Ermutigung aus Amoris laetitia* (FS W. Kasper) (Freiburg, 2018).

[38]   Stefan Heid, *Zölibat in der frühen Kirche. Die Anfänge einer Enthaltsamkeitspflicht für Kleriker in Ost und West* (Paderborn, 1997); Gerhard Kardinal Müller, *Ihr sollt ein Segen sein. 12 Briefe über das Priestertum* (Freiburg, 2018), 165–80.

[39]   Gerhard Ludwig Müller, *Gemeinschaft und Verehrung der Heiligen. Geschichtlich-systematische Grundlegung* (Freiburg, 1986); Müller, *Maria – die Frau im Heilsplan* Gottes (Regensburg, 2002); Gerhard Kardinal Müller et al., eds., *Heilige und Heiligenverehrung in Ost und West* (Bonn-Sibiu, 2018).

[40]   Pope John Paul II, *Die menschliche Liebe im göttlichen Heilsplan. Eine Theologie des Leibes*, ed. N. and R. Martin (Kisslegg, 2008); Eng.: *The Theology of the Body: Human Love in the Divine Plan* (Boston: Pauline Books and Media, 1997).

[41]   Aristotle, *Metaphysics*, 1003a.

[42]   Aristotle, *Nicomachean Ethics*, 1094a.

embrace the Christian Faith against his own will. This doctrine is contained in the word of God and it was constantly proclaimed by the Fathers of the Church.[43]

Christians turn to God and pray, "Our Father who art in heaven, hallowed be thy name, thy kingdom come, thy will be done on earth as it is in heaven" (cf. Matt 6:9–10). *In the service* of the coming of God's kingdom and rule is the community of his disciples called by Jesus; as a result of the sending of the Spirit at Pentecost, this community manifests itself as the Church of God. The Dogmatic Constitution on the Church of the Second Vatican Council, issued in 1964, begins with the following words:

> Christ is the Light of nations. Because this is so, this sacred synod gathered together in the Holy Spirit eagerly desires, by proclaiming the Gospel to every creature (cf. Mark 16:15), to bring the light of Christ to all men, a light brightly visible on the countenance of the Church. . . . The Church is in Christ like a sacrament or as a sign and instrument both of a very closely knit union with God and of the unity of the whole human race.[44]

Her confession (*credo*) of the Triune God, which goes back to her apostolic and biblically well-attested origins, is summarized in the Roman Baptismal Symbol (*Apostolicum*) and the Great Creed according to the Ecumenical Councils of Nicaea (AD 325) and Constantinople I (AD 381). In it, the individual Catholic professes along with the whole Church his faith in God the Father, the Son, and the Holy Spirit, in whom he is baptized and through whom he has become a son or daughter of God in Christ and a citizen of God's kingdom (i.e., a member of the Church).

Personal faith in the Triune God also includes knowledge of his saving work in the history of all humanity and especially of his chosen people, Israel. With the historical appearance of Jesus of Nazareth as the promised Messiah (Greek/Latin: *Christus*), the Church of the end time emerged as his foundation and includes the faithful from God's chosen people and from all the Gentile nations who are now also called to salvation (cf. Eph 2:16). The reconciliation of mankind with God through Christ's redemptive death on the Cross, his Resurrection from the dead, and the universal outpouring of the Pentecostal Spirit of God "upon all flesh" (Acts 2:17) was followed, as its first effect, by the

---

[43]   Vatican II, *Dignitatis Humanae*, §10.

[44]   Vatican II, *Lumen Gentium*, §1.

reconciliation of "Jews and Gentiles" and their fellowship of faith, hope, and love in the one Church of Christ:

> [F]or through him both of us have access in one Spirit to the Father. So then you are no longer strangers and aliens, but you are citizens with the saints and also members of the household of God, built upon the foundation of the apostles and prophets, with Christ Jesus himself as the cornerstone. In him the whole structure is joined together and grows into a holy temple in the Lord; in whom you also are built together spiritually [in the Spirit] into a dwelling-place for God. (Eph 2:18–22)

And even before the final confession of the resurrection of the dead and of eternal life, the *one, holy, catholic, and apostolic Church* appears as the universal community of salvation and the universal means of salvation, the vaccine against the meaninglessness of existence.

She is even identified by outsiders with the name "Catholic Church" and distinguished with this attribute from other Christian communities, non-Christian religions, and other worldviews. Emperor Constantine († AD 337), after recognizing general religious freedom in the Roman Empire, including for the Christians, already speaks in a letter to Pope Miltiades (r. AD 311–314), the "Bishop of Rome" of the "legitimate Catholic Church."[45]

In modern democratic states that are based on human rights, the Church is recognized in law as a public corporation. This means she has the natural right to regulate her own affairs, i.e., to be free from state and ideological pressures on her liturgy, her teaching on faith and morals, and her sacramental order established by divine law.

The qualities and predicates attributed to her in the Creed are not claims that the Church makes towards her members, let alone towards outsiders, but rather inner effects of "the source of your life in Christ Jesus, who became for us wisdom from God, and righteousness and sanctification and redemption" (1 Cor 1:30).

The Church is the work of the Father. As the body of Christ, his Son, she is intimately united to the Father through Christ as he carries out his mission for the salvation of the world in history. Based on the Pauline statement that all the baptized are "one in Christ Jesus" (Gal 3:28), i.e., one indivisible mystical

---

45 Eusebius of Caesarea, *Historia ecclesiastica* 10.5.18; 20, https://www.newadvent.org /fathers/250110.htm.

person, St. Augustine coined the felicitous formulation "head and body, the one and whole Christ [caput et corpus, unus et totus Christus]."[46]

This also brings to nothing the accusation raised by the Protestant Reformation that the Church, in the shape of priests and sacraments as human-creaturely agencies, had "forced itself between God and man." Behind this accusation lies the fear that the Church's dogma is an impediment to the personal act of faith towards God, or that the sacramental rite turns the presence of grace in the word of God into a kind of magical usurpation of salvation, with the human priest taking the place of Jesus Christ, the only divine priest. This, they argue, impedes people's immediacy in faith and conscience and renders "the laity" dependent on the whims and claims to power of "the priests." Contrasted to this is the universal priesthood given in Baptism: this means that everyone has in the same sense a teaching and preaching office and that the "priest" is just a mandate holder of the community of equals. This is what Martin Luther militantly claimed in his main Reformation writings published in 1520: *An den christlichen Adel deutscher Nation von des christlichen Standes Besserung* (To the Christian Nobility of the German Nation); *Von der babylonischen Gefangenschaft der Kirche* (On the Babylonian Captivity of the Church); and *Von der Freiheit eines Christenmenschen* (On the Freedom of a Christian).

The body of Christ that is the Church, in the community of the faithful *and* their shepherds, cannot—in the Catholic view—force itself between God and man, because Christ as its head is the only mediator between God and us but works through and in his body. People live from the word that comes from the mouth of God and from his divine Son, Jesus, who offers himself to them as the Bread of Life; but to the disciples the Word says with respect to the hungry, "You give them something to eat" (Luke 9:13). So they do not interpose themselves between God and the people like, to put it crudely, the waiter between the chef and the guest in a restaurant.

The ecclesial community of believers, in the multiplicity of its members, is the Church of God in which Christ appointed his servants and gave them gifts, so that

> some would be apostles, some prophets, some evangelists, some pastors and teachers, to equip the saints for the work of ministry, for building up the body of Christ, until all of us come to the unity of the faith and of the knowledge of the Son of God, to maturity, to the measure of the full stature of Christ. (Eph 4:11–13)

---

[46] St. Augustine, *Sermo* 341.1; cf. Joseph Ratzinger, *Volk und Haus Gottes in Augustins Lehre von der Kirche. Die Dissertation und weitere Studien zu Augustinus und zur Theologie der Kirchenväter* (= JRGS 1) (Freiburg, 2011).

The supposed opposition between ecclesial-sacramental mediation, and the personal immediacy of the Christian to God, was the real reason that long held back St. John Henry Newman (1801–1890) from converting from the Anglican Church of England—a product of the Reformation—to the Catholic Church. In the end, he said:

> Only this I know full well now, and did not know then, that the Catholic Church allows no image of any sort, material or immaterial, no dogmatic symbol, no rite, no sacrament, no saint, not even the Blessed Virgin herself, to come between the soul and its Creator. It is face to face, "solus cum solo," in all matters between man and his God. He alone creates; He alone has redeemed; before his awful eyes we go in death; in the vision of him is our eternal beatitude.[47]

St. Thomas Aquinas already made it clear that the act of the believer "is terminated" directly in God, whereas the dogmatic teaching of the Church is merely its conceptual form, which, however, a finite mind cannot do without even when natural knowledge is mediated by science: "Actus credentis non terminatur ad enuntiabile, sed ad rem"[48]—just as my thirst is quenched by water, but I can only draw it and drink from the spring by using a vessel. Or as Cardinal Newman could say with regard to the dogma of the Immaculate Conception of Mary, Virgin and Mother of God—Maria Immaculata (1854): "It is a simple fact to say, that Catholics have not come to believe it because it is defined, but that it was defined because they believed it."[49]

Hence it is not necessary for our salvation to believe in the dogma of the Incarnation as a definition per se. Rather, personally surrendering our intellect and will, we believe in the Triune God who became man in his Son since this is, of course, infallibly and inerrantly stated in the dogma. For this reason, when we receive the sacraments and at every Holy Mass on Sundays and feast days, we recite the Creed together with the whole congregation in the (enunciable) form of explicit propositions, addressing it directly to God.[50]

Since the ecclesial-sacramental mediation of salvation places the human being in a personal immediacy to God in the acts of knowing God and being united with him in love, it makes use of the corporeal-social nature of man

---

[47] St. John Henry Newman, *Apologia pro vita sua* (London: Longmans, Green, 1890), ch. 4, no. 2, p. 195, https://www.gutenberg.org/files/22088/22088-h/22088-h.htm.

[48] St. Thomas Aquinas, *Summa theologiae* II-II, q. 1, a. 2, ad 2, https://www.ccel.org/a/aquinas /summa (hereafter, *ST*).

[49] St. John Henry Newman, *Apologia pro vita sua*, ch. 5, p. 255.

[50] St. Thomas Aquinas, *ST* II-II, q. 1, a. 1.

as its medium. Because of its embodiedness, the human mind always begins with sense perception. It uses the words of human language to communicate with others and also with God. Since man is a social being, he cannot exist and develop on his own, either physically or mentally or spiritually, unless he is accepted into a community, grows up in it, participates in its culture, and promotes it through his own contributions. Personal, meaningful communication with God presupposes the linguistic, sensory, social processes of human nature. And that is why God did not relate man, whom he created in this way, directly to himself, bypassing his nature and his reason, but founded the Church as a community of salvation in word and sacrament. If the Word became flesh, it also dwells visibly, audibly, and sensibly among us in the Church as the house and people of God (cf. Matt 13:13–17):

> We declare to you . . . what we have *heard*, what we have *seen* with our eyes, what we have *looked at* and *touched* with our hands, concerning the word of life . . . so that you also may have *fellowship* with us; and truly our fellowship is with the Father and with his Son Jesus Christ. We are writing these things so that our joy may be complete. (1 John 1:1–4, emphasis added)

Since Jesus is the reason and source of the Church's being and mission, the essential attributes of the Church come about as effects and representations of God's salvific will, which communicates itself to humanity as truth and life. Just as Christ is the Son of the living God, the community called by him is "the church of the living God, the pillar and bulwark of the truth" (1 Tim 3:15), and the revelation of "God the Father . . . in truth and love" (2 John 3).

In the unity of the Church, as the one body of Christ in the multiplicity of its members, is represented the unity of the Triune God (Rom 12:4; 1 Cor 10:17; 12:4, 12); in the same way, God makes his holiness shine forth in the Church through the Gospel, through Baptism and the Eucharist. The catholicity (i.e., universality) of the Church results from the universal salvific will of God, who wants all people to be saved and to come to the knowledge of the truth: "For there is one God; there is also one mediator between God and humankind, Christ Jesus, himself human, who gave himself a ransom for all—this was attested at the right time. For this I [Paul] was appointed a herald and an apostle . . . a teacher of the Gentiles in faith and truth" (1 Tim 2:4–7). And her apostolicity (apostolic = missionary) the Church receives from Jesus, "the apostle and high priest of our confession" (Heb 3:1). He is the messenger (i.e., apostle) of the Father, who passes on his mission and authority to his messengers, his apostles chosen by him. The Risen Lord says to the disciples, and thus also to the bishops as the successors to the apostles, "'As the Father has sent me, so I send you.' When he had said this, he breathed on them and said to them, 'Receive the Holy Spirit. If you forgive the sins of any, they are forgiven them; if you retain the sins of any, they are retained'" (John 20:21–23).

Offenses and scandals

Of course, there is still a difference between the Church, inasmuch as she is the body of Christ, and the Church in her members, who on their earthly pilgrimage will also become sinners again and damage the credibility of the whole Church through scandals. Therefore, "the Church, embracing in her bosom sinners, at the same time holy and always in need of being purified, always follows the way of penance and renewal."[51] All members of his body, the Church (cf. Col 1:18), and especially the priests (i.e., bishops and presbyters)—as "examples to the flock" (1 Pet 5:3) in faith and life—have supreme responsibility for the eternal salvation of those inside and outside the Church.

They go against their mission and authority if they become a cause for offense and outrage to their neighbors through an unchristian lifestyle and immoral behavior. Like the step at the doorway of the house of God, the credibility of its witnesses is the human gateway to divine faith. An unchristian life on the part of the witnesses can become a stumbling block and pitfall for many. The words of Jesus must ring in the ears of every servant of the Church:

> If any of you put a stumbling block before one of these little ones [simple people] who believe in me, it would be better for you if a great millstone were fastened around your neck and you were drowned in the depth of the sea. Woe to the world because of stumbling-blocks! (Matt 18:6–7)

The priest must be the good shepherd, the well-prepared teacher, and the wise householder and not the hired hand, who "does not own the sheep, sees the wolf coming and leaves the sheep and runs away" (John 10:12). But conversely, the faithful are also urged not to disturb the peace and unity of the community with pseudo-emancipatory behavior. "Obey your leaders and submit to them, for they are keeping watch over your souls and will give an account. Let them do this with joy and not with sighing—for that would be harmful to you" (Heb 13:17).

---

51 Vatican II, *Lumen Gentium*, §8.

The Church, as an end-time community of salvation born of God's Word and Spirit, has neither boundaries in the way of a state, nor a specific purpose like a manufacturing plant or international business corporation. Her bishops are neither ideologically biased secular potentates nor oligarchs lobbying for their ideology of world improvement (re-education programs with managed thinking; funding abortion programs in poor countries to regulate the growth of the world's population; combatting poverty by decimating the poor).

But unlike a community of ideas or interests, the Church does not lack a visible social structure. And unlike an ideology (*weltanschauung*), she does not owe her existence to the theoretical speculation of an inspired philosopher—e.g., Plato, Aristotle, Plotinus, Kant, Hegel, Marx, Heidegger—who influences the history of ideas with a prodigious system of thought and a school, or who has a "transformative" impact on the development of society. Nor is the Church a "religion" founded by a prophet or mystic in order to resolve man's relationship to the transcendent God or to an a-personal ground of being. And she is certainly not to be confused with some national or international coalition following the call of an ideologue or guru in urging the proletariat of every country, the believers in progress and science of all times, the idealistic utopians and illuminators of existence, or the materialistic do-gooders and builders of an earthly paradise to finally unite in order to create the New Man with a Great Reset, and to bring about the consummation of history immanently within the world in their idea of a paradise on earth. Finally, the salvation community of the Church has nothing to do with the gnostic-esoteric practices of meditative self-redemption (New Age) or the spiritual dissolution of the self in nirvana, beyond the opposition of being and nothingness.

In the personal encounter with God in the world and in history, what comes about is not a *dissolution* of the human being's personhood, created in God's image, but rather a *redemption* of it from sin, and with this a knowledge of God as the goal of the created being's entire spiritual and moral existence. In the most dramatic hour of his earthly life, the Passion, Jesus's prayer to God his Father revealed to us the center and goal of the Christian life:

> Father, the hour has come; glorify your Son so that the Son may glorify you, since you have given him authority over all people, to give eternal life to all whom you have given him. And this is eternal life, that they may know you, the only true God, and Jesus Christ whom you have sent. (John 17:2–3)

But the Church remains the humble community of "lambs" and "sheep" (cf. John 21:15–17), who recognize Jesus by his voice (John 10:2, 14). As the Good

Shepherd of Israel, he gathers them like God's flock by "lay[ing] down his life for the sheep" (John 10:11). Jesus's first beatitude refers to "the poor in spirit, for theirs is the kingdom of heaven" (Matt 5:3). The knowledge that the Father and the Son are one remains hidden from "the wise and the intelligent" of this world, as does the fact that Jesus reveals the Father to us and reveals himself as the Son of the Father (Matt 11:25–30). The Church does not appear among the nations triumphantly and with imperial gestures but in the foolishness of proclaiming the Gospel of the Cross of Christ:

> [W]e proclaim Christ crucified, a stumbling-block to Jews and foolish-ness to Gentiles, but to those who are the called, both Jews and Greeks, Christ the power of God and the wisdom of God. For God's foolishness is wiser than human wisdom, and God's weakness is stronger than human strength. (1 Cor 1:23–25)

The Church is the community of believers called by the word of God, a community for which God has made his house and his people, who bear witness to his universal salvific will and serve its realization in history until he comes again at the end of time. A person becomes a disciple of Jesus, and is incorporated into his ecclesial body, through Baptism, when he "commits his whole self freely to God, offering the full submission of intellect and will to God who reveals,' and freely assenting to the truth revealed by Him." In doing so, he must not forget:

> To make this act of faith, the grace of God and the interior help of the Holy Spirit must precede and assist, moving the heart and turning it to God, opening the eyes of the mind and giving "joy and ease to everyone in assenting to the truth and believing it." To bring about an ever deeper understanding of revelation the same Holy Spirit constantly brings faith to completion by His gifts.[52]

To the faith that springs from the revelation and grace of God belongs the conviction of the Church's supernatural origin in God's universal salvific will, which through Jesus Christ entered definitively and incorruptibly into the space and time of creation. In the doxology at the end of his Letter to the Romans, the apostle Paul opens up to us "my gospel and the proclamation of Jesus Christ" as "the revelation of the mystery that was kept secret for long ages but is now disclosed, and through the prophetic writings is made known to

---

52   Vatican II, *Dei Verbum*, §5.

all the Gentiles, according to the command of the eternal God, to bring about the obedience of faith" (Rom 16:25–26).

Christ, the Son of God and Savior of the world, is thus in his Person and teaching unsurpassable and unassailable and for the thinking of the faith irreducible (*unhintergehbar*). "I believe, therefore I live," one could say in a loose adaptation of Descartes. And Kant's categorical imperative, which refers only to the secondary "Ought," is preceded in Christian terms by the categorical indicative of the primary "Is" in God:

> For through the law I died to the law, so that I might live to God. I have been crucified with Christ; and it is no longer I who live, but it is Christ who lives in me. And the life I now live in the flesh I live by faith in the Son of God, who loved me and gave himself for me. (Gal 2:19–20)

In the second century, St. Irenaeus of Lyons opposed the esoteric promises of salvation made by the Gnostics and established the irreducible (*unhintergehbar*) newness of the human relationship with God. In answer to the question "What new thing did the Lord bring to us by his advent?" he replied: "Know that he brought all [possible] novelty, by bringing himself, who had been announced. For this very thing was proclaimed beforehand, that a novelty should come to renew and quicken mankind."[53] Christ is God's most sustainable innovation and investment in his creation. And the Church is the executive body that puts into practice God's infinite commitment to our happiness and salvation. She is in Christ "the universal sacrament of salvation"[54] of the world. For through the apostles and "through the Church the wisdom of God in its rich variety might now be made known . . . in accordance with the eternal purpose that he has carried out in Christ Jesus our Lord" (Eph 3:10–11).

The Catholic Church is thus a worldwide community sui generis. Unlike natural human forms of community, her origin lies in an initiative undertaken not by human beings but by God, who alone is the origin and goal of the whole universe, of history, and of every person. She is "a people made one with the unity of the Father, the Son, and the Holy Spirit,"[55] the (social) body of Christ, the temple of the Holy Spirit, "a chosen race, a royal priesthood, a holy nation, God's own people, in order that you may proclaim the mighty acts of him who

---

53 St. Irenaeus, *Adversus haereses* 4.34.1.

54 Vatican II, *Lumen Gentium*, §48; *Gaudium et Spes*, §45)

55 Vatican II, *Lumen Gentium*, §4.

called you out of darkness into his marvelous light" (1 Pet 2:9; cf. Rev 5:10; Exod 19:6; Isa 43:20).

The inner connection between the foundation of the Church in the Incarnation and life being breathed into her in the Holy Spirit with the sacraments and charisms of the Church is described by Vatican II as follows:

> In the human nature united to Himself the Son of God, by overcoming death through His own death and Resurrection, redeemed man and remolded him into a new creation (cf. Gal 6:15; 2 Cor 5:17). By communicating His Spirit, Christ made His brothers, called together from all nations, mystically the components of His own Body.
>
> In that Body the life of Christ is poured into the believers who, through the sacraments, are united in a hidden and real way to Christ who suffered and was glorified. Through Baptism we are formed in the likeness of Christ: "For in one Spirit we were all baptized into one body" (1 Cor 12:13). In this sacred rite, a oneness with Christ's death and Resurrection is both symbolized and brought about: "For we were buried with Him by means of Baptism into death"; and if "we have been united with Him in the likeness of His death, we shall be so in the likeness of His resurrection also" (Rom 6:4–5). Really partaking of the body of the Lord in the breaking of the Eucharistic bread, we are taken up into communion with Him and with one another. "Because the bread is one, we though many, are one body, all of us who partake of the one bread" (1 Cor 10:17). In this way all of us are made members of His Body (cf. 1 Cor 12:12) "but severally members one of another" (Rom 12:5).
>
> As all the members of the human body, though they are many, form one body, so also are the faithful in Christ (cf. 1 Cor 12:12). Also, in the building up of Christ's Body various members and functions have their part to play. There is only one Spirit who, according to His own richness and the needs of the ministries, gives His different gifts for the welfare of the Church (cf. 1 Cor 12:1–11). What has a special place among these gifts is the grace of the apostles to whose authority the Spirit Himself subjected even those who were endowed with charisms (cf. 1 Cor 14). Giving the body unity through Himself and through His power and inner joining of the members, this same Spirit produces and urges love among the believers. From all this it follows

that if one member endures anything, all the members co-endure it, and if one member is honored, all the members together rejoice (cf. 1 Cor 12:26).

The Head of this Body is Christ. He is the image of the invisible God and in Him all things came into being. He is before all creatures and in Him all things hold together. He is the head of the Body which is the Church. He is the beginning, the firstborn from the dead, that in all things He might have the first place (cf. Col 1:15–18). By the greatness of His power He rules the things in heaven and the things on earth, and with His all-surpassing perfection and way of acting He fills the whole body with the riches of His glory (cf. Eph 1:18–23).

All the members ought to be molded in the likeness of Him, until Christ be formed in them (cf. Gal 4:19). For this reason we, who have been made to conform with Him, who have died with Him and risen with Him, are taken up into the mysteries of His life, until we will reign together with Him (cf. Phil 3:21; 2 Tim 2:11; Eph 2:6; Col 2:12, etc.). On earth, still as pilgrims in a strange land, tracing in trial and in oppression the paths He trod, we are made one with His sufferings like the body is one with the Head, suffering with Him, that with Him we may be glorified (cf. Rom 8:17).

From Him "the whole body, supplied and built up by joints and ligaments, attains a growth that is of God" (Col 2:19). He continually distributes in His body, that is, in the Church, gifts of ministries in which, by His own power, we serve each other unto salvation so that, carrying out the truth in love, we might through all things grow unto Him who is our Head (cf. Eph 4:11–16).

In order that we might be unceasingly renewed in Him (cf. Eph 4:23), He has shared with us His Spirit who, existing as one and the same being in the Head and in the members, gives life to, unifies, and moves through the whole body. This He does in such a way that His work could be compared by the holy Fathers with the function which the principle of life, that is, the soul, fulfills in the human body.

Christ loves the Church as His bride, having become the model of a man loving his wife as his body (cf. Eph 5:25–28); the Church, indeed, is subject to its Head (Eph 5:23–24). "Because in Him dwells all the fullness of the Godhead bodily" (Col 2:9), He fills the Church, which is His body and His fullness, with His divine gifts (cf. Eph 1:22–23), so that she may expand and reach all the fullness of God (cf. Eph 3:19).[56]

---

[56] Vatican II, *Lumen Gentium*, §7.

Catholic—in the "post-metaphysical age"

In his two-volume masterpiece entitled *Auch eine Geschichte der Philosophie* (This Too a History of Philosophy [2019]), Jürgen Habermas, one of the most important contemporary social analysts of the "Frankfurt School," develops the whole of European intellectual history up to the emergence of today's dominant *post-metaphysical thinking* via the *connecting thread of faith and reason*.

In Habermas's account, the *hub* of this controversial discourse is the *Catholic Church*, insofar as it created and played a crucial role in shaping Western Christianity in the cultural sphere of the Roman Empire.

Of course, Christianity must not be restricted to the Middle Ages in Western Europe. For in the course of the Christian mission, it was very early on taken beyond the bounds of Mediterranean culture. And since the great discoveries in the sixteenth century, the Catholic Church, in accordance with Jesus's Great Commission, has been present not only intentionally but also factually and essentially throughout the world and in every culture. The nature and mission of the Catholic Church cannot therefore be defined using either coordinates of time and epoch—Christian antiquity and the Middle Ages,[57] the "end of the modern age"[58]—or those of space and culture—the "Christian Occident"[59] or, in secular terms, "the West."[60] Rather, her unique nature can only be understood in a universal-historical perspective based on God's relationship to his all-embracing salvific will.

In the truest sense of the word, the Catholic Church alone is rightly considered the first and to this day the only "global player" on the stage of human history, and the densest "social network" for two thousand years. However, her goal is not the "One World" which, according to the rules of its materialistic view of mankind, is to be totally controlled by political ideologues and billionaire oligarchs with the help of a digital dictatorship. Only in God's Spirit can human beings become conscious of their dignity as persons, strive after goodness in freedom, and be perfected in love. The economic globalism of social Darwinism, with its total mainstreaming of thought and behavior, must combat the mind/spirit and freedom as its arch-enemies. Here it is that the poisonous root of a deadly hatred of all things Catholic burgeons.

Modernity, from the Latin *modus*, as the mode of consciousness of the respective latest generation—in which we all place ourselves for good or

---

[57] Theodor Steinbüchel, *Christliches Mittelalter*, Leipzig, 1935.

[58] Cf. Romano Guardini, *Das Ende der Neuzeit. Ein Versuch zur Orientierung* (Würzburg, 1950).

[59] Theodor Haecker, *Vergil—Vater des Abendlandes* (1931); Haecker, *Werke* 5 (Munich, 1967), 9–1142.

[60] Cf. Heinrich August Winkler, *Geschichte des Westens. Von den Anfängen in der Antike bis zum 20. Jahrhundert* (Munich, 2016).

ill—cannot be the embodiment of epochal decadence, or a marker of a philosophy or worldview, that is decisionistically imprinted on the present as a result of our relating to the latest state of social, cultural, and technical development. Even after the Enlightenment and criticism of religion, it cannot be apodictically ruled out that the broadest horizon of the human condition is to be found in supernatural revelation, just as, according to Immanuel Kant's *Critique of Pure Reason* (1781), metaphysics is possible as the First Philosophy as long one challenges the time-conditioned premises of its thinking and cognitive principles.

"Modern" is the same as "up-to-date," or the suitable answer sought to the basic existential questions regarding the meaning of being and the ground of my person—in the flexible context of historical experiences, social conditions, and scientific knowledge of the microcosm and macrocosm. Since man is a finite and time-limited being living in this world, his happiness—if the circumstances of my life correspond to its goal—cannot be guaranteed or his longing fulfilled by the transient riches of money, being respected by the powerful, conforming to the spirit of the times and the "media gossip," i.e., "but that's what people say and do nowadays," or living a hedonistic lifestyle. Jesus's words remain irrefutable: "For what will it profit them to gain the whole world and forfeit their life? Indeed, what can they give in return for their life? Those who are ashamed of me and of my words in this adulterous and sinful generation, of them the Son of Man will also be ashamed when he comes in the glory of his Father with the holy angels" (Mark 8:36–38).

The Church of Christ is always up-to-date in her anticipation of what is to come through the firm belief "that Christ, who died and was raised up for all, can through his Spirit offer man the light and the strength to measure up to his supreme destiny."[61]

Christ is the "new Adam" (1 Cor 15:45), the Son, by whom in these last days—*novissime*—God has spoken to us (Heb 1:2). He is therefore unassailably the most up-to-date man—the *homo modernissimus*.

He is the future in person and hence the present of the goal towards which man is heading on the journey of life.

The modernity of the Church is co-extensive with her catholicity, her mission to gather all people in Christ. Catholic universalism has its origin in the Pentecostal outpouring of the Spirit of divine love on all people. In the Spirit's "tongues as of fire" (Acts 2:3), everyone can communicate with everyone else in their own and others' languages and cultures. What the Church aims for is not an imposed, unitary culture but rather the freely chosen unity

---

61   Vatican II, *Gaudium et Spes*, §10.

of civilizations. For without freedom there is no culture. It is not a world government or surveillance states that contrive to bring about peace through brainwashing and the use of force; rather, it is God's peace, with the conversion of hearts, that brings those responsible in politics, business, and science to reason and to a respect for the dignity and freedom of every human being.

Undoubtedly, Catholic theology, in its endeavor to understand the deeper logic of the Christ event, has offered the rational potential of revealed faith, combined with a critical reception of philosophy since its Greek beginnings, as an answer to the challenges of our fragile existence in the finite world. When we die, however, reason sinks into the bottomless pit. And no one has up to now been able to pull themselves up by their own hair from the abyss of death. It is cold comfort to think that we shall no longer notice anything when we are dead, or that our memory "lives on" in our children, or that in woodland burials our ashes "live on" as fertilizer for the trees.[62]

For the question of the meaning of being does not sink with us into the grave. It continues to echo through history, as a cry for justice for the dead. Man is more than the sum of his biological parts and the neurophysiological and psychological functions of his brain. After death, where is the spiritual and moral added value of my person, which existed just once?

Our species survives through the birth of other individual human beings. The contents of my consciousness may be stored materially on a hard drive or a USB stick. Yet, the uniqueness of my person cannot be kept alive merely in the shadowy memory of mortals but rather in the absolute Spirit alone. But what is the ontological status of my person, which in its ontological uniqueness is far above all material constellations and constructions? Here divine reason comes to the aid of human reason in revealing the ultimate mystery of man between being doomed to die and longing for immortality:

> When this perishable body puts on imperishability, and this mortal body puts on immortality, then the saying that is written will be fulfilled: "Death has been swallowed up in victory." "Where, O death, is your victory? Where, O death, is your sting?" The sting of death is sin, and the power of sin is the law. But thanks be to God, who gives us the victory through our Lord Jesus Christ. (1 Cor 15:54–57)

This is why Christian theology has never reduced Christianity to a new human self-understanding. As Habermas rightly observed, the Christological

---

[62] Quirin Huonder, *Das Unsterblichkeitsproblem in der abendländischen Philosophie* (Stuttgart, 1970); Josef Pieper, *Tod und Unsterblichkeit* (Munich, 1979).

paradigm shift shaped the course of Western intellectual history and, in its wake, of all human history in the polarity of *faith and reason*—but only, we Christians add, within the higher nexus of *faith and love*. Not the law of the jungle, the "struggle of all against all," but love—which in the will-to-good transcends eros and integrates it into its *woraufhin* (upon-which)—is the mysterious law of world history.

> And now faith, hope, and love abide, these three; and *the greatest* of these is *love.* (1 Cor 13:13, emphasis added)

What is original about Christianity is not only the new interpretation of the world or changing it but rather the hope of its complete transformation into "a new heaven and a new earth" (Rev 21:1). Faith opens up a view of "the new Jerusalem, coming down out of heaven from God" (Rev 21:2). This "holy city" is not built of "the blood, sweat and tears of human beings," because a human being made in "the image and likeness" of God (Gen 1:26; 5:1; 9:6;), a new man transformed into the image of Christ (Rom 8:15; 1 Cor 15:49; 2 Cor 3:18, Col 3:10; 2 Pet 1:4), can never be a thingly (*dinglich*) building material but only a personally respected fellow-citizen in the city of God. The new Jerusalem comes from God like a Bride adorned for her husband. *Christ* is the *head of his body* and the *Bridegroom of his Church*, which he has chosen in love to be his bride (John 3:29; 1 Cor 11:2; Eph 5:21–32). The Church is a gift of the Holy Spirit and not a work, however artful, of human beings. Those who belong to her and remain faithful to Christ in all the trials of life and death hear

> a loud voice from the throne saying, "See, the home of God is among mortals. He will dwell with them; they will be his peoples, and God himself will be with them; he will wipe every tear from their eyes. Death will be no more; mourning and crying and pain will be no more, for the first things have passed away." (Rev 21:3–4)

But where could a well-meaning alien (from the Latin *alienus*), traveling to the earth from some far-distant galaxy, land on our planet if there were no suitably equipped landing site? Where can the message from the transcendence of God, who in classical theological language is called *totaliter aliter* (completely other) compared to us, find someone to receive it here on earth, if the earthlings have disabled their radio stations? If, when he is thinking about being and asking about the meaning of being in general, and his own personal existence in particular, man's horizon is blocked towards the transcendent origin of the world and if, in his moral action, he does not recognize an authority superior to the world as a measure of good and evil, then we have arrived at post-metaphysical thinking. Reason is limited to the world and self-referentially only its own ground and measure. "Post-metaphysical" means in "a secular age"[63] that the transcendental reference to God as the origin and goal of all creation does not exist in most people's consciousness, is blanked out as irrelevant, or is even negated as harmful.

In "post-metaphysical thinking," a historical self-revelation on the part of God does not represent a point of reference that could offer any orientation to "modern man's" self-understanding and relation to the world. The Gospel of Christ, in the Church's preaching and in the Bible, is then no longer "God's word in the mouth of man" (cf. 1 Thess 2:13) but, at most, convoluted knowledge on the part of man about himself, the aesthetic and ethical content of which needs to be "unraveled."

Following Immanuel Kant (1724–1804), philosophy is "the science of the relation of all cognition and all use of reason to the ultimate end of human reason, to which, as the highest, all other ends are subordinated."[64] In this "cosmopolitan" sense, it can be brought down to four questions; the first three of these questions (on metaphysics, morals, religion) are contained in the fourth (on anthropology) and summed up in it:

1. What can I know?
2. What ought I to do?
3. What may I hope?
4. What is man?

It is easy to detect the Christian heritage here, with its parallel to the three divine virtues of faith, love, and hope, which transform man from a lost sinner and slave to the elemental forces—destructive violence, evil, death—into a son and friend of God.

Kant, however, in focusing on the coldly moral in the *categorical imperative*, forgets the all-important question: *Do we have something to celebrate or will we end up laughing on the other side of our face?*

---

[63] Charles Taylor, *A Secular Age* (Cambridge, MA: Harvard University Press, 2007); Jocelyn Maclure and Charles Taylor, *Laïcité et liberté de conscience* (2010); Eng.: *Secularism and Freedom of Conscience* (Cambridge, MA: Harvard University Press, 2011).

[64] Immanuel Kant, *Logik, Einleitung A 26: Werke in zehn Bänden 5*, ed. W. Weischedel (Darmstadt, 1968), 448. English quoted from: Immanuel Kant, *Lectures on Logic*, ed. J. Michael Young, The Cambridge Edition of the Works of Immanuel Kant (Cambridge, England: Cambridge University Press, 1992), 536.

Man cannot quit this earth complacently, only confident of having done his duty. And we certainly cannot escape the nihilistic feeling of ultimate meaninglessness in the sensual enjoyment of life, a brimful bank account, or the concentration of power in our shabby egos when the "Forbes list of the richest people in the world" replaces the calendar of saints.

Life is only joyful when "love is strong as death, passion fierce as the grave. Its flashes are flashes of fire, a raging flame. Many waters cannot quench love, neither can floods drown it" (Song 8:6–7).

The Christian is someone convinced that no one will perish who places his hope in God, "who gives life to the dead and calls into existence the things that do not exist" (Rom 4:17). For, "If for this life only we have hoped in Christ, we are of all people most to be pitied. But in fact Christ has been raised from the dead, the first fruits of those who have died" (1 Cor 15:19–20). So Christians have every reason to celebrate and not to "grieve as others do who have no hope" (1 Thess 4:13).

In this miserable world—our *historia calamitatum*—what is there to celebrate? To this the Catholic faith community of all Christians answers: *Well, joy in God.*

The redeemed rejoice with the Messiah, the Lord's Anointed:

> I will greatly rejoice in the LORD, my whole being shall exult in my God; for he has clothed me with the garments of salvation, he has covered me with the robe of righteousness, as a bridegroom decks himself with a garland, and as a bride adorns herself with her jewels. For as the earth brings forth its shoots, and as a garden causes what is sown in it to spring up, so the Lord GOD will cause righteousness and praise to spring up before all the nations. (Isa 61:10–11)

The "medicine of immortality"[65] offered in the Eucharist, which is Christ, the Son of God himself, works not just for the moment and for the next time but for ever and ever.

Worshipping God in the liturgical ministry of prayer and serving one's neighbor through Christ as the liturgist, "the mediator and high priest of the new covenant" (cf. Heb 8:1–6; 9:1, 26), becomes the source and expression of human happiness: joy in God. This is our reasonable worship (*latreia*), "by the mercies of God, to present your bodies as a living sacrifice, holy and acceptable to God, which is your spiritual worship" (Rom 12:1).

---

[65] St. Ignatius of Antioch, *Epistola ad Ephesios* 20.2.

The quality of being Catholic is the categorical indicative of the affirmation of being

The Catholic liturgy is the *categorical indicative* that makes the categorical imperative of morality acceptable and bearable. What world enlightener and would-be reformer could ever equal Jesus, who withholds from the "wise and intelligent" what he revealed to "infants"?

> All things have been handed over to me by my Father; and no one knows the Son except the Father, and no one knows the Father except the Son and anyone to whom the Son chooses to reveal him. Come to me, all you that are weary and are carrying heavy burdens, and I will give you rest. Take my yoke upon you, and learn from me; for I am gentle and humble in heart, and you will find rest for your souls. For my yoke is easy, and my burden is light. (Matt 11:27–30)

Yet Kant's questions prove that, even in post-Christian times, a person shaped by Christianity in Western culture and humanity who has lost God may well reject the answer from faith but still cannot dismiss as irrelevant the questions it raises.

Compared to pre-industrial times, it has been possible to improve and ensure provision for existential needs such as food, housing, clothing, and healthcare, and for consumption and entertainment to an incredible degree. And yet every individual still remains threatened by sudden great misfortune, by the despotism of the powerful, and by a technology that has gotten out of control, as well as by economic, ecological, and political catastrophes; or by a tiny Covid-19 virus that has unleashed the Corona pandemics with their devastating psychological and economic consequences.

And the questions—What is the exact meaning of *my* individual being in particular? and "Why does the universe go to all the bother of existing?"[66]— remain unresolved.

Provision for intellectual and spiritual existential needs, on the other hand, is still lying on the table as unfinished homework. Does "the act of the liberating decision to be oneself already [follow] from the revolutionary overcoming of natural societies?" When man emancipates himself from "self-imposed immaturity in the form of repression and exploitation and overcomes his depressive loss of self," it has to be asked whether, if "post-metaphysical thinking has shaken confidence in the promise of a saving justice," is the happy ending of

---

66   Stephen Hawking, *A Brief History of Time: From the Big Bang to Black Holes* (New York: Bantam, 1988), 174.

his psychodrama and mental acrobatics ultimately just something man himself has orchestrated in his favor?[67]

What remains of life with all its sufferings and struggles, hopes, and disappointments, of the tremendous efforts and tragic or miserable failures, if there is no justice in the world to come? No matter how high an amount the factors within the parenthesis add up to, if they are multiplied by the zero of transience outside them, the resulting sum is only absolute meaninglessness. Only when we recognize God as the origin and goal of all being, and as the meaning of our lives, is it all not in vain. Then our ears hear "a voice from heaven saying . . . 'Blessed are the dead who from now on die in the Lord.' 'Yes,' says the Spirit, 'they will rest from their labours, for their deeds [life's work] follow them'" (Rev 14:13).

The idea of "secular modernity without God" obviously did not work if it is forced into the sheepish admission:

> But reason would itself atrophy with the disappearance of every thought that transcends that which exists in the world as a whole. The defense against this entropy is a point of contact of post-metaphysical thought with religious consciousness, as long as the latter is embodied in the liturgical practice of a community of believers and thus asserts itself as a present form [*Gestalt*] of the spirit. The rite claims to establish the connection with a power breaking into the world from transcendence.[68]

Jürgen Habermas impresses very clearly on the Christians that their relationship to God cannot be just faith as doctrine (with its reflection in theology); it is realized in an actual and not merely virtual way above all in the liturgy of the Church as worship of God (i.e., *religio*) and as a community of life with him (i.e., *communio*). In addition to the witness and profession of faith (i.e., *martyria* and *leiturgia*) (Acts 13:2; Heb 8:2, 6), the Church's *diakonia* (i.e., *caritas* as service rendered to one's neighbor out of love for God) is also an essential part of the living unity of the believer with God. For God carries out the Last Judgment on "all the nations" when Jesus says to us with regard to the good works we have done or failed to do: "[J]ust as you did it [or did not do it] to one of the least of these who are members of *my* family, you did it to *me*" (Matt 25:40, 45).

The defense of the Christian faith (i.e., apologetics) against philosophical objections and life-world polemics is not achieved just with reason but also by living a life of practiced discipleship in following Christ. When Fr. Maximilian

---

[67] Jürgen Habermas, *Auch eine Geschichte der Philosophie II*, 803.
[68] Habermas, *Auch eine Geschichte der Philosophie II*, 897.

Kolbe (1894–1942) offered his life in the hell of Auschwitz to save a husband and father, Franciszek Gajowniczek (1901–1995), taking upon himself the most dreadful death in the starvation bunker for the love of Christ, then such a martyrdom was and is the highest form of *apologia* of the Logos (i.e., rational proof of the hope of all Christians [cf. 1 Pet 3:15]). In the "message [*logos*] about the cross" (1 Cor 1:18), the higher power and reason of God is demonstrated. "For God's foolishness is wiser than human wisdom, and God's weakness is stronger than human strength" (1 Cor 1:25).

In Cremona, the city in Italy most affected by the Corona crisis, the seventy-two-year-old priest Don Giuseppe Berardelli let a fellow patient have his respirator and died on March 16, 2020, from the effects of the insidious disease, as a witness to Christ, the Good Shepherd who "lays down his life for the sheep" (John 10:11). Christian witness to Christ in his Cross and Resurrection is worship of God in the martyrdom of the Word and the offering of life (Rev 6:9). "[F]or the Father seeks such as these to worship him. God is spirit, and those who worship him must worship in spirit and truth" (John 4:23–24).

A faithful Catholic—and not one who just belongs out of convention—will always have the words of Vatican II ringing in his ears and heart:

> Taking part in the Eucharistic Sacrifice [i.e., Holy Mass], which is the fount and apex of the whole Christian life, they offer the Divine Victim to God, and offer themselves along with it. . . . Strengthened in Holy Communion by the Body of Christ, they then manifest in a concrete way that unity of the people of God which is suitably signified and wondrously brought about by this most august sacrament.[69]

It is not only in the thin atmosphere of the heights of brooding speculation that man can experience the transcendence of his hopes and allow himself to be seized by the glory of the Creator but also on the plains of his everyday needs: "Ever since the creation of the world his eternal power and divine nature, invisible though they are, have been understood and seen through the things he has made [invisibilia Dei, per ea quae facta sunt, intellecta, conspiciuntur]" (Rom 1:20).

With a depression-free sense of self-worth, or more accurately a *creaturely joie de vivre*, he cries out to the Lord: "What is man that *you* should keep him in mind, or the son of man that *you* should care for him? Yet *you* have made him little lower than the angels, with glory and honour *you* crowned him" (Ps 8:5–6, RNJB, emphasis added).

---

[69] Vatican II, *Lumen Gentium*, §11.

Joy in God is the Christian's lifeblood: "My soul magnifies the Lord, and my spirit rejoices in God my Saviour" (Luke 1:46–47), Mary shouts out for joy on learning that the Son whom she will bear "in the city of David [is] a Saviour, who is the Messiah, the Lord" (Luke 2:11).

For faith, which comes from *hearing the word* of Christ (Rom 10:17), not only expands our understanding of ourselves and the world in the light of the Gospel. It also brings about a new relationship to oneself and the world because of the fundamental new beginning of all our thinking and acting, giving us joie de vivre and creative power. From the comprehensive orientation of the ego towards God in faith, hope, and love follows love of neighbor and responsibility for the world, both our planet and the cosmos. Through Christ's redeeming death on the Cross with the overcoming of death, sin, and distance from God, every one of those baptized "in the name of Jesus Christ so that your sins may be forgiven ... will receive the gift of the Holy Spirit" (Acts 2:38) and become a "new creation" (Gal 6:15).

Nothing could change the world more sustainably than God becoming a man in Jesus Christ: the *Incarnation of the Logos*, the Word who was with God from the beginning and who is God (John 1:1, 14).

Contained in this is its redeeming arrival in the center of the human person, the *justification of the ungodly* (*iustificatio impii*) through his merciful grace. It is *God's greatest work*, the *opus Dei maximum*, which, as Thomas Aquinas says,[70] is even greater than the work of creation and reveals its first and last meaning. "[J]ust as he chose [*elegit*] us in Christ before the foundation of the world to be holy and blameless before him in love. He destined [*praedestinavit*] us for adoption as his children through Jesus Christ, according to the good pleasure of his will, to the praise of his glorious grace" (Eph 1:4–6).

On the stage of the theatre of the world, the inexorable law of the "right of the strongest" seems to hold sway. But the inner direction is performed in his providence by God alone, who "so loved the world that he gave his only Son, so that everyone who believes in him may not perish but may have eternal life" (John 3:16). Only love of God above all else, and of our neighbor as ourselves, leads us safely along the path to full freedom. Love "rejoices in the truth" (1 Cor 13:6).

Pagan-minded philosophers cannot help but draw the bitter conclusion—from the endless loop of power struggles, massacres, corruption, vices, betrayal, war, genocide, and all the crimes against humanity—that "man is a wolf to man [*homo homini lupus*]," as Plautus († 184 BC) says in the comedy *Asinaria*.

---

[70] St. Thomas Aquinas, *ST* I-II, q. 113, a. 9.

Or also *Homo homini deus*, "Man to man is a god," as Thomas Hobbes in the dedication of his work *De cive* (1642) to the Earl of Devonshire.[71]

With respect to his actions, the Roman emperor Severus Alexander (AD 222–235) was praised by Niccolò Machiavelli—albeit under the dominant influence of Severus's mother Julia Mamaea—as the ideal ruler, because a careful examination will show him to be "a most valiant lion and a most cunning fox."[72] And it is no coincidence that imperialist states, with the deliberate intention of intimidating others, display predators on their coats of arms: the Roman she-wolf, the imperial eagle, the royal lion, the Russian bear, or the Chinese dragon. Wherever people idolize themselves, they become demons and devils to their fellow human beings.

The mystery of God's kingdom, on the other hand—unlike "all the king-doms of the world" with "their glory and all this authority" (Luke 4:5–6)—is revealed in the mediation of salvation and the overcoming of evil, not through violence and deceit, but in the patience of the Lamb that is slaughtered. Jesus tells the Pharisees, who inform him of Herod Antipas's intention to kill him, "Go and tell that fox for me, 'Listen, I am casting out demons and performing cures today and tomorrow, and on the third day I finish my work'" (Luke 13:32).

Christ Jesus, the Son of God, "did not regard equality with God as something to be exploited, but emptied himself. . . . And being found in human form, he humbled himself and became obedient to the point of death—even death on a cross" (Phil 2:6–8). The Son of God does not ride into the holy city on a warhorse—and with "more than twelve legions of angels" (Matt 26:53) behind him sent by his Father. He arrives in Jerusalem on a donkey, a harmless beast of burden, that is, not on a warhorse at the head of legions and with war elephants. He is a king of peace. When he saw Jesus coming towards him, John the Baptist pointed to him and declared: "Here is the Lamb of God who takes away the sin of the world!" (John 1:29).

The final battle for man takes place between the beast that devours all things, the dragon that looks "like a leopard, its feet were like a bear's, and its mouth was like a lion's mouth" (Rev 13:2), and the Lamb who has ransomed the redeemed for God (cf. Rev 14:3–4). The whole drama of history between the earthly rule of tyranny and the divine rule of grace is reflected in the scene where Jesus stands powerless before Pilate, the Creator of life in the hands of a creature who usurps the decision over life and death. Jesus's kingship is not based on coercive power but on truth (John 18:37) that sets free (John 8:32).

---

[71] Johannes Hirschberger, *Geschichte der Philosophie II* (Freiburg, 1965), 197.

[72] Niccolò Machiavelli, *Il Principe*, ch. 19; Eng.: *The Prince*, trans. W. K. Marriott (Project Guten-berg, 1998), https://www.gutenberg.org/files/1232/1232-h/1232-h.htm#chap19.

In contrast to others who, according to the logic of the use of force, seize power over others unjustly, "Worthy is the Lamb that was slaughtered to receive power and wealth and wisdom and might and honour and glory and blessing!" (Rev 5:12). Christian theology, bearing in mind that the purpose of Christ's kingship was to testify to the truth (cf. John 18:37), draws its own conclusion from the "positive dialectic of history," with its equally unbroken succession of the devoted sacrifices of parents for their children, the selfless caring for the sick and dying, the works of corporal and spiritual mercy: in the end, love triumphs over hate, and life over death.

Since Christ's Cross and Resurrection, man is no longer the enemy of man but has become his brother and friend. Because man's natural goodness, which is corrupted by original sin, was restored through grace, the following statement applies: every man is naturally every man's friend in universal human empathy (homo homini naturaliter amicus).[73] This love, however, is perfected in the personal love between thou and thou found in spouses, parents and children, etc., and most profoundly in the grace-borne reciprocal love of God and man.

The goal and consummation of freedom is the full possession of eternal life in the beatific vision of God and the communion of the saints. Reconciliation as the way and goal of history is the victory of God's reason. His mercy is the triumph of love. For just as unreason was the inheritance of the loss of the knowledge of God that existed in the gracious and natural first beginning of being human, because of the sin of Adam as original and hereditary sin, so, too, moral evil is the thorn in the flesh of the struggle for righteousness. On the path of her earthly pilgrimage, the Church (*ecclesia militans*) fights with the spiritual "weapons of righteousness" (Rom 6:13) in the service of God against sin and all the injustices of this world. The Christian remains vigilant and equips himself for the spiritual battle by putting on "the breastplate of faith and love, and for a helmet the hope of salvation" (1 Thess 5:8). "Take the helmet of salvation, and the sword of the Spirit, which is the word of God" (Eph 6:17).

The Christian does not gain his faith, which is infused by the Holy Spirit and conveys salvation, from philosophical speculation on the idea of God but rather from the historical experience of God's loving care for his people, from God's witness to himself in word and deed, and from God's liberation of mankind from the slavery and desolation of all programs of self-redemption. God reveals himself as the one who exists in himself, from himself, and for himself (ipsum esse per se subsistens), who is not determined or limited by reference to the world. He is not born of the spontaneity of finite reason and constructed and postulated as our idea of God. He does not stand in a

---

[73] St. Thomas Aquinas, *ST* II-II, q. 114, a. 1, ad 2.

dialectical relationship to the world, and he is not in some pantheistic way the designation for universal, all-encompassing nameless being. He reveals himself absolutely freely and makes himself known sovereignly, without our finite mind being able to comprehend him, i.e., to conceptualize him and reduce him to a human denominator.

When asked by the Israelites for the name of the one who sent him, Moses is told to give them God's answer: that he reveals himself in his word: "I AM WHO I AM" (Exod 3:14), involving himself actively and powerfully in history in his free and unreserved commitment to his chosen people.

> "I am the LORD your God, who brought you out of the land of Egypt, out of the house of slavery." (Exod 20:2)

Jesus Christ, the Word made flesh, is visibly God the Redeemer and Deliverer in his freely assumed humanity and destiny. Indeed, in him we have been transformed from enemies to friends of God, from slaves of this world to freemen, from strangers to sons and heirs of God (Rom 5:12; 8:15; John 3:1). "[C]reation itself will be set free from its bondage to decay and will obtain the freedom of the glory of the children of God" (Rom 8:21). "For freedom Christ has set us free" (Gal 5:1), and this freedom transcends political, social, and private freedom, while at the same time containing the potential to progressively bring it about amid the changing conditions of history and the growing possibilities of science, technology, and communication. "The Church, or, in other words, the kingdom of Christ now present in mystery,"[74] in the faithful and their pastors plays her part in the spreading and growth of the kingdom of God in time and history. It is "a kingdom of truth and life, a kingdom of holiness and grace, a kingdom of justice, love and peace."[75]

In contrast to the growing kingdom of God, Nietzsche's lament for the "death of God"[76] and the "eternal return of all things"[77] offers just imperialist, expansionist, nationalist, and racial ideological egoisms. Over and over again, their titanic-demonic concentrations of power plunge like avalanches into the vale of tears, their debris of unreason and wickedness dragging millions of people with them into ruin.

---

[74] Vatican II, *Lumen Gentium*, §3.

[75] Vatican II, *Lumen Gentium*, §36.

[76] Friedrich Nietzsche, *Die fröhliche Wissenschaft*, 343: *Sämtliche Werke 3*, eds. G. Colli and M. Montinari (Munich, 1980), 480–82; 573–74.

[77] Friedrich Nietzsche, *Also sprach Zarathustra. Ein Buh für alle und Keinen III. Der Genesende: Sämtliche Werke 4* (Munich, 1980), 276.

The Christian, on the other hand, does not put his hope in dull-witted and often wicked people who claim ideological leadership and total control. He prays that God's kingdom of justice and freedom will come, for "he has rescued us from the power of darkness and transferred us into the kingdom of his beloved Son, in whom we have redemption, the forgiveness of sins" (Col 1:13–14). Christ is the reconciliation and peace of God in his own Person for this world and the next (Col 1:20). The apostles and the whole Church have been given "the ministry of reconciliation" (2 Cor 5:18) and entreat the people to "be reconciled to God" (2 Cor 5:20) and to one another.

And this is the Church that in the Creed is called the one, holy, catholic, and apostolic community of salvation. Theologically, the history of God's people, from its beginnings as witnessed in the Old Testament, encompasses humanity since Abel—*ecclesia ab Abel*—and empirically-historically the period of the last four thousand years in the region of the Holy Land.[78] And Christ's Gospel has been proclaimed and witnessed by the Catholic Church in the power of the Holy Spirit for two thousand years—"in Jerusalem, in all Judea and Samaria, and to the ends of the earth" (Acts 1:8).

The history of the Catholic Church began with her foundations laid in the Christ event, then proceeding through all the peaks and troughs of time, along with changing social and cultural conditions, to the globalized world civilization we have today.

For some, the Church is a relic from the past with impractical ideas about finding theoretical and practical answers to the gigantic challenges of the present, or quite simply the killjoy that spoils an egomaniacal enjoyment of life without remorse. She does not seem to them to be compatible with a future that will be characterized by a total scientification of thought and a socialization of subjects in which the person is reduced to a function. The dynamic propelling the world towards trans- and post-humanism seems unstoppable, making the basic proposition of the inalienable dignity of every human being as a person, and his or her being created in the image and likeness of God, grow dim like some pious myth from the infancy of humanity.

The Church is a thorn in the flesh of the materialist and atheist criticism of religion. The star of popular Enlightenment philosophy, Voltaire, has engraved his mantra on the history of modern hostility towards the Church and persecution of Christians: "*Écrasez l'infâme* [crush the infamous thing]," i.e., the Church. Aggressive "New Atheism" is merely an unchanged and uncorrected reprint of the polemics and prejudices of its forerunners. And the rejection of (Christian) religion as a dangerous illusion, an empty flight from the world

---

[78]   LG, §2.

with the promise of an imaginary hereafter, as per Feuerbach, Marx, Comte, Nietzsche, and Freud, has been the master employed by all political-ideological attempts—liberal, communist, fascist, and consumerist—to more or less brutally exclude the Church from the public sphere (motto: religion is a private matter); or from people's thinking altogether and to discredit the remnant of the faithful as "diehard reactionaries, living in the past, stuck in the Middle Ages," and to throw them to the "emancipated and enlightened" as cheap fodder for their ridicule and sarcasm. At the same time, in the tradition of the Romantics but also misunderstanding Schleiermacher's definition of "religion as a feeling of absolute dependence"[79] on the infinite, religion is dismissed as mere sentiment (*Gefühlssache*). "The feeling of absolute dependence . . . is not to be explained as a *Mitgesetztsein* [co-presence, co-positedness, co-existence] of the world, but only as a *Mitgesetztsein* of God, as the absolute unthought [*ungedacht*]) unity."[80] What the father of liberal Protestant theology was concerned with was an equally valid a priori origin of world consciousness alongside intellect (*Verstand*) and will, metaphysics, and morality.

In the Catholic theological tradition, the religious disposition will be defined in relation to the orientation of reason towards truth and of the will towards the good, even more primordially as the joy of being, which is grasped in the ground of the intellectual soul (*Geistseele*) as the gift of the Creator and experienced as the unity of love. For intellect (*Verstand*) and will are only realizations (faculties) of the intellectual soul, which is the bearer of my substantial existence as a person. Therefore, its grounding in being is the (still pre-reflexive) becoming aware that it exists through the loving creative will of God. In the human being as a unity of body and mind, physical and spiritual creation meet and interpenetrate one another. Therefore, the intellectual soul is the horizon and border (*horizon et confinium*)[81]—of the intellectual grasp of the meaning of the world's existence and of God as its origin and goal. Philosophical contemplation of the world begins with wonder. Theological understanding (*Erkenntnis*) begins with the joyful recognition that "[i]n him [God] we live and move and have our being" (Acts 17:28) and of God's saving presence in Jesus Christ: "Then the disciples *rejoiced* when they saw the [Risen] Lord" (John 20:20, emphasis added).

The starting point—behind which it is impossible to go back (*unhintergehbar*) for a finite intellect's cognizing and willing—is therefore positivity of being, which rejects nothingness as a mere thought thing or as the insubstantial

---

79 Friedrich Schleiermacher, *Der christliche Glaube I. Einleitung*, §8, ed. M. Redeker (Berlin, 1960), 28.

80 Schleiermacher, *Der christliche Glaube*, vol. 1, §32, p. 173.

81 St. Thomas Aquinas, *Summa contra Gentiles* II, ch. 68 (hereafter abbreviated as SCG).

appearance of nothingness. Man exists through a creative act of God and knows that he is both given and tasked. With respect to God, man knows that human existence in the world is both a gift and a task. Even those who are damned for their abuse of freedom do not fall back into non-existent nothingness, because God's promise of being to rational creatures is irrevocable and the grace of the Creator (*gratia Creatoris*) would only be taken back in eternity at the cost of self-contradiction in God. For divine omnipotence must not be thought of as arbitrariness but rather as the infinite active capacity to lead the purpose of his creation to its goal, even in the face of the decay of the finite and, more so still, despite the obstruction brought about by sin and, in the extreme case of the damned, to demonstrate to them his eternal justice.

However, under the powerful and seductive ideological-political pressure of the capitalist-cum-vulgar-Marxist mainstream, the tendency has also developed among Catholics and other Christians to adapt Christianity to all-powerful modernity and to enable it to survive into the modern age as a religion of reason, feeling, or humanity without dogmas and sacraments. For the Western "elites," who have themselves lost their faith, it serves in the form of a civil religion as a convenient social-bonding agent for the state in a pluralistic society. It is all too easy for many people to be drawn into thinking in stereotypes which, since the French Revolution, has divided "modern society" ideologically into conservatives and liberals. Anyone wishing to learn from history should recall the fate of the quasi-state church in Gallican-minded France. Polarizations in the seventeenth and eighteenth centuries between the *parti dévot* (pius party) (Cardinal Pierre de Bérulle) and the *parti politique* (political party) (Cardinal Richelieu), and the struggles between the "rigorist" Jansenists and "laxist" Jesuits, had almost completely paralyzed the Church in the face of the new attitude to life of the popular Enlightenment; and they ultimately brought about the disaster experienced by the Church during the French Revolution.[82] The devastating consequences of a modernist and a traditionalist reception of Vatican II are there for all to see, because both parties are not merely unwilling to engage in dialogue either with God in his revealed word or with each other but they also fight each other tooth and nail. They then claim the Church to have been victoriously saved or reformed when their respective opponents are "driven out of the Church" or at least "neutralized." And they do not even shy away from using such terms.

However, it is part of Catholics' spiritual hygiene to always protect themselves—in the existential questions of human existence—from ideological viruses and ecclesiological pandemics and, beyond traditionalism and

---

[82] Gustav Schürer, *Katholische Kirche und Kultur in der Barockzeit* (Paderborn, 1937), 503–766.

progressivism, to take their bearings solely from God's truth in the Gospel of Christ. This is the word of God in Sacred Scripture and the Apostolic Tradition, especially in the Creed and the Divine Liturgy, and in the binding witness and interpretation of it by the Church's Magisterium.

Ideology arises from the absolutization of an intellectually grasped partial aspect of reality—possibly even grasped correctly—which those who discover it, or their followers, fanaticize politically and/or ideologically. Faith, on the other hand, comes from the Word of God, who is himself the truth and guarantees that it will be freely received in a finite intellect. The believer does not have God's truth at his command (*verfügen über*), but he allows himself to be seized by it both intellectually/spiritually and affectively. The believer knows that God, also in his revealed word, is always greater than anything we can ever comprehend. *Deus semper maior*—"God ever greater"—is the motto of St. Ignatius of Loyola. "For now we see in a mirror, dimly, but then we will see face to face. Now I know only in part; then I will know fully, even as I have been fully known" (1 Cor 13:12).

In the intellectual appropriation of the revealed truths, scientific theology performs a mediating role in the discussion of the real and hypothetical insights of the humanities and natural sciences—not of their ideological contamination—that is commensurate with the metaphysical and epistemological conditions of finite reason, which is nevertheless open to transcendence. A synthesis of understanding of the faith and knowledge about the cosmos, the evolution of living things and the neurology of the brain, is necessary and must be constantly updated because there can never be, either a priori or a posteriori, any dichotomy between them. Everything we understand in the faith and in our knowledge of the world originates in God's infinite knowledge of himself and the world of his creation. When matter is viewed from the aspect of quantity and motion, as opposed to the metaphysical understanding of it as the ground of possibility (*Möglichkeitsgrund*) of what concretely exists and is empirically knowable, it is the subject of research in the natural sciences. However, if it were not intelligible, i.e., already formed by mathematical logic (*more geometrico*), then it could also not be grasped by our intellect in the four fundamental forces of the universe—i.e., gravity, electromagnetism, and the weak and the strong atomic energy—and described and communicated in the scientific community. "The mathematical letters with which the book of nature is written" are therefore traces of the divine reason that the Creator has implanted in the world he called into existence out of nothingness, into its grounds of possibility (i.e., energy/matter). They belong to the effects from which God's being-there (*Da-sein*)—but not the being which is his essence—can be demonstratively inferred as the cause of their realization in the world and the goal of their motion.

Supernatural, revealed faith is not about the worldview of physics, a weltanschauung, or merely coping with contingency by using transferable components from historical Christianity. For surrogates are deceptions, like the placebo drugs that only help hypochondriacs and plunge the (mentally alert) sick into despair.

The Christian faith is the personal relationship with God, who reveals himself in salvation history in Jesus Christ. Who God is for us is no longer mediated to us via Moses. Here the man Jesus himself expresses revelation in his divine Word, which he is himself: "I am the *way*, and the *truth*, and the *life*" (John 14:6, emphasis added). So belief in the Triune God, in the Incarnation of the Logos, and in the justification of the sinner remains independent of the current state of knowledge in astronomy, physics, biology, chemistry, psychology, the humanities, and the social sciences. The human intellect did not create either the cosmos or the structure and mode of action of matter, and has no original insight into them (is not an *intellectus archetypus*), but only recognizes them a posteriori with difficulty, not without error, and never perfectly. For this reason, too, the accumulating and differentiating empirical knowledge of the human intellect does not contradict the fact that the whole, the general, and the individually existing of finite being owe themselves to the infinite power of God. Man's being-in-the-world, the *condition humaine*, does not exclude but rather includes God's communicating himself to mankind in a human way in his word and actions, and dwelling among humankind in the God-man Jesus Christ, his Word made flesh (John 1:14), so that we dwell in the house of the Father of the Son (John 14:2). Indeed, even more, God inhabits our innermost hearts (inhabitatio Dei in anima christiana), as Jesus, the Son of God, says: "Those who love me will keep my word, and my Father will love them, and we will come to them and make our home with them" (John 14:23).

Curiosity about communication with extra-terrestrial humanoid beings fires the imagination of both researchers and science-fiction lovers. But how much more interesting than communicating with creatures in other galaxies must it be for spiritual and free creatures to communicate with their Creator?

In a time of intellectual and moral loss of orientation and global crises, we are challenged to reorient ourselves in the Church and the world in the light of the Gospel. What is needed is the courage to continue on the path of following Christ with more confidence and a greater willingness to *cooperate* with God's universal will for salvation. To be sure, man does not cooperate with God in work that is his alone and of which only he is capable—such as creation and redemption, or the justification of the sinner. Only Mary, in her

50

very own way, played a part in God's plan of salvation through her "yes" to God's being conceived in her womb as a human being—"sed sola Maria cooperante dispositioni."[83] Through Mary's obedience, made possible by grace, she became the cause of salvation for herself and for all humanity: "et sibi et universo generi humano causa facta est salutis."[84] It is God's Incarnation through the Holy Spirit and birth from Mary that give rise to the Marian character of Catholic piety. The Catholic gives "'the obedience of faith' (Rom 16:26; cf. 1:5; 2 Cor 10:5–6) '. . . to God who reveals, an obedience by which man commits his whole self freely to God, offering the full submission of intellect and will to God who reveals.'"[85] Catholics let themselves be guided by the "mother of my Lord" (Luke 1:43)—as Elizabeth greets her—taking the Blessed Mother's response to the angel's message as the yardstick for their own relationship with God: "Here am I, the servant of the Lord; let it be with me according to your word" (Luke 1:38).

Initial justification by grace alone is what makes subsequent cooperation possible. It is by virtue of grace that Christians cooperate of their own free will in the building up of the kingdom of God in time and history, in the way that is proper to them and assigned to them by God.[86] No one who asks about the meaning of his or her life, and wants to know the truth about man's place in the world in relation to the ultimate truth of being, can fail to be moved by the Catholic Church's message that God desires to bring about the salvation and happiness of all people through Jesus Christ.

The Catholic Church's divine mission to bear witness to a belief in the self-communication of the Father, and the Son, and the Holy Spirit as life and truth to all people is expressed by the Second Vatican Council:

> First, the council professes its belief that God Himself has made known to mankind the way in which men are to serve Him, and thus be saved in Christ and come to blessedness. We believe that this one true religion subsists in the Catholic and Apostolic Church, to which the Lord Jesus committed the duty of spreading it abroad among all men. . . . On their part, all men are bound to seek the truth, especially in what concerns God and His Church, and to embrace the truth they come to know, and to hold fast to it.
>
> This Vatican Council likewise professes its belief that it is upon the human conscience that these obligations fall and exert their

---

[83] St. Irenaeus, *Adversus haereses* 3.21.7.

[84] St. Irenaeus, *Adversus haereses* 3.22.4.

[85] Vatican II, *Dei Verbum*, §5.

[86] St. Thomas Aquinas, *Contra errores Graecorum*, ch. 23.

binding force. The truth cannot impose itself except by virtue of its own truth, as it makes its entrance into the mind at once quietly and with power.[87]

The Church on the playing field of the world?

In his *Epistle to Diognetus*, an unknown second-century Christian author wrote, "For the Christians are distinguished from other men neither by country, nor language, nor the customs which they observe. For they neither inhabit cities of their own, nor employ a peculiar form of speech, nor lead a life which is marked out by any singularity."[88]

So they do not form a state within a state, a special group hermetically separated from the rest of society, a closed circle of initiates, or an alternative society to hold up a critical mirror to the rest or to spoil their natural enjoyment of life.

Rather, the Catholic Church is made up of people of both sexes, of all nations and languages, and of all ages and levels of education. She takes as given the realities of man's spiritual, corporeal, and social nature as created by God, and she knows it to be elevated and perfected by the grace of the Savior and involved in the service of supernatural salvation. A dynamic relationship exists between God's creation and his historically realized work of salvation. Man is designed for God, and human reason displays a natural desire to know the truth and to see God "face to face" (1 Cor 13:12; 1 John 3:2). And human freedom is ultimately the will to become one with the innermost mystery of being, which is the Triune God in his very being and will: "Whoever does not love does not know God, for God is love. . . . [A]nd those who abide in love abide in God, and God abides in them" (1 John 4:8, 16).

The Catholic faith rules out any kind of positive or negative dialectic between God and his creation. God gains nothing and loses nothing by freely relating creation to himself and in man relating an autonomous/self-determined subject of created freedom to his universal salvific will, and by eternally predestining us, out of pure grace, to eternal fellowship with him through the cooperation of our free will. God creates the world and communicates himself to us in his Word made flesh, not in order to fill his emptiness or to finally escape his loneliness, but solely in order to reveal his glory.[89] The exclusion in Catholic thinking of any kind of dualism—as well as monism—in

---

[87]   Vatican II, *Dignitatis Humanae*, §1.

[88]   Mathetes, *Epistle to Diognetus*, 5.

[89]   St. Irenaeus, *Adversus haereses* 4.4.3.

Catholic thinking, both in the mild form of "Platonism" and in the radical form of Gnostic myth and Manichaean ideology, is expressed in the way that God in his goodness makes all that he creates *very good* in the internal grounds of its being and allows created being to share in his goodness (Gen 1:31). This is why it was possible for Tertullian to state as a basic principle in his anti-Gnostic work—*On the Resurrection of the Flesh* (written around AD 210)—that the flesh, i.e., the body, which is essentially linked to the soul, shows itself to be the *lynchpin* of the salvation event (Incarnation) and of the ecclesial-sacramental mediation of salvation: *caro salutis est cardo*.[90]

Thirty years earlier, St. Irenaeus of Lyons had already criticized what he called the nonsense of the Gnostic-Manichaean contempt for the body, which, in effect, also applies to the "Platonic" despair regarding the ability of the flesh to resurrect, as seen in writers like Kelsos, Porphyry, and Julian the Apostate: "Complete nonsense is spoken by those who have only contempt for the whole plan of God's salvation and deny that the flesh participates in salvation, and find its rebirth contemptible."[91] And with regard to the Flesh and Blood of Christ in the Eucharist of the Church, he adds, "If therefore both the cup (containing wine and a little water) and the prepared bread receive the Word of God and become the Eucharist, the Body and Blood of Christ, and if these nourish and support the substance of our flesh, how then can they deny that the flesh is capable of receiving God's gift, which is eternal life [caro capax vitae aeternae]?"[92]

This ordering of man in his spiritual-moral nature towards God also manifests itself in that, when people surrender themselves in faith to God with both their reason and their will, they find their true home in God. Faith does not alienate man from himself but rather overcomes the feeling of being lost in nothingness and being exposed in a hostile world. Thus, Tertullian was able to see the spontaneous invocations of a higher power by the pagans of his time, e.g., "God sees it" or "May the departed rest in peace," as also bearing witness to their belief in the unity, goodness, and justice of God, his judgment in the hereafter, and the continued existence of the souls of the departed.[93] Supernatural faith is not a foreign body to human nature. Human nature becomes the testimony of a soul designed for grace: "O testimonium animae naturaliter christianae."[94]

---

[90] Tertullian, *De resurrectione carnis* 8.6–7.

[91] St. Irenaeus, *Adversus haereses* 5.2.2.

[92] St. Irenaeus, *Adversus haereses* 5.2.3.

[93] Tertullian, *De testimonio animae* 2–5.

[94] Tertullian, *Apologeticum* 17.

Those who persecute the Christians persecute themselves in the questions and hopes that are shared by the common nature of all human beings.[95] Similarly, Theophilus of Antioch (ca. AD 170) counters the accusation that reason and faith contradict one another by formulating the relationship between nature and grace: "If you say to me, 'Show me your God,' then I say to you, 'Show me the man in you, and I will show you my God.'"[96]

The guiding principle running through all Catholic theology is the inner ordering of all created things towards God as their origin and goal. And the natural world—for the embodied, rational, and will-centered human being—remains the time-space and medium of a knowledge of and encounter with God in the word, the sacraments, and the community life of the Church. Even though faith, which is based on God's authority alone, cannot be proved by natural reason in philosophy and the empirical sciences—and thus cannot be reduced to immanent factors or eliminated altogether along the lines of naturalism and rationalism—man's spiritual-moral nature, elevated by the light of revelation, is nevertheless the addressee of the word of God to us. Thomas Aquinas puts it thus: "Since therefore grace does not destroy nature but perfects it, natural reason should minister to faith as the natural bent of the will ministers to charity [gratia non tollit sed perficit naturam]."[97]

The supernatural acts and divine virtues of faith and love, which are infused by the Holy Spirit, are not spiritual and moral acts in contrast to human reason and willpower but rather the elevation of natural knowledge into a knowledge and love of God. Universal orientation towards God and concrete responsibility for the world, transcendental reference (*Verwiesenheit*) and immanent goals, belong together like the bread and the nourishment we draw from it. Where the Church's members are most profoundly united with Christ and each other is at the celebration of the Eucharist.

In his *First Apology* defending Christianity against a hostile environment, which he addressed in Rome to the pagan emperors Antoninus Pius (AD 138–161) and Marcus Aurelius (AD 161–180), the philosopher Justin of Samaria—St. Justin Martyr (ca. AD 100–163)—who came to the Christian faith only as an adult, sets out the spiritual and moral preconditions for full membership in the Church:

> And this food is called among us Eucharist, of which no one is allowed to partake but the man who believes that the things which

---

[95] Tertullian, *De testimonio animae* 6.
[96] Theophilus of Antioch, *To Autolycus* 1.2.
[97] St. Thomas Aquinas, *ST* I, q. 1, a. 8, ad 2.

we teach are true, and who has been washed with the washing that is for the remission of sins, and unto regeneration [i.e., Baptism], and who is so living as Christ has enjoined.[98]

So the Christians do not cut themselves off from people of other religions, and they do not avoid the company of their family, friends, neighbors, fellow villagers, and townspeople.

Catholics live together with people of other faiths in the midst of society, at both a national and an international level. And they participate in serving the common good in the public life of the state, the economy, philosophy, the humanities, the natural and social sciences, culture (theatre, literature, the fine arts), and everyday life with their work and celebration, in joy and sorrow, within the family circle and among friends.

Even though they understand their faith as a gift of God's grace and base their confession on the authority of the self-revealing God, they are nonetheless always ready to give every fellow human being reasonable information to explain the inner logic—the meaning and ground—of the hope that fills them. Because they have a clear conscience and out of love for God display "good conduct in Christ" (1 Pet 3:16), they give their answers "with gentleness and reverence" (1 Pet 3:16), not arrogantly and hurtfully, always respecting the dignity of every person and their respective conscience, where the truth can only be freely accepted. Although people are divided in their knowledge of truth, they are united in the search for truth.[99] But all Christians belonging to the Catholic faith are united beyond the bounds of different times and spaces by their confession of Jesus of Nazareth, "the Saviour of the world" (John 4:42). They confess him as the ground of hope in both life and death. They recognize him as the only mediator between God and mankind. For he is the Word of God the Father, the Son in the Triune Godhead who assumed our human nature, taking on its mortality and ability to suffer.

Christ does not live without the community of his disciples, which, after his Resurrection and through the sending of the Holy Spirit by the Father and the Son, became the Church. In the Church, Christ is present as the head of the body and in all its members, the individual baptized. And so the Church is historically the mediator of Christ's salvation in the proclamation of the word of God, in the sacramental bestowing of grace, and in her prayer and community life. The Second Vatican Council, as the highest teaching authority of the Catholic Church, provided a fundamental description of the nature and

---

[98] St. Justin Martyr, *First Apology* 66.
[99] Vatican II, *Dignitatis Humanae*, §1.

universal mission of the Church: "The Church is in Christ like a sacrament or as a sign and instrument both of a very closely knit union with God and of the unity of the whole human race [intimae cum Deo unionis totiusque generis humani unitatis]."[100]

So it is characteristic of the Catholic faith that an inner connection exists between the divine self-revelation in Jesus Christ and the presence of Christ *in* the Church (*Christus praesens*) and *as* the Church in that she is sacramentally his body.

The sacramental visibility of the Catholic Church follows from the true Incarnation of God and the revelation of his universal/catholic salvific will (1 Tim 2:4). The Church is, according to her inner nature, the pilgrim people of God and his house, the body of Christ and the temple of the Holy Spirit, the Lord's vineyard and field, God's flock, the Bride of Christ, our Mother, the heavenly Jerusalem.[101]

One mark that everyone knows today—aside from whether people rightly or wrongly call themselves Catholics—is whether they recognize the Roman Pontiff as the successor of the apostle Peter and as the visible head or principle of her worldwide unity:

1. in the confession of faith;
2. in the worship of God and the mediation of salvation (liturgy and sacraments); and
3. in her social constitution, insofar as the bishops, along with their priests and the pope at the head of the College of Bishops, are appointed as shepherds, liturgists, and teachers of the faithful (Matt 16:18; 18:18; John 21:15–18; Acts 6:4; 20:28; Eph 4:11; 1 Tim 5:17; Tit 1:9; 1 Pet 2:25; 5:1–4; Heb 13:7, 13, 24; etc.).

It should be noted here—to already mention an important controversy that has been ongoing between Catholics and the ecclesial communities of the Reformation since the sixteenth century, and which reflects the whole antithesis—that, according to Catholic belief, Christ is the real head of the Church from whom alone, as the sole cause, all graces overflow onto the body and its members. On the other hand, the bishops for their particular churches, and the pope for the universal Church, are only called heads because, within the bounds of their jurisdiction and term of office, they sacramentally convey the grace of Christ in visible, liturgical, symbolic actions and represent the unity

---

[100] Vatican II, *Lumen Gentium*, §1.
[101] Cf. Vatican II, *Lumen Gentium*, §6.

of the Church as a visible community. They act in Christ's stead and with his authority in the Holy Spirit by proclaiming the word of God and, as "servants of Christ and stewards of God's mysteries" (1 Cor 4:1), by communicating the grace of Christ to the faithful in the sacraments (2 Cor 2:10; 2 Cor 5:20).[102] "But the ministers of the Church [bishops, priests] do not give the grace of the sacraments, but only give the sacraments of grace."[103]

St. Ambrose of Milan (AD 339–397) formulated the indispensable criterion for a Christian to be in visible and full communion with the Catholic Church: "Where Peter is, there is the Church [ubi Petrus, ibi ecclesia]."[104] When the authority of Pope St. Damasus I (r. AD 366–384) was questioned, the same Church Father wrote to the Roman Emperor Gratian, beseeching him "not to allow the Roman Church, the head of the whole Roman world, and the sacred Faith of the apostles to be disturbed; for from thence flow all the rights of venerable Communion to all persons [churches]."[105] The universally operating Catholic Church is divided into dioceses, i.e., local Catholic churches, which are led by a bishop as the head and principle of unity of their members. The community of local churches and their bishops together form the Catholic Church, with the pope as the symbol and principle of her worldwide unity and communion. The dioceses are, in turn, divided into local parishes, which are cared for pastorally by a priest—i.e., a presbyter, pastor, or parish priest—through preaching the word of God, administering the sacramental means of grace, and looking after the personal welfare and salvation of the faithful. He is not a religious-social functionary but rather, like Jesus, the Good Shepherd who is willing to lay down his life for his sheep (John 10:11). Alongside this, there are globally or regionally active religious orders and various Church-run institutions in the fields of science, education, and social services (e.g., universities, schools, hospitals, and institutions for the disabled, sick, and elderly). The charitable, cultural, and political work of the Catholic Church, and of individual Catholics in secular professions, is not restricted to their own co-religionists, but extends to everyone who is in need of spiritual, psychological, and physical help and attention.

Hence the first definition of the Catholic faith—as distinguished from members of all other Christian communions, members of other religions, and all who are seekers after truth and strive for more justice in this world—is

---

[102] Cf. St. Augustine, *In Johannis Evangelium Tractatus* 46; St. Thomas Aquinas, *ST* III, q. 8, a. 6.

[103] St. Thomas Aquinas, *ST* suppl., q. 36, a. 3.

[104] St. Ambrose, *Enarrationes in Psalmos* 40 [41].30.

[105] St. Ambrose, *Epistula* 11.4.

contained in the Vatican II statement about Catholics who belong fully to the Church both inwardly and outwardly:

> They are fully incorporated in the society of the Church who, possess-
> ing the Spirit of Christ, accept her entire system and all the means of
> salvation given to her, and are united with her as part of her visible
> bodily structure and through her with Christ, who rules her through
> the Supreme Pontiff and the bishops. The bonds which bind men to
> the Church in a visible way are profession of faith, the sacraments,
> and ecclesiastical government and communion.[106]

The Church is necessary for everyone who has freely—and with conviction—embraced the Catholic faith to attain eternal salvation. Faith is a gift
from above, and being a Christian is a matter of divine election and calling, but
not so as to exalt oneself above others and make claims before God but rather
a calling to give thanks to God and serve others inside and outside the Church.

In its lengthiest constitution, the Second Vatican Council presents a
definition of the Catholic Church's position and task in the modern world:

> The joys and the hopes [*gaudium et spes*], the griefs and the anxieties
> of the men of this age, especially those who are poor or in any way
> afflicted, these are the joys and hopes, the griefs and anxieties of the
> followers of Christ. Indeed, nothing genuinely human fails to raise
> an echo in their hearts.[107]

Because God in Jesus, his Son, took on our human nature and lived a real
life laden with suffering here on earth, the Church, as the pilgrim people of God
journeying on the steep and stony road towards their heavenly home, cannot
intellectually and morally separate herself from the drama of history and the
tragedies taking place in the lives of millions of people. The Church is either
missionary or else shrivels into a religious sect with or without social activism.

Through the Incarnation, the Son of God became our brother. Every
human being is created in the image and likeness of God (Gen 1:27). Those
who believe in Christ are the messengers of the Gospel of infinite mercy and
human dignity. This is the foundation of our worldwide solidarity with the
poor, the sick, the persecuted, and the despised but also of our struggle for
social justice, the life of the unborn, and the right of the elderly to live until

---

[106] Vatican II, *Lumen Gentium*, §14.
[107] Vatican II, *Gaudium et Spes*, §1.

they die a natural death and have a dignified burial, as well as to have their memory preserved. In a theological sense, not superficially in an ideological one, the Church is a Church of the poor and for the poor.[108]

Here the word "Church" does not mean just the hierarchical offices but rather the whole Church, with all the faithful and their pastors, who have been called to serve the people of God. "Though they differ from one another in essence and not only in degree, the common priesthood of the faithful and the ministerial or hierarchical priesthood are nonetheless interrelated: each of them in its own special way is a participation in the one priesthood of Christ."[109] Thus priests, religious, and laity form the *communio* of the one people of God, and, in the power of the Holy Spirit, they continue the mission of Christ in *martyria, leiturgia,* and *diakonia.*[110] The early Church of Jerusalem, which was founded through the preaching of the apostles, the acceptance of the faith, and through Baptism and the Eucharist, "devoted themselves to the *apostles' teaching* and *fellowship,* to the *breaking of bread* and the *prayers*" (Acts 2:42, emphasis added). And it remains the essential task of the apostles, and thus of their episcopal successors, to devote themselves "to prayer and to serving the word" (Acts 6:4). The teaching of the apostles—the deposit of faith (*depositum fidei*) entrusted to their successors in episcopal office (1 Tim 6:20)—is present in the living Tradition of the Church, in her proclamation of doctrine and her liturgical praxis, and in the sense of faith (*sensus fidei*) of the people of God. The community (i.e., *koinonia* or *communio*) is the ecclesial unity of the faithful in faith, hope, and love, and in word, sacrament, and life. The breaking of bread (Luke 24:30) and the Lord's Supper/table of the Lord (1 Cor 10:14–22; 11:17–34) are early expressions meaning the same thing, namely, what is later called the Sacrament of the Altar, the Divine Liturgy, or Holy Mass. When we think of common prayer, we think first of the Lord's Prayer, which Jesus taught to his disciples (Matt 6:9–15; Luke 11:2–4; Mark 11:25).[111] It is the basic Christian prayer and the pattern and model for all our praying and calling out to God, our heavenly Father: "Abba, Father" (Rom 8:15; Gal 4:6) through Jesus Christ, the incarnate Son of God, in the Holy Spirit, who has been poured into our hearts (Rom 5:5).

---

[108] Gerhard Ludwig Müller, *Iglesia. Pobre y para los Pobres. Con escritos de Gustavo Gutiérrez y de Josef Sayer* (Madrid, 2014).

[109] Vatican II, *Lumen Gentium,* §10.

[110] Paul Babin, *Le Sacerdoce Royal des Fidèles dans la Tradition ancienne et modern* (Paris, 1950); Christoph Binninger, "*Ihr seid ein auserwähltes Geschlecht." Berufen zum Aufbau des Gottesreiches unter den Menschen. Die Laienfrage in der katholischen Diskussion in Deutschland um 1800 bis zur Enzyklika „Mystici corporis"* (St. Ottilien, 2002).

[111] Heinz Schürmann, *Das Gebet des Herrn* (Freiburg, 1981).

The goal of proclamation is at all times the living encounter with Jesus Christ. Because he is the Word of God made flesh, the Son of the eternal Father made man, Jesus is, as our Creator and Redeemer, the only way to the Father, to communion in the Triune Godhead, the origin and goal of all humanity. Christ is the revealed meaning of our life and the whole history of the world. He reveals himself as the Son of God, thus also revealing the mystery of his Person and his mission as Savior of the world, when he says to the disciples, "I am the way, and the truth, and the life. No one comes to the Father except through me" (John 14:6).

The popes of recent times have issued frequent and insistent calls for a re-evangelization of the countries with an ancient Christian culture.[112] This can also be applied to those countries that have had a deep Christian culture for five hundred years. The poor churches outside the prosperous zones in Europe, North America, and large parts of Asia are not located on the periphery of God's attention. Christ is the ground and center of every human being, no matter where and under what circumstances they live. Every local church forms a significant part of the history of the universal Church. Mission does not mean indoctrination and manipulation of consciences. The mission that comes from Christ is a mandate which calls on his messengers to promote the real-life encounter of every human being with Christ in the community of believers. Being human becomes theocentric and Christological in personal acts of faith, hope, and love, and it is humanized in the cardinal virtues of prudence, justice, fortitude, and temperance (*temperantia*). Being a Christian proves itself and matures in the corporal and spiritual works of mercy. Then, at the Last Judgment, the righteous enter into eternal life and hear Jesus's words: "Truly I tell you, just as you did it to one of the least of these my brothers, you did it to me" (Matt 25:40, 46).

Being a Christian does not lie either in the will to preserve external stocks of tradition, or in a cozy accommodation to changing intellectual and political fashions. The Church is not a civil religion. For no matter how often people allow themselves to be seduced by self-proclaimed saviors, experience teaches us the irrefutable truth that human beings and human products—such as science, technology, economics and monetary systems, forms, and styles of government—cannot answer or solve the existential challenges we face. God alone, who addresses us directly in his Word, in Christ, is the solution to the riddle that man is to himself. Notwithstanding the most profound ideas of intellectual history, grand narratives of history and sociological analyses, and

---

[112] Georg Schwaiger, *Papsttum und Päpste im 20. Jahrhundert. Von Leo XIII. Zu Johannes Paul II* (Munich, 1999).

the subtlest hermeneutics and critiques of knowledge, every individual is still left alone in his or her distress with the naked fundamental questions: "What is man? What is the meaning of sorrow, of evil, of death? . . . What can man offer to society, what can he expect from it? What follows this earthly life?"[113]

Here, where no third thing remains between life and death, the Catholic Church professes her belief in the dignity and mystery of man, which is illuminated in the light of Christ:

> The Church firmly believes that Christ, who died and was raised up for all, can through his Spirit offer man the light and the strength to measure up to his supreme destiny. Nor has any other name under the heaven been given to man by which it is fitting for him to be saved. She likewise holds that in her most benign Lord and Master can be found the key, the focal point, and the goal of man, as well as of all human history.[114]

Trusting in him, following Jesus, and becoming like him in life and in death—this is the Christian's elucidation of existence and overcoming of contingency from the word of God and the power of his grace. Faith is at the same time the gift of the Spirit from above, the knowledge of God infused into our understanding, the free surrender of the whole person to God, and willing collaboration in the building and growth of the kingdom of God in this world-time. God is not a partial truth of this world. He is the first and universal truth himself, which puts into perspective all the particular truths and secondary causes of the insights of natural reason in philosophy and science. God's love is not like a tiny ray of the sunshine in a cold corner but rather the source of light and warmth that fills our whole heart. Christ is the true light that enlightens every human being. But to all who receive him he gives power to become children of God (cf. John 1:9, 12).

As in every age, today, too, there are will-o'-the-wisps trying to lure us with false lights into the mire of relativism and materialism. There should, they say, be no truth at all that lays claim to us and imposes an objective yardstick on us, for man is only free when everyone maintains their own truth and lets others have theirs. This would be true if there were no transcendence of truth and man alone were man's light and redeemer. But God, who does not *have* truths and offer them to us but who *is* truth, frees mankind from the dungeon

---

[113] Vatican II, *Gaudium et Spes*, §10.

[114] Vatican II, *Gaudium et Spes*, §10.

of egocentricity. His creatures, endowed as they are with spirit and will, are not enslaved in the idolatry of the lords of this world.

Polytheism and atheism offer many paths that lead round and round in the circle of immanence, without any prospect of escaping the labyrinth. But they fail to find the one way that leads from God to man with the divine nature of Christ, and guides human beings to God with the human nature of Christ, for, as Jesus says, "No one comes to the Father except through me" (John 14:6).

Money makes the world go round, says a proverb, expressing a bitter and blood-stained truth. But it is equally true that money has always done a bad job of this. It is true what Paul wrote to his co-worker and successor Timothy: "For the love of money is a root of all kinds of evil, and in their eagerness to be rich some have wandered away from the faith and pierced themselves with many pains" (1 Tim 6:10). The gifts of the earth are plentiful and there for all. The luxurious life of a few at the expense of others; corruption as shameless self-enrichment; lack of respect for the dignity of one's own body, which is a temple of the Holy Spirit; and lack of respect for the physical, mental, and spiritual dignity of children, young people and adults—all these evils and vices come from greed, from the love of money, which is the root of all evil. This demon of cupidity and thinking only of ourselves can only be driven from our hearts by the spirit of Christ's love.

Jesus Christ is the straight path through time and the only door into the eternity of truth and freedom. Christ is not an authoritarian character who enslaves people under the pretext of caring for them. He is our friend, our Savior and liberator from the omnipotence of totalitarian mainstreaming and the deep-seated fear of being ostracized if we do not conform. The false illusion of an inner-worldly salvation, and the spurious hope of an earthly paradise in the all-providing totalitarian surveillance state, also seduce Christians into giving up their "birthright" as God's children for the "mess of pottage" (Gen 25:34) of transient needs and pleasures.

The light of faith in the living God, the Creator of heaven and earth, and in Jesus Christ his Son, our Lord and God, and in the Holy Spirit, the Spirit of truth and love, dispels the eclipse of God in our thought and action. The light of faith gives the warmth of the genuine love of God and neighbor to hearts that are numb with cold. Christ, the "sun of righteousness" (Mal 4:2) rips open the cloud cover that shrouds our future.

The inward and outward mission of the Church, in both past and future, is not futile and never was. In his first encyclical, Pope Francis spoke of the light of the Gospel that belongs to faith:

There is an urgent need, then, to see once again that faith is a light, for once the flame of faith dies out, all other lights begin to dim. The light of faith is unique, since it is capable of illuminating *every aspect* of human existence. A light this powerful cannot come from ourselves but from a more primordial source: in a word, it must come from God. Faith is born of an encounter with the living God who calls us and reveals his love, a love which precedes us and upon which we can lean for security and for building our lives. Transformed by this love, we gain fresh vision, new eyes to see; we realize that it contains a great promise of fulfillment, and that a vision of the future opens up before us.[115]

The crucial question for humanity: is Jesus really the Son of God?

"Long ago God spoke to our ancestors in many and various ways by the prophets, but in these last days he has spoken to us by a Son" (Heb 1:1–2).

All Christianity, in doctrine and life, hangs on a single question: Is Jesus really the Son of the eternal God who took on our humanity, spoke to us in a human way, and irreversibly changed our destiny for the better through his death and Resurrection?

Even within the Church, it has been and still is a matter of dispute whether Christ is the Son of God and, hence, whether this Sonship is grounded in the divine Trinity. The main proponent of liberal Protestant theology, Adolf von Harnack (1851–1930), reduced Christianity to trust in the fatherly God and the infinite value of the human soul, stating in his lectures on *The Essence of Christianity* (1899): "Not the Son, but the Father alone belongs in the Gospel as Jesus proclaimed it."[116]

He maintains that, even though Jesus did indeed have a uniquely intimate consciousness of God and had become in his Person the model of pure love of God and neighbor, it was only under the influence of the Hellenistic thinking of the Church Fathers that he rose substantially to the rank of equality with God.[117] In this way, as in the case of Hans Küng, the Christian faith becomes a cultural phenomenon which, with the religious ferment of ideal Christianity, manages to take the lead in the development of humanity.[118] However,

---

[115] Pope Francis, *Lumen Fidei*, §4.

[116] Adolf von Harnack, *Das Wesen des Christentums*, lect. 8, 1 (Munich, 1964), 92.

[117] Gunther Wenz, *Der Kulturprotestant. Adolf von Harnack als Christentumstheoretiker und Kontroverstheologe* (Munich, 2001).

[118] On the debate within Catholicism, cf. Peter Seewald, *Benedikt XVI. Ein Leben* (Munich, 2020), 552.

it is completely mistaken to use, of all things, the content of the Gospel of God's grace as a basis for reducing historical Christianity to a stimulant for the kind of ennobled humanity anticipated by bourgeois believers in progress or socialist-revolutionary notions of creating paradise on earth. There are neither empirical nor transcendental-philosophical grounds for the possibility of man's self-redemption. God alone is man's Creator and Redeemer, which is exactly why all man's spiritual and moral powers are only released to allow him to help bring about the coming of God's kingdom in this world and in the world to come.

In the European tradition, doubts about the divinity of Christ, as it is understood in the Catholic Creed, essentially go back to the variant of Enlightenment philosophy that rejected the idea of a supernatural self-revelation on the part of God in the history of Israel and in the historical individual humanity of Jesus of Nazareth. This meant that there was nothing left in a natural religion that could be taken over into a state-controlled civil religion except the elements of morality. Kant's reduction of Jesus to a moral preacher, or as symbolizing "the ideal of the Son of God which is set up before us as our model" for morality,[119] follows the pattern already established by the pagan philosopher Celsus in his work *Alethes logos* (ca. AD 176–180).[120]

If the Neoplatonic concept of God as an idea, rather than as a Person, is taken as a basis, talk of the Incarnation of the Word of the living God is illogical, offensive, or ridiculous. Nor can this God conceived of as the first principle or mover intervene by his own free action in the course of the cosmos or in the mechanistically constructed mathematical-logical laws according to which it runs. In a conception of reality that is determined by the coordinates of a deistic-pantheistic image of God and a mechanistic image of the world, there can be a priori neither a self-revelation of God in the Word, nor his becoming flesh, nor a self-testimony of the divinity of Christ in his powerful miracles and his glorious Resurrection from the dead.

Jean-Baptiste le Rond d'Alembert (1717–1783), an enlightened free thinker and famous editor of the *Encyclopédie*, enthused in a letter of November 30, 1770, to his friend King Frederick II of Prussia (1712–1786) about "a Christianity without dogmas, church fathers and councils, just as Jesus wanted it, as spiritual worship of God and noble humanity."[121]

In a cosmic course determined once and for all by divine wisdom, there is no room for a free and spontaneous encounter of God with man in the

---

[119] Immanuel Kant, *Die Religion innerhalb der Grenzen der blossen Vernunft* (B 76): *Werke in zehn Bänden 7*, ed. W. Weischedel (Darmstadt, 1968), 714.
[120] Cf. Origen, *Contra Celsum* (= FC 50/1–5) (Freiburg, 2011–2012).
[121] Johannes Hirschberger, *Geschichte der Philosophie II* (Freiburg, 1965), 249.

world and in history. The same Prussian king was a great friend of Voltaire (1694–1778), who categorically denied the deity of Christ and, along with the Socinians, Jews, Muslims, etc., considered the idea of a God-man "monstrous."[122] Frederick himself regarded the doctrine of the vicarious suffering of the Son of God as having been exposed as a mere work of man, because it does not befit God's greatness that his Son should become a man and sacrifice himself on the Cross in order to save the corrupt human race, even though the world obviously continues in its wickedness and unredeemed state as if nothing world-shattering had happened. "Only limited and narrow minds dare to ascribe to God a conduct so unworthy of his adorable providence and make him undertake through one of the greatest miracles a work that is nevertheless unsuccessful."[123]

Spinoza, Voltaire, Lessing, and Rousseau, and later Comte, Feuerbach, Marx, and Freud all saw themselves confirmed in their rejection of Christ's divinity by the literary-critical interpretations of the Bible that emerged with the rise of historical thinking and for which, incidentally, the Catholic priest-scholar Richard Simon was the inspiration.[124] Such interpretations claim Christology is, ultimately, no more than a transfer of socially and culturally conditioned thought patterns and experiential categories onto a personality who is historically difficult to grasp. It comes down to the same thing whether it subjectively impressed the first witnesses and their followers without their critically reflecting on the cause of their projections, or whether the disciples falsified the figure of Jesus in crude self-interest, a view advanced by Hermann Samuel Reimarus (1694–1768) and the anonymous treatise *De tribus impostoribus*.[125]

The task of historical criticism seems little more than the deconstruction of a construct of ideas and feelings held by the disciples and the early Church. But historical criticism can also be applied to the biblical and early-Christian sources to work out the true humanity of Jesus and the human circumstances of the testimony about him. This is precisely how it is possible in revealed faith to cognize the mystery of the Person and history of Jesus, a mystery that is grounded in God.

---

[122] Voltaire, *Art. Divinité de Jésus*; id. *Dictionnaire philosophique* (1761) (Paris, 1331), 454–551.

[123] Quoted in German from Ernst Walter Zeeden, *Martin Luther und die Reformation im Urteil des deutschen Luthertums I* (Freiburg, 1950), 300.

[124] Sacha Müller, *Richard Simon (1638–1712). Exeget, Theologe, Philosoph und Historiker. Eine Biographie* (Würzburg, 2005); Müller, *Kritik und Theologie. Christliche Glaubens- und Schrifthermeneutik nach Richard Simon* (St. Ottilien, 2002).

[125] Cf. Henning Graf Reventlov, *Epochen der Bibelauslegung*, 4 vols. (Munich, 1990–2001).

An inexperienced ski jumper will come to grief taking off from a high ramp, whereas it enables the professional to lift off and fly high above the precipitous slope to land safely at the bottom of it. Those who, in the light of reason enlightened by the Spirit (1 Cor 12:3; Rom 12:1 [*rationabile obsequium*]), truly believe in God's Incarnation are by no means disquieted by knowing the human conditions and circumstances of Jesus's message but instead find themselves actually confirmed in their approval of Jesus, the Son of God and Savior of the world. They will encounter God in following the Crucified and Risen Lord. In rationalism, which a priori considers a supernatural revelation unlikely and anyway unknowable to us, what remains is, at most, an existential interpretation of the biblical message of God's saving action in Christ, which has to be salvaged from the by-products of being clothed in the mythology of an obsolete worldview.[126]

It is, of course, true that the worldview and historical context at the time of Jesus and the early Church do not belong to divine Revelation. But whether a woman knows the biological processes of embryonic development professionally as a biologist, or from reading about them as general knowledge, or has no idea about them at all, the miracle of the mother-child relationship cannot be rationalized away because it is irreducibly (*unhintergehbar*) grounded in the mystery of love. Similarly, a weltanschauung cannot be the measure and criterion of the faith that is a participation in the cognition through which God knows himself and makes himself known: "no one knows who the Son is except the Father, or who the Father is except the Son and anyone to whom the Son chooses to reveal him" (Luke 10:22).

After ideological and political atheism, with its pride in reason, had been set on a brutally aggressive collision course with the Christian faith community for the past three centuries, Umberto Eco (1932–2016) recently tried to do the same with candyfloss in his tale of a "son of God" made man that focuses not on his challenging truth but rather on the enchanting beauty of its illusion. Our meta-poet puts himself in the role of a space traveler from another galaxy, who makes a stopover here on earth. Evidently, the stranger shares with the human species of the earthlings the insight that the existence of a thinking being, who is aware of the randomness of its being thrown into the contingent world, is like a mortal wound that cannot be healed but can be anaesthetized with essential oils. The long-distance traveler would, so Eco thinks, realize that he has unexpectedly fallen among a "miserable and vile race," but he would admire its "theogonic energy," i.e., its god-birthing imagination with

---

[126] Rudolf Bultmann, *Neues Testament und Mythologie. Das Problem der Entmythologisierung der neutestamentlichen Verkündigung* (1941) (Munich, 1985).

which it has succeeded, in a poetic flight of fancy, in "conceiving the model of the Christ, the model of universal love, of forgiveness for enemies and of life sacrificed to save someone else."[127] He would think the Incarnation of God and the redemption of lost man from the world's injustice and hopelessness of existing without meaning to be merely figments of human imagination, bereft of rhyme or reason.

Eco's parable is beguilingly circular, because it is not correct at the beginning and does not add up at the end. Even his space tourist is not allowed simply to pretend to be stupid. For if he passes moral judgment on people's behavior and finds their stories true or beautiful, then he shares with them a spiritual nature. A spiritual being, who necessarily asks about the origin and goal of being as the uncaused principle of the material and moral world, cannot ascribe his existence to non-existent metaphysical chance; nor can he endure the abysmal wickedness of the world without the prospect of a supernatural justice. Umberto Eco's story is too beautiful to be true. The story of God saving the world is only beautiful if and because it is true.

A more weighty objection to the possibility of distinguishing between a real word of God to us and an imagined revelation is that raised by Immanuel Kant. "For if God should really speak to man, man could still never *know* that it was God speaking. It is quite impossible for man to apprehend the infinite by his senses, distinguish it from sensible beings, and *recognize* it as such."[128] He maintains that any claimed revelation can only be exposed negatively as a deception if it contradicts the moral law. However, faith cannot be transformed into knowledge, which, according to Kant's epistemology, is only phenomenal and admits God only as a speculative idea of pure reason. Kant was a concrete inhabitant of Königsberg who really existed and not a phenomenon and mere object of the cognition of someone else's mind. He encountered his contemporaries as the subject of his reason and freedom in the unfathomable depth of the mystery of his Person. Even as an epoch-making epistemologist, he was unable to grasp the unity of the "two sources [*Stämme*] of our knowledge (which probably spring from a common, but to us unknown root), namely, sense and understanding."[129]

[127] Umberto Eco, *Wenn der andere ins Spiel kommt, beginnt die Ethik. Carlo M. Martini and Umberto Eco, Woran glaubt, wer nicht glaubt?* (Vienna, 1998), 83–93, at 92. See "When the Other Appears on the Scene," http://www.crosscurrents.org/ocofolloa.htm

[128] Immanuel Kant, *Der Streit der Fakultäten* (1798) A 102; Eng.: *The Conflict of the Faculties*, trans. Mary J. Gregor (New York: Abaris, 1979), 143, https://dokumen.tips/documents/immanuel-kant-the-conflict-of-the-faculties.html?page=4.

[129] Immanuel Kant, *Kritik der reinen Vernunft* (1787) B 30; Eng.: *The Critique of Pure Reason*, trans. J. M. D. Meiklejohn (Project Gutenburg, 2003), https://www.gutenberg.org/files/4280/4280-h/4280-h.htm.

Although intellectual communication in language presupposes the sound of the voice, the intended meaning that is grasped in my mind can nevertheless also be translated into another language system. The words of language are not merely sounds that elicit in us signals of joy at having found food, anger at predators, fear of danger, or warning of enemies. They are signs that convey an intellectual content and thus enable communication within the horizon of the meaning of being. In every individual cognition, the whole of the cognizable is always implicitly cognized as well. Only within the infinite horizon of being can that which concretely is, be recognized as being and as a concrete individual.

Language is undoubtedly "the house of Being in which man exists by dwelling, in that he belongs to the truth of Being, guarding it,"[130] but certainly not its prison, where I would have to saw in vain at the bars of my cell. Language dwells beneath the canopy of an *open* sky. Not only receptive cognition takes place in language; on the productive side, there is also a consummation of the freedom that wants and is able to communicate itself.

What do I do when I give a theological lecture not in my mother tongue but in a foreign language? I can make the essence of what I want to say understood, even if not all the nuances come across to the listener. My nationally formed tongue can set no absolute limit to my will to communicate. In God, the will to communicate in words is fulfilled by the Holy Spirit, who causes the word of God which is spoken and speaks in Christ to reach our inner ear. An educated Italian will recognize me as a German not only by my accent but also by the German educational canon that comes through unmistakably, in spite of all my references to international literature. Even though he might greet these circumstances that limit and define me with an ironic smile, speaker and listener will nevertheless achieve a level of intellectual exchange and understanding that constitutes a unity of the cognizer and the cognized in cognition. Thus, through the Holy Spirit, a common understanding of the word of God is possible and real in the variety of languages of the one Catholic Church and in her Creed.

I have no difficulty reading the interpretation of Kant by the philosopher Marcello Pera in his book *Critica della Ragione secolare. La modernità e il cristianesimo di Kant* (Critique of Secular Reason: Kant's Modernity and Christianity)[131] in Italian, grasping its content, and even judging it on the basis of my reading in German of Immanuel Kant's work on the philosophy of religion, *Die Religion innerhalb der Grenzen der blossen Vernunft* (Religion within

---

[130] Martin Heidegger, *Über den Humanismus* (1949) (Frankfurt a.M., 1975), 22, http://timothyquigley.net/cont/heidegger-lh.pdf.

[131] Marcello Pera, *Critica della Ragione secolare. La modernità e il cristianesimo di Kant* (Florence, 2019).

the Bounds of Bare Reason) (1793), and then discussing it with him in public. But in music, too, people of different languages understand each other, even if they do not understand the language of the composer or the composer has long since died. People also understand the message of paintings and buildings, even if they have never seen the artists or architects, or do not even know their names. And archaeologists can decipher from their findings not only the practical living conditions of people who belong to vanished civilizations but also their knowledge of the world and their ways coping with contingency.

If God created the world through his Word and everything that has come into being exists through his divine intellect and, insofar as it has being, is therefore intelligible in itself, then God can also make himself known to the human mind of his prophets in his word of being (*Wesens-Wort*): by elevating human reason's natural power of comprehension through the illumination of the Holy Spirit and bringing it into line with the divine intellect. He shapes the content of his communication through the system of concepts and categories in the Hebrew or Greek language, which he employs in the minds and powers of the prophets' expressions. This produces in them the mental cognitive image through which they grasp the word that he wants to communicate to them, and pass on orally or in writing to the people of God. When—analogous to the creation of the world in the Word and Spirit (Gen 1:2–3), and God breathing life into man, who was formed from the dust of the ground (Gen 2:7)—the Spirit of God was in the last days "poured out upon all flesh" (Acts 2:17), the Church was formed into a community of many languages and cultures by the Spirit of the Father and the Son. "All of them were filled with the Holy Spirit and began to speak in other languages, as the Spirit gave them ability" (Acts 2:4). In the individual languages, it is the one language of the Spirit and of love, that of the Holy Spirit as the bond uniting Father and Son in the Trinity, that brings together the diversity of cultures to complement and enrich one another, and prevents the division of humanity into imperialistic and expansionist nations. Hence the faithful are of one mind: "Now the whole group of those who believed were of one heart and soul" (Acts 4:32).

The highly diverse language groups gathered for the feast of Pentecost in Jerusalem, the historical origin of the visible Church, asked in amazement: "[H]ow is it that we hear, each of us, in our own native language?" (Acts 2:8). The answer is quite simple: because the Holy Spirit is the interpreter who, from the absolute meta-level of the divine Word, guarantees the complete accuracy of the simultaneous translation (John 14:26). "When the Spirit of truth comes, he will guide you into all the truth; for he will not speak on his own, but will speak whatever he hears, and he will declare to you the things that are to come" (John 16:13). After the universal outpouring of the Holy Spirit on all mankind, the many nations could say of the apostles, "in our own languages we hear them speaking about God's deeds of power" (Acts 2:11). After many were won for Christ through Peter's preaching, baptized in his name for the forgiveness of sins, and received the Holy Spirit individually (Acts 2:38), all who believed "had all things in common" (Acts 2:44).

God does not want to spare us the trouble of using experience and reason to help us recognize the created world and ourselves in our physical, historical, and social form of existence as part of the cosmos. Knowledge of the world through natural reason (*lumen naturale*), including knowledge of God's existence (cf. Rom 1:19–20), is essentially different from the knowledge communicated through the grace of God and his transcendental and universal relation to creation which gives the world its being (*lumen fidei*).

In the historical revelation of the word, God communicates himself to human beings as the content and goal of their search for truth and their desire for eternal happiness and a blessed life in God.[132] Jesus, the Son of God, "who is close to the Father's heart, who has made him known" (John 1:18), reveals to his disciples: "The words I have spoken to you are spirit and life" (John 6:63). The communication of his truth becomes self-communication when the Word who is God subsists in the human nature of Jesus or lived as the concrete, historical man Jesus of Nazareth in the time of the Roman emperors Augustus and Tiberius, and was crucified under Pontius Pilate. Jesus is the identity of the one Word of God with the many words of his human communication (hypostatic union). "You have the words of eternal life" (John 6:68), Peter says to the "Word [who] became flesh and lived among us" (John 1:14). He is the "word of life," and "we declare to you what was from the beginning, what we have heard, what we have seen with our eyes, what we have looked at and touched with our hands, concerning the word of life" (1 John 1:1).

Although there is a continuity of historical revelation from the prophets of Israel to Jesus, the absolute novelty of Jesus's mission cannot be ignored. It is not just that God spoke through him. He *is* the Word, who became flesh and dwelt among us.

To believe in Jesus, the Son of God and Savior of the world, does not mean recognizing God's outward "will to command" (*Gebotswille*) but rather recognizing God himself in his Word and Spirit (his will to be [*Wesenswille*]). To be sure, by way of clarification as against voluntarism, God's temporal will to command has its rational, Logos-like ground in his eternal will to being.

Faith is more than just trusting in God. Faith, even already in the hiddenness of the pilgrim state, is participation in the mutual knowledge of the

---

[132] Wilhelm Korff, *Wie kann der Mensch glücken? Perspektiven der Ethik* (Munich, 1985).

70

Father and the Son in the Holy Spirit, and thus the elevation of our being, thinking, and acting to God's level, and the foundation of unity with him. For we are "called children of God; and that is what we are" (1 John 3:1). Christ's Sonship of God is faithfully confessed by the Church, speaking in the person of St. Peter, based on the revelation by the heavenly Father (Matt 16:16). It is preceded by Jesus's self-revelation as "the Father's Son" (2 John 3): "All things have been handed over to me by my Father; and no one knows the Son except the Father, and no one knows the Father except the Son and anyone to whom the Son chooses to reveal him" (Matt 11:27; cf. Luke 10:22).

It is obvious that this is not a question of insight into a set of facts, e.g., the structure and mode of operation of matter, the course of human history, the social interactions in society; rather, it is about the consciousness permeating the divine Persons in the love that knows and wills itself and which "the only true God" (John 17:3) is himself in his essence and life (1 John 4:8, 16). Jesus's disciples are drawn into the divine inner life through faith and love, and they are permeated and carried by it in their spirit, reason, and will. It is only in this way that we can understand Jesus's words to the Father at the end of his high priestly prayer before his Passion: "I made your name known to them, and I will make it known, so that the love with which you have loved me may be in them, and I in them" (John 17:26).

In the hypostatic—i.e., personal—union of the divine and human natures of Christ in the Person of the divine Word, the gap is bridged between "accidental truths of history and necessary truths of reason." This is what Gotthold Ephraim Lessing (1729–1781), the eminent representative of German Enlightenment philosophy and great representative of German literature, despaired of being able to do: "That, then, is the ugly broad ditch which I cannot get across, however often and however earnestly I have tried to make the leap. If anyone can help me over it, let him do it, I beg him, I adjure him. He will deserve a divine reward from me."[133]

Quite immodestly, I would like to wish myself such a reward with my deliberations on how to make "reasonable worship" of God (Rom 12:1) comprehensible to my contemporaries at the beginning of the twenty-first century. For we believers in Christ should always be ready to communicate the rational reasons for our hope in the God of Jesus Christ to anyone who asks (cf. 1 Pet 3:15). For faith presupposes reason, elevates it, and perfects it in the revealed knowledge of God.[134] Faith never requires a negation of our natural knowledge

---

[133] Gotthold E. Lessing, *Über den Beweis des Geistes und der Kraft* (1777): *Lessings Werke III*, ed. K. Wölfel (Frankfurt a.M., 1967), 311; Eng.: *On The Proof of the Spirit and of Power* (London: A. and C. Black, 1956), https://faculty.tcu.edu/grant/hhit/Lessing.pdf.

[134] Michael J. Marmann, *Praembula ad gratiam. Ideengeschichtliche Untersuchung über die Entstehung des Axioms gratia praesupponit naturam*, Beau Bassin and Mauritius, 2018.

(a *sacrificium intellectus*)—at most it requires a more differentiated hermeneutics of the relationship between natural (in principle falsifiable) knowledge of the world and supernatural (infallible) knowledge of God, which is grounded in the basically infallible reason, i.e., logos, of God.

The tensions are basically insurmountable between, on the one hand, revealed religion as it was conceived among the philosophers and natural philosophers of antiquity and the Middle Ages and, on the other hand—since Copernicus, Galileo, Kepler, Newton, and Darwin in the context of dualistic or monistic system philosophy (rationalism-idealism, empiricism-materialism)— the New Science with its mathematical method (*more geometrico*). But any approach to the philosophy of religion must come to realize that man is a possible hearer of a self-revelation by God that has actually taken place in history. According to one of the great theologians of the twentieth century, Karl Rahner (1904–1984), man is a *hearer of the word*.[135]

Then it also becomes clear that the Christ of dogma and the Jesus of history are the same Person, and that only to the dualistically squinting eyes of naturalists or supernaturalists did the Son of God and the Son of the human being Mary suddenly appear to be two individuals.

But the Fathers of the Council of Chalcedon (AD 451)

> unanimously teach to confess one and the same Son, our Lord Jesus Christ, the same is perfect in divinity and perfect in humanity, the same truly God and truly man composed of rational soul and body, the same one in being with the Father as to the divinity and one in being with us as to the humanity, like unto us in all things but sin (cf. Heb 4:15). The same was begotten from the Father before the ages as to the divinity and in the latter days for us and for our salvation was born as to his humanity from Mary the Virgin and Mother of God.[136]

The incarnational reality of God's self-revelation in the spatio-temporal continuum of humanity's being-in-the-world is part of its content; and this cannot be de-fleshed until all that is left is either a bloodless idea or the tragic or heroic existential of a psychodrama. The image of the world and history is undoubtedly itself subject to constant change and has as its carrier only the finite, error-prone reason of the individual human being in his or her own way of viewing it. Faith, however, owes itself to the illumination of the Holy

---

[135] Karl Rahner, *Hörer des Wortes. Zur Grundlegung einer Religionsphilosophie* (1941) (= SW 4) (Freiburg, 1997), 2–281.
[136] DH 301.

Spirit, through which we come to the rational judgment of the act of faith and voluntary assent to God: this man Jesus does not subsist in the will to create (*Schöpfungswille*), whereby God establishes a relationship to his creature which constitutes the human person; rather, he exists in the consubstantial Person-Word, which is the Triune God in the relationship of the Son to the Father in the Holy Spirit.

Belief in Jesus does not begin nominalistically with deliberations on the possibility and conceivability of revelation, or on the question of whether an Incarnation of God can be reconciled with an a priori idea of God. On no account can we set ourselves up as the guardians of God's majesty, thinking we must protect it from the filth and nausea of matter:

> Has not God made foolish the wisdom of the world? For since, in the wisdom of God, the world did not know God through wisdom, God decided, through the foolishness of our proclamation, to save those who believe. For Jews demand signs and Greeks desire wisdom, but we proclaim Christ crucified, a stumbling-block to Jews and foolishness to Gentiles, but to those who are the called, both Jews and Greeks, Christ the power of God and the wisdom of God. (1 Cor 1:20–24)

In reality, faith results from the historically contingent encounter with the historical man Jesus of Nazareth, and it cannot be derived from the thinking of finite human reason. This Jesus stands within the irreducible (*unhintergehbar*) open horizon of God's self-attestation as Creator of the world and historical liberator of his covenant people of Israel. But even in the natural interpersonal sphere, every human being remains free to open up to another person or to reject that person. No one can be forced by the recognized laws of the mechanical working of nature, or compelled by the rules of psychology, to open his heart to another person and entrust himself completely to that person in love. Much less can all the reasons derived from our knowledge of the world, or from a philosophical or even theological knowledge of God, compel us to open our minds and hearts to God. Let those who are hesitant about making a decision on the whole of their lives, or weary of God's constant wooing of them, be comforted by the tenderness of his invitation: "Listen! I am standing at the door, knocking; if you hear my voice and open the door, I will come in to you and eat with you, and you with me" (Rev 3:20).

The innermost essence of faith is eucharistic (i.e., thanksgiving) love, in which we give ourselves to the infinite love of God. This is the sense in which one must understand the words of the great Blaise Pascal, which are directed against the rationalism of popular philosophy but equally have no desire to encourage irrationalism and fideism: "Le cœur a ses raisons que la raison ne connaît point [the heart has its reasons, of which reason knows nothing]."[137]

What is at issue is the truth of God's historical self-revelation in Jesus Christ. It is not a matter of literary criticism examining the appropriateness of metaphors or fictions of the aesthetic, ethical, existential, and social usefulness of myths, narratives, paradigms, and models. The truth of the Incarnation is the salvation of mankind in time and eternity. Christianity as just one more of the countless different ways of making sense of the senseless would be self-deception. "If for this life only we have hoped in Christ, we are of all people most to be pitied" (1 Cor 15:19).

"Jesus Christ" is the name of the only revolution that deserves to be called one: not just because he made *something* better for the next time but because he made *everything* good and new forever. He is the eschatological and definitive paradigm shift that renders the salvation-mediating faith even of ordinary people independent of reinterpretations, in which theology as the science of faith descends into an ideology of mastery of the world. Christ is "the home of God . . . among mortals" (Rev 21:3; cf. John 1:14). He says, "I am the Alpha and the Omega, the beginning and the end. To the thirsty I will give water as a gift from the spring of the water of life. Those who conquer will inherit these things, and I will be their God and they will be my children" (Rev 21:6–7; cf. Rom 8:14–17; Gal 4:4, 7).

A person does not come to believe in Jesus because a literary reconstruction brings Jesus's personality to life virtually in the consciousness of one who reads the Bible or exegetical commentaries. The Risen Lord lives in God and not as a phantasm in the transient consciousness of a mortal man. As the Word made flesh, Jesus himself is the Father's exegete, who "has made him known" (John 1:18). His life and death are the event and the historical presence of God's self-communication in the word and sacrament of the Church as the truth and life of every human being.

The Catholic Church: God's foundation or a global welfare organization?

But how can I, as someone living in the twenty-first century, after all the light and many shadows of the Church's history and in the context of the digitalized culture of a global world society, enter into the faith of the Church in such a way that I do not let her two-thousand-year history weigh on me like a burden and drag me down into the depths of nostalgia and traditionalism

---

137 Pascal, *Pensées*, frag. 277.

but rather allow it to bear me along like a living stream from its source and on into God's eternity?[138]

The place where you encounter Catholic believers is in the Church, which is the addressee of the word of God given in history to his people. In her faith consciousness (*Glaubensbewusstsein*), which remains identical yet grows continuously from generation to generation, she is the witness and conveyer of God's final gift to us. Christ, as her head, is the actual subject of her proclamation, of the celebration of the sacramental means of grace and the apostolic authority of bishops, priests, and deacons. For it is Christ himself who speaks the divine word of salvation to us in the preaching of the apostles (1 Thess 2:13), who baptizes and confirms, and who makes present in the Eucharist his Sacrifice on the Cross as the high priest of the New Covenant. Jesus Christ is "the shepherd and guardian of your souls" (1 Pet 2:25), "the chief shepherd" (1 Pet 5:4), in whose name the bishops/presbyters "tend the flock of God" (1 Pet 5:2), "of which the Holy Spirit has made you overseers, to shepherd the church of God" (Acts 20:28).

The historical Jesus had gathered around him the band of disciples, from whom the post-Easter Church was to emerge. In and for the Church *he* appointed the apostles to share in his messianic consecration and mission, to proclaim his Gospel and collaborate in building up the kingdom of God in this world—with a view to humanity's eternal perfection upon his return at the end of time. Through the Great Commission, beginning with the preaching of the apostles, Jesus historically constituted the pilgrim Church as the sacrament of salvation for the world. The Church is not a man-made institution for the betterment of the world or the creation of the New Man in the image and likeness of a mortal and sinful man; she is the people of God made one with the unity of the Father, the Son, and the Holy Spirit and united in faith, hope, and love.[139]

The Church is not born of human ideas and utopias—not even those of the holiest and most pious of people—but of God. According to her very nature and meaning, the Church is the body of Christ and the temple of the Holy Spirit; and the faithful are the members of this body and the living building blocks of this temple of God, and are to become so more and more through living lives conformed to Christ. Even though the history of divine Revelation

---

[138] Walter Brandmüller, *Licht und Schatten. Kirchengeschichte zwischen Glaube, Fakten und Legenden* (Augsburg, 2007); Walter Brandmüller and Ingo Langer, *Der Fall Galilei und andere Irrtümer. Macht, Glaube und Wissenschaft* (Augsburg, 2006); Arnold Angenendt, *Toleranz und Gewalt. Das Christentum zwischen Bibel und Schwert* (Münster i.W., 2007); Manfred Lütz, *Der Skandal der Skandale. Die geheime Geschichte des Christentums* (Freiburg, 2018).

[139] Vatican II, *Lumen Gentium*, §4.

reached its focus and climax once and for all in Christ and is therefore con-cluded for evermore, God nevertheless speaks to a twentieth-century Christian just as personally and immediately as to the centurion Cornelius, who became a believer with his whole household in response to Peter's preaching and was baptized in the name of Jesus (Acts 10:48).

The growing distance in time does not distance us from the Person of Christ, who is more present to my consciousness in faith and closer to my heart in love than I can be to myself; and in him we put our hope as the coming Lord.

Thus we are connected vertically and synchronously with the exalted Lord, as well as linked horizontally and diachronically with the historical Jesus in his earthly life in the Holy Land two thousand years ago through the living Tradition of the Church. The means by which the Apostolic Tradition is passed on are the liturgy in the seven sacraments as well as the prayer and teaching community of the Church. Those who received the Holy Spirit in Jerusalem had come to believe in *Jesus the Lord* through "the apostles' teaching" (Acts 2:42). The belief in Jesus, the "Author of life" (Acts 3:15) who is infused by the Holy Spirit, must not be confused with a scientific-theological conception that is subordinate to faith. First comes faith, then theological understanding ("primum credere, deinde theologari; fides quaerens intellectum").

The "apostles' teaching" is nothing less than the word of God in the tes-timony of the early Church, just as the "teaching of the Church" is nothing other than the word of God put into the Creed (dogma). Peter's first sermon at Pentecost already contains the whole of the apostles' teaching, which was merely elaborated later in the Church's rule of faith and Creed. Peter formu-lates its core message in the name of the Church of all times: "Therefore let the entire house of Israel know with certainty that God has made him both Lord and Messiah, this Jesus whom you crucified" (Acts 2:36).

The bishops as their successors are entrusted with the faithful proclama-tion of the apostles' teaching in the "doctrine of the Church," the *depositum fidei* (1 Tim 6:20). However, unlike the apostles, the bishops are not the recipients of revelation and its original witnesses. In them, apostolic authority and apostolic teaching are relatively separate. In terms of content, they rely on the revelation that took place once and for all and its expression in Sacred Scripture in the Apostolic Tradition. Therefore, the bishops have to take their bearings as far as content is concerned from the original testimony of the apostles, which is reproduced in the writings of the New Testament. These, together with the Holy Scriptures of the Old Covenant, make up the one treasure of the word of God that has been entrusted to the Church to pass on.[140]

---

[140] Vatican II, *Dei Verbum*, §10.

The post-Apostolic Tradition is therefore the form in which the word of God is passed on; its content is the word of God in the apostolic witness of Sacred Scripture and Sacred Tradition. The later dogmatic decisions of the popes and the ecumenical councils, or the universally recognized particular synods, do not add anything to the content of divine Revelation and its original testimony in Sacred Scripture and Sacred Tradition. For, as St. John Henry Cardinal Newman said regarding the dogma of Mary's having been conceived without original sin in her mother's womb (1854), "it is a simple fact to say that Catholics have not come to believe it because it is defined, but that it was defined because they believed it."[141] This is clear from an analysis of the act of faith. It is directed towards God as the first and universal truth, who is present in the truths expressed in the individual statements of the Church's Creed. The one truth does not multiply itself into truths but imprints itself on our discursively working finite minds—in the succession and juxtaposition of the cognitive aspects of the one and same truth that is God himself in the multiplicity of the human words of Jesus and, derived from them, also of the Church.

Thus we do not formally believe in the dogmatic proposition, which is only the propositional form of the truth that is believed, while the act of faith is focused on the content and thus on God.[142] However, the act of faith, the only suitable context for which is the ecclesial community of believers, needs to have the identifiably same propositional form to shape a concept in the consciousness that enables us to communicate in the community.

In summary, the Second Vatican Council states the hermeneutics of the Catholic faith, as developed by the earliest Church Fathers against the Gnostics and other heretics:[143]

> Sacred Tradition and Sacred Scripture form one sacred deposit of the word of God, committed to the Church. Holding fast to this deposit the entire holy people united with their shepherds remain always steadfast in the teaching of the apostles, in the common life, in the breaking of the bread, and in prayers (cf. Acts 2:42, Gk), so that holding to, practicing and professing the heritage of the Faith, it becomes on the part of the bishops and faithful a single common effort.
>
> But the task of authentically interpreting the word of God, whether written or handed on, has been entrusted exclusively to the living teaching office of the Church, whose authority is exercised in

---

[141] St. John Henry Newman, *Apologia pro vita sua*, ch. 5, p. 255.

[142] St. Thomas Aquinas, *ST* II-II, q. 1 a. 2, ad 2.

[143] Comprehensively presented in Michael Fiedrowicz, *Theologie der Kirchenväter. Grundlagen frühchristlicher Glaubensreflexion* (Freiburg, 2007).

the name of Jesus Christ. This teaching office is not above the word of God, but serves it, teaching only what has been handed on, listening to it devoutly, guarding it scrupulously, and explaining it faithfully in accord with a divine commission and, with the help of the Holy Spirit, it draws from this one deposit of faith everything which it presents for belief as divinely revealed.

It is clear, therefore, that Sacred Tradition, Sacred Scripture, and the teaching authority of the Church, in accord with God's most wise design, are so linked and joined together that one cannot stand without the others, and that all together and each in its own way under the action of the one Holy Spirit contribute effectively to the salvation of souls.[144]

Christ is the Light of nations. Because this is so, this Sacred Synod gathered together in the Holy Spirit eagerly desires, by proclaiming the Gospel to every creature (cf. Mark 16:15), to bring the light of Christ to all men, a light brightly visible on the countenance of the Church. Since the Church is in Christ like a sacrament, or as a sign and instrument both of a very closely knit union with God and of the unity of the whole human race, it desires now to unfold more fully to the faithful of the Church and to the whole world its own inner nature and universal mission. This it intends to do following faithfully the teaching of previous councils.

The present-day conditions of the world add greater urgency to this work of the Church so that all men, joined more closely today by various social, technical, and cultural ties, might also attain fuller unity in Christ.[145]

This description of the Catholic Church's divine origin, and her central task of connecting all people with God's salvific will (which forms the introduction to Vatican II's Dogmatic Constitution on the Church), will only make sense to those who understand her nature from within. Those who can only understand the Church from the outside as one among many man-made socio-religious organizations will be wary or bored, suspecting that there are few noble interests behind this self-understanding or ascribing such a dogmatic claim to the dreamworld of religious idealists.

But the Church's divine mission stems from the divinity of Christ, who is her head. Since he joins himself to the community of believers as the members

---

[144] Vatican II, *Dei Verbum*, §10.
[145] Vatican II, *Lumen Gentium*, §1.

of our body are joined to each other and form one unit of life from the head, the Church is analogously the body of Christ. The various metaphors used in the New Testament to describe the nature of the Church always express the one and same truth that the multitude of believers are united in Christ: on the one hand, inwardly through faith, hope, and love and, on the other hand, visibly and externally through the Creed, the sacraments, and the community built up by the apostles or their successors as the "body of Christ" (Eph 4:12) and the "temple of the Holy Spirit" (1 Cor 6:19): "There is one body and one Spirit, just as you were called to the one hope of your calling, one Lord, one faith, one baptism, one God and Father of all, who is above all and through all and in all" (Eph 4:4–6).

The Church comes from the historical revelation of God. Man is already created as a communal being and so God redeems us humans inasmuch as we, as the sum of the individuals, form the community but are also carried by it.[146] The people of God who already existed in the Old Covenant is gathered anew by Jesus and transformed into the messianic community of the New Covenant, which he anticipated in the Upper Room and established in his sacrificial death on the Cross. The Church of the New Covenant is open to everyone who accepts faith in Jesus and is baptized in the name of the Father and of the Son and of the Holy Spirit. The Risen Lord appears to the disciples he had gathered as the nucleus of the end-time people of God. Jesus's community of disciples enters world history with the Pentecost event. Now the Church continues Jesus's mission from the Father until the end of the world. In this way, the kingdom of God that Jesus had proclaimed is being continuously turned into a reality. The Church happens as the continual passing on of the word of God and the grace of Christ so that people are redeemed from sin and death and rejoice that they are now called and are sons and daughters of God in Christ. But God also speaks to people personally, coming directly near to them in prayer and conscience, even though they live many hundreds of years after Jesus and the apostles, or thousands of miles away from Palestine. They do not have to content themselves with a CD or a video, on which voices can be heard and the face of the long since deceased can be seen. Christ himself speaks to us through the Church's media. He speaks to us in the assembly of the Church through the medium of the words of Scripture and in the Creed and prayers of the Church. If he is present when just two or three of his disciples are gathered together, then he is certainly so when thousands and millions are gathered in his name (Matt 18:18; 28:20).

---

[146] Vatican II, *Lumen Gentium*, §9.

God himself is the subject and content of the apostolic and ecclesial Tradition (*paradosis; traditio*) of the Gospel of grace.

Therefore Sacred Scripture cannot stand in opposition to the Church as a legally enforceable norm. It is inwardly bound to the community of faith as the soul is to the body:

> Tradition is the living word, perpetuated in the hearts of believers. To this sense, as the general sense, the interpretation of Holy Writ is entrusted. The declaration, which it pronounces on any controverted subject, is the judgment of the Church; and, therefore, the Church is judge in matters of faith [*judex controversiarum*]. Tradition, in the objective sense, is the general Faith of the Church through all ages, manifested by outward historical testimonies; in this sense, Tradition is usually termed the norm; the standard of scriptural interpretation—the rule of faith.[147]

It is obvious that faith as a salvific relationship with God cannot depend on a knowledge of hundreds and hundreds of folios of texts written by the Church Fathers and millions of theological books. It is not this objective Tradition—except, at least in outline, for the episcopal and theological teachers of the faith—that is important for Catholics for their relationship to God and to the Church but rather the subjective Tradition of the supernatural sense of faith (*sensus fidei*) of God's people:

> That discernment in matters of faith is aroused and sustained by the Spirit of truth. It is exercised under the guidance of the sacred teaching authority, in faithful and respectful obedience to which the people of God accepts that which is not just the word of men but truly the word of God (1 Thess 2:13). Through it, the people of God adheres unwaveringly to the Faith given once and for all to the saints (Jude 3), penetrates it more deeply with right thinking, and applies it more fully in its life.[148]

It is precisely because the Church takes her bearings from the Apostolic Tradition that she is protected from any dissipation of the revealed faith, from arbitrary new interpretations, from lapsing into assuming a more mystical and

---

[147] Johann Adam Möhler, *Symbolik*, §38; Eng.: *Symbolism*, trans. J. B. Robertson (New York: E. Dunigan, 1844), 352.

[148] Vatican II, *Lumen Gentium*, §12.

sentimental aura, from the dissolution of dogma into subjectively experienced new contexts of meaning and the existential significances of fictional narratives, or from any inner change in the function of the Catholic Church that would turn her into a politico-religious movement. For the Gospel that the apostles proclaimed to us, and which we accepted in faith, is the foundation on which we stand (1 Cor 15:1). Paul had already stated this in a letter to the Church of God in Corinth, "to those who are sanctified in Christ Jesus, called to be saints" (1 Cor 1:2). He goes on to say that they are also being saved by the Good News he proclaimed to them:

> if you hold firmly to the message that I proclaimed to you, unless you have come to believe in vain. For I *handed on* to you as of first importance what I in turn had *received*: that Christ died for our sins in accordance with the Scriptures, and that he was buried, and that he was raised on the third day in accordance with the Scriptures, and that he appeared to Cephas, then to the twelve. (1 Cor 15:2–5, emphasis added)

This is the Church's primitive confession, which makes visible her origin and enduring original ground (*Anfangs-Grund*) in God's universal-catholic salvific will.[149]

---

[149] Karl Lehmann, *Auferweckt am dritten Tag nach der Schrift. Früheste Christologie, Bekenntnisbildung und Schriftauslegung im Lichte von 1 Kor 15, 3–5* (= QD 38) (Freiburg, 1968).

Chapter 2

CATHOLIC LIFE WITH GOD
IN HIS CHURCH

How does one come to the Catholic faith?

During my time as Bishop of Regensburg, a parish priest visited me one day and asked me to receive a young couple. They were migrants who had managed with great difficulty to escape persecution in their home country. During their visit, they told me about the torture the husband had suffered in prison, and that his pregnant wife had been severely abused in the refugee camp. She lost her child in the process. As both were now preparing for Baptism, I asked them about their motives for wanting to become Catholics. They explained to me that, in the parish where they lived, they had for the first time in their lives met people who did not impose any conditions or ask for anything in return for the generous help they received. People had simply been good to them.

They felt accepted for their own sakes and respected in their human dignity. When trying to find out what motivated this selfless love of neighbor, they had come upon the unconditional love of God that lies at the heart of the Christian faith. The God in whose existence they already believed had revealed himself to them, not as a superior power (*Über-macht*) that arouses fear and demands slavish submission but rather as the omnipotence that is love and affords justice to the humiliated. They had recognized the God whom Jesus made known as his Father, and as whose Son he revealed himself to his disciples in the Holy Spirit (Matt 11:25–30).

Their experience was like that of the seventy-two disciples of Jesus at the beginnings of the Church. When they returned from their mission, they reported *full of joy* that *in the name of Jesus* even the demons were forced to submit to them (see Luke 10:17). In the New Testament, "demons" refers to "the principalities and powers"[1] that weigh us down and make the human spirit swerve from its natural dynamic towards good or incite it to evil. But Jesus directed their rejoicing away from their triumph over evil and towards man's final destiny, fellowship with God, telling them to "rejoice that your names are written in heaven" (Luke 10:20).

At the beginning of the faith (*initium fidei*)[2] that the Holy Spirit awakened in them, these two spouses took the decisive step from a religious and philosophical belief in God, the almighty Creator of the world, to a Christian-supernatural belief in the Triune God.

A Christian is someone who feels the joy of the Holy Spirit, through whom "God's love has been poured into our hearts" (Rom 5:5). Since joy is the direct emanation of the love that is perfect in God, no one who loves God can perish from despair at the nothingness of our existence and all the injustices in a world that is alienated from God.[3]

For this is the basic Christian attitude: "Rejoice in the Lord always; again I will say, Rejoice. Let your gentleness be known to everyone. The Lord is near. . . . And the peace of God, which surpasses all understanding, will guard your hearts and your minds in Christ Jesus" (Phil 4:4–7).[4]

The great mystic and Doctor of the Church St. Teresa of Avila (1515–1582) kept a note in her breviary which was found after her death.[5] On it she wrote a principle that comforts everyone who trusts in God alone:

> *Nada te turbe*
> *Nada te espante,*
> *Todo se pasa,*
> *Dios no se muda,*
> *La paciencia*
> *Todo lo alcanza;*
> *Quien a Dios tiene*
> *Nada le falta:*
> *Sólo Dios basta.*[6]

---

[1] Heinrich Schlier, *Mächte und Gewalten im Neuen Testament* (= QD 3) (Freiburg, 1958).

[2] Second Council of Orange (AD 529), can. 5 (DH 375).

[3] St. Thomas Aquinas, *ST* II-II, q. 28, a. 2.

[4] Kurt Cardinal Koch, *Gottes Freude und Freude an Gott. Perspektiven heutiger Verantwortung* (Freiburg, 2019).

[5] Cf. Theresia von Avila, *Die Seelenburg* (= *Sämtliche Schriften V*) (Munich, 1973), 342.

[6] Santa Teresa de Jesús, *Obras Completas* (= BAC 212) (Madrid, 1986), 667.

Let nothing disturb you,
Let nothing frighten you,
All things pass away:
God never changes.
Patience obtains all things.
He who has God
Finds he lacks nothing;
God alone suffices.

The believer recognizes God because God himself makes himself known to the believer in the eternal unity of Father and Son through and in Jesus of Nazareth, the Messiah, i.e., Christ, of Israel and the *Lord's Anointed* in the Holy Spirit. Mark begins his testimony and confession: "The beginning of the good news [Gospel] of Jesus Christ, the Son of God" (Mark 1:1).

In his own words, Jesus explains to us—at a key point in the Bible—the mystery of the Triune God. God, who through the act of creation is the author of the world and mankind's existence, is the same God who revealed himself in Jesus, his Son:

> At that same hour Jesus rejoiced in the *Holy Spirit* and said, "I thank you, Father, Lord of heaven and earth, because you have hidden these things from the wise and the intelligent and have revealed them to infants; yes, Father, for such was your gracious will. All things have been handed over to me by my Father; and no one knows *who the Son is* except the Father, or *who the Father is* except the Son and anyone to whom the Son chooses to reveal him." (Luke 10:21–22, emphasis added)

> Long ago God spoke to our ancestors in many and various ways by the prophets, but in these last days [eschatologically] he has spoken to us by a Son, whom he appointed heir of all things, through whom he also created the worlds. He is the reflection of God's glory and the exact imprint of God's very being, and he sustains all things by his powerful word. When he had made purification for sins, he sat down at the right hand of the Majesty on high. (Heb 1:1–3)

Here the Church is not professing revealed truth couched in elaborate terminology, as she was forced to do at the first councils when countering the heretical denial of the Trinitarian and Christological mysteries. What is important here is the act of personal faith, which is addressed directly towards God as the first truth. It should never be forgotten that the Church's confession does not emerge from a theoretical construct and cannot therefore be confused with a weltanschauung. Her Creed is essentially a framing in language of the revelation of God in his Son Jesus Christ and in the Holy Spirit, who bring about our salvation. Faith conveys a knowledge of God as the origin of our being and the goal of our longing. Only in this light is the reason of faith capable of a synthesis with our knowledge of the world and history.

Progress in our knowledge of man, society, and nature and the practical application of it in technology, medicine, economics, and ecology is by no means forcing belief in God as the origin and goal of all creation into perpetual retreat, thus rendering it increasingly meaningless, both theoretically and practically:

> For the view is wrong of those who maintain that what we know [with natural reason] of the creature [i.e., our created nature] has nothing to do with the [supernatural] truth of faith.... For error concerning creatures, by subjecting them to causes other than God, spills over into false opinion about God, and takes men's minds away from him, to whom faith seeks to lead them.[7]

Faith does not come from marveling at the world's existence[8] and from our reflection on the first principles of being and the absolute intellect, which in the act of thinking thinks itself, the unmoved mover.[9] Faith comes from the grace of God, who reveals himself to us in the word of Christ (Rom 10:17):

> "The word is near you" ... (that is, the word of faith that we proclaim); because if you confess with your lips that Jesus is Lord and believe in your heart that God raised him from the dead, you will be saved. For one believes with the heart and so is justified, and one confesses with the mouth and so is saved. (Rom 10:8–10)

Well-prepared both catechetically and mystagogically (cf. Heb 6:1–4), the two spouses were now able to descend into the fount of eternal life and be cleansed "with the washing of water by the word" (Eph 5:26), being "buried with him by baptism into death, so that, just as Christ was raised from the dead by the glory of the Father, so [they] too might walk in newness of life" (Rom 6:4).

---

7 St. Thomas Aquinas, *SCG* II, ch. 3.
8 Albert Schirnding, *Am Anfang war das Staunen. Über den Ursprung der Philosophie bei den Griechen* (Munich, 1978).
9 Aristotle, *Metaphysics*, 1005a; 1071b.

At the Easter Vigil, before receiving Baptism, each of the two candidates answered, when asked whether they renounced sin and evil, with a clear "I do," promising to live in the freedom of the children of God and base their whole lives on the love of the gracious and merciful God. For, having become a "new creation" (Gal 6:15) in Christ, every Christian lives by the faith professed at his or her baptism. The bishop then confirms the personal confession with the words:

> *This is our faith. This is the faith of the Church. We are proud to profess it in Christ Jesus our Lord.*

In accordance with Baptism's "in the name of the Father and of the Son and of the Holy Spirit" (Matt 28:19), most versions of the Creed are tripartite-trinitarian.[10] Behind the idea (since Rufinus of Aquileia) that each one of the twelve articles goes directly back to a single apostle lies the conviction that the faith of the present-day Church accurately and completely reflects the original "teaching of the apostles" (Acts 2:42), as it is witnessed in its entirety and undivided by each individual apostle and by the College of Apostles.

The "I" or "We" with which the confession of faith begins is the "I" and "We" of the Church, which is the body of her head, Jesus Christ: "The confession of faith is drawn up in a symbol in the person, as it were, of the whole Church, which is united together by faith [ex persona totius ecclesiae, quae per fidem unitur]."[11]

Thus the candidate for Baptism enters the Church and participates in the faith through which we are saved. Using the Old Roman Baptismal Symbol in the version of the Apostles' Creed,[12] the newly baptized then prays:

> *I* believe in *God,*
> *the Father* Almighty,
> Creator of heaven and earth,
>
> and in *Jesus Christ,* his only *Son,* our Lord,
> who was conceived by the Holy Spirit,
> born of the Virgin Mary,
> suffered under Pontius Pilate,
> was crucified, died, and was buried;

---

[10]   Peter Bruns, *Lexikon der antiken christlichen Literatur* (Freiburg, 1998), 575–77.

[11]   St. Thomas Aquinas, *ST* II-II, q. 1, a. 9, ad 3.

[12]   Cf. (relying on St. Cyril of Jerusalem) the first complete text of the Apostles' Creed in Latin (ca. AD 400) in Rufinus of Aquileia, *Commentarius in Symbolum Apostolorum* (CCL 21).

he descended into hell;
on the third day he rose again from the dead;
he ascended into heaven,
and is seated at the right hand of God the Father Almighty;
from there he will come to judge the living and the dead.

I believe in *the Holy Spirit*,
the Holy *Catholic* Church,
the communion of saints,
the forgiveness of sins,
the resurrection of the body,
and life everlasting. Amen.

Having professed their faith, the two spouses were now baptized into the faith of the Church at the sacred Easter Vigil, in accordance with Jesus's universal commission to the apostles and the whole Church:

All authority in heaven and on earth has been given to me. Go therefore and make disciples of all nations, *baptizing them in the name of the Father and of the Son and of the Holy Spirit*, and teaching them to obey everything that I have commanded you. And remember, I am with you always, to the end of the age. (Matt 28:18–20, emphasis added)

Anyone who is baptized and believes in the Triune God does not just have a *new understanding* of God based in the word of his revelation. The Christian also has a *new relationship* to God, which creatively re-grounds his whole being and definitively changes his life for the better. This also brings a new understanding of our existence in the world and a new constructive and critical relationship to the world.

In a personal relationship from person to person, the baptized individual, as a child and friend of God, relates his or her "I" to the "thou" of God. The innermost part of faith is the "I-thou" relationship to God the Father through Jesus Christ, his Son, in the love of the Holy Spirit. What is more, the person knows and grasps his or her "I" both as naturally constituted by God the Creator and also supernaturally constituted as a *son or daughter* and *friend* of God, their Redeemer and Perfecter. Inserted into the community of disciples, the newly baptized may now say to God, *"Our Father*, who art in heaven." As Jesus, the Son of God, taught his disciples (Matt 6:9–13), so, too, Christians pray daily in "perfect love," which "casts out fear" (1 John 4:18).

Before they receive Holy Communion, the bishop invites the newly baptized and confirmed and the whole worshipping assembly to join in the Lord's Prayer with the words, "At the Savior's command and formed by divine teaching, we dare to say":

Our Father, who art in heaven,
hallowed be thy name;
thy kingdom come,
thy will be done
on earth as it is in heaven.
Give us this day our daily bread,
and forgive us our trespasses,
as we forgive those who trespass against us;
and lead us not into temptation,
but deliver us from evil.

When adults are baptized, they receive Confirmation in the same ceremony, through the bishop or a priest designated to act on his behalf. Following the example of the apostles, the bishop lays his hands on their heads as a sign of clothing them "with power from on high" (Luke 24:49), a strengthening and internalization of their relationship with God in the Holy Spirit (Acts 8:17). But before the bishop lays his hands on the confirmands and anoints their foreheads with the holy chrism, saying, "N., be sealed with the Gift of the Holy Spirit," he asks in the epiclesis for the seven gifts of the Holy Spirit, the Comforter and Helper (John 14:16–17, 26; 16:13–14): "Give them the spirit of wisdom and understanding, the spirit of right judgment and courage, the spirit of knowledge and reverence" (cf. Isa 11:2, LXX). Connected with these are the different and distinct charisms by which the Church of Christ is built up in the Holy Spirit (Rom 12:3–10; 1 Cor 12:4–11; Eph 4:17; 1 Pet 4:10–11). In order to avoid from the outset any aggressive tensions between clergy, religious, and laity, who have all become one body through Baptism, let us recall the words of the apostle: "For as in one body we have many members, and not all the members have the same function, so we, who are many, are one body in Christ, and individually we are members one of another" (Rom 12:4–5).

By fully participating for the first time at the Eucharist, in the sacramental making present of Christ's Sacrifice on the Cross, and thus receiving his Body and Blood as food and drink for eternal life, the newly baptized are now fully incorporated into the one, holy, catholic, and apostolic Church, which we know as the Bride of Christ and our Mother in faith.[13]

In their personal thanksgiving after receiving Holy Communion, everyone can pray individually:

> Thou, Almighty Master, didst create all things for the sake of thy name, and hast given both meat and drink, for men to enjoy, that we might give thanks unto thee, but to us thou hast given spiritual meat and drink, and life everlasting, through thy Son. Amen.[14]

> O sacrum convivium—O sacred banquet!
> in which Christ is received,
> the memory of his Passion is renewed,
> the mind is filled with grace,
> and a pledge of future glory to us is given.[15]

> My Lord and my God, take everything from me that keeps me from you.
> My Lord and my God, give everything to me that brings me near to you.
> My Lord and my God, take me away from myself and give me completely to you.[16]

Being a child of God and a member of the Church are the two inseparable relationships that unite us with God and incorporate us into the community and prayer life of his Church. They are not the same as voluntary membership of a club or state with whose aims I identify myself but which I can also leave.

The third-century martyr-bishop St. Cyprian of Carthage († AD 258) had already impressed on those, who wanted to put together "their" church according to their own taste, that the Catholic Church is not an organization founded by human beings which propagates religious ideas and carries out moral rearmament and social programs in the manner of an NGO; rather, it is "the universal sacrament of salvation"[17] of the world and was founded by Christ. The Church consists in the fellowship of "the one shepherd and the one flock," and is represented "in Christ's seamless robe" (John 19:23), which no one who tears apart the Church of Christ can ever possess. Whoever forsakes

---

[13]   Second Vatican Council, *Lumen Gentium* (1964), §§52–69.

[14]   *Didache* 10.3.

[15]   St. Thomas Aquinas, "Office of Corpus Christi."

[16]   Nicholas of Flüe (1417–1487).

[17]   Vatican II, *Lumen Gentium*, §48; *Gaudium et Spes* (1965), §45.

the Church cannot "attain to the rewards of Christ. . . . *He can no longer have God for his Father, who has not the Church for his mother.*"[18]

And Cyprian calls out to his confreres in the College of Bishops, whose unity begins with St. Peter and the Roman Church:

> And this unity we ought firmly to hold and assert, especially those of us that are bishops who preside in the Church, that we may also prove the episcopate [*episcopatus*] itself to be one and undivided. . . . The Church also is *one*, which is spread abroad far and wide into a multitude [i.e., the particular or local churches] by an increase of fruitfulness.[19]

Bishops are consecrated, i.e., set aside for a sacred task, reflecting that they do not act out of worldly calculations of power and profit like politicians and business managers but are instead appointed by the Holy Spirit to lead the Church of God (Acts 20:28). In the spirit of Christ, "the shepherd and guardian [*episcopos*] of your souls" (1 Pet 2:25), they are to "to tend the flock of God that is in your charge, exercising the oversight, not under compulsion but willingly, as God would have you do it—not for sordid gain but eagerly" (1 Pet 5:2). "Now as an elder myself and a witness of the sufferings of Christ" (1 Pet 5:1), Peter exhorts the bishops and priests, "[d]o not lord it over those in your charge [*in cleris*], but be examples to the flock. And when the chief shepherd appears, you will win the crown of glory that never fades away" (1 Pet 5:3–4). But being a Christian does not mean leading a tranquil life in the religious idyll of the garden of the soul; rather, it is a battle as a follower of Jesus for the truth and righteousness of God. We do not fight against other people for religious-political supremacy but "against the wiles of the devil. For our struggle is not against enemies of blood and flesh, but against the rulers, against the authorities, against the cosmic powers of this present darkness, against the spiritual forces of evil in the heavenly places" (Eph 6:11–12). We have to put on "the whole armour of God" so as to be able to withstand on the evil day, and to do everything and stand firm, we are told to

> fasten the belt of truth around your waist, and put on the breastplate of righteousness. As shoes for your feet put on whatever will make you ready to proclaim the gospel of peace. With all of these, take the

---

[18] St. Cyprian, *De unitate Ecclesiae* 6, emphasis added.

[19] St. Cyprian, *De unitate Ecclesiae* 5.

shield of faith, with which you will be able to quench all the flaming arrows of the evil one. Take the helmet of salvation, and the sword of the Spirit, which is the word of God. (Eph 6:13–17)

The war against the dragon of evil is won by "those who keep the commandments of God and hold the testimony of Jesus" (Rev 12:17).

Whoever is not content with just being entered in the parish's baptismal register but also wants to be, think, and live as a Catholic, must put into practice everything that constitutes being a Christian and its ecclesial mediation. This is concretely present in:

1. The word of God, witnessed in the Sacred Scriptures of the Old and New Testaments and in the Apostolic Tradition, *that is*, "the Word living enduringly in the hearts of the faithful."[20]

2. The Creed and the Ten Commandments, which are summed up in the commandments to love God and neighbor: only that faith justifies which is "made effective through love" (Gal 5:6). It is, of course, the love poured into our hearts by the Holy Spirit (Rom 5:5) that frees the human will from being arrested by sin, thus perfecting in God those justified by faith through fulfilling God's will in his commandments (cf. Rom 13:10). Love of God and love of neighbor are inextricably interlocked in Christ, the God-man, in grace and discipleship (Christian mysticism and ethics) [1 John 4:21]. In the light of the two greatest commandments Jesus proclaimed (Mark 12:29–34), the Ten Commandments (Exod 20:1–17; Deut 5:1–22) are now also to be understood within a belief in the liberating and merciful God (first tablet of the Decalogue), and realized in the Christian life (second tablet of the Decalogue):

I am the LORD your God, who brought you out of the house of bondage.
1. You shall have no other gods before me.
2. You shall not take the name of the LORD your God in vain.
3. Remember the sabbath day, to keep it holy.
4. Honor your father and your mother.
5. You shall not kill.
6. You shall not commit adultery.
7. You shall not steal.
8. You shall not bear false witness against your neighbor.
9. You shall not covet your neighbor's wife.
10. You shall not covet your neighbor's goods.

---

[20] Johann Adam Möhler, *Symbolik*, §38, 415.

So that the will of God is not obeyed simply according to the letter but rather in the spirit of Jesus, the Christian understands and lives God's commandments in the light of the Beatitudes of Jesus's Sermon on the Mount (Matt 5:1–12):

> Blessed are the poor in spirit, for theirs is the kingdom of heaven.
> Blessed are those who mourn, for they shall be comforted.
> Blessed are the meek, for they shall inherit the earth.
> Blessed are those who hunger and thirst after righteousness, for they shall be satisfied.
> Blessed are the merciful, for they shall obtain mercy.
> Blessed are the pure in heart, for they shall see God.
> Blessed are the peacemakers, for they shall be called sons of God.
> Blessed are those who are persecuted for righteousness' sake, for theirs is the kingdom of heaven.
> Blessed are you when men revile you and persecute you and utter all kinds of evil against you falsely on my account. Rejoice and be glad, for your reward is great in heaven, for in the same way they persecuted the prophets who were before you.

3. In the signs and means of salvation: the seven sacraments:[21]

Baptism and Confirmation,
The Most Holy Eucharist—source and summit of the whole Christian life—
Penance and the Anointing of the Sick, and
Holy Orders (three degrees) and Matrimony.

> In the community of the faithful under the leadership of the bishops and especially the Bishop of Rome, the Successor of Peter.

Catholic in daily life

> Father, . . . [g]ive us daily the bread that we need. (Luke 11:2–3; cf. Matt 6:9–11)
> I am the living bread that came down from heaven. Whoever eats of this bread will live for ever. (John 6:51)

---

[21]   Vatican II, *Lumen Gentium*, §11.

Christian faith is not to be confused with a metaphysical anticipation of being, or with religious reverence for life in general, or with a worldview belonging to the human or natural sciences. Nevertheless, because of its origin in divine reason (word; *logos*), which is reflected in its logic and systematics, it is essentially related to these overall schemes of human existence.[22] Consequently, the positive structure of grace and nature, or of faith and reason, is always reflected in the relationship of the believer to God, the Creator of the world and Perfecter of man.

Faith is about the Christian's personal relationship with God in the here and now. What is needed to explain the world is not formally God as the idea of ideas, or "the thinking of thinking," the "unmoved mover,"[23] the "absolute spirit,"[24] or the hypothetically assumed demiurge of astrophysics and evolutionary biology but rather the living God of Israel. He is "the God and Father of our Lord Jesus Christ" (Eph 1:3), who taught his disciples to pray to him in this way: "Our Father ..." (Matt 6:9).

Jesus was no prince of poets and popular philosopher who compressed the pleasure and pain of being in the world into aphorisms and pithy points. Even less did he present himself as a guru and master of the art of living (*Lebenskünstler*) who amazed and enchanted his audience with platitudes and commonplaces.

In faith, his disciples recognize him as the Son of God, the Creator and Lord of heaven and earth. Jesus revealed his unity and identity with God, his Father, in the Holy Spirit, not to the intellectually and politically wise elite and to rulers of this world but rather to "little children," i.e., to the mass of simple people: "All things have been handed over to me by my Father; and no one knows who the Son is except the Father, or who the Father is except the Son and anyone to whom the Son chooses to reveal him" (Luke 10:22).

The "mass" here does not mean the myriads of uprooted people who long for a "leader" and irrationally project onto such a person their resentments and utopias, whose "revolt"[25] should be feared and whose "psychology"[26] should without fail be studied. The mass of "little ones" is the "great multitude that no one could count, from every nation, from all tribes and peoples and languages"

---

[22] Gerhard Ludwig Müller, *Den Horizont der Vernunft erweitern. Zur Theologie von Benedikt XVI* (Freiburg, 2013).

[23] Aristotle, *Metaphysics*, 1026a; 1072b (in bks. 6 and 12).

[24] Georg W. F. Hegel, *Enzyklopädie der philosophischen Wissenschaften im Grundriss* (1830), §577 (= Ph 33), ed. F. Nicolin and O. Pöggeler (Hamburg, 1969), 463.

[25] José Ortega y Gasset, *La riginsn de las masas* (1930); Eng.: *The Revolt of the Masses* (New York: W. W. Norton, 1932).

[26] Gustave Le Bon, *Psychologie des Foules* (1895); Eng.: *The Crowd: A Study of the Popular Mind* (New York: Macmillan, 1896), https://archive.org/details/crowdastudypopuoobongoog/page /n21/mode/2up?.

eryone
s, their
m and

AS-30

0/Gky93ynbQ/-1 of 1-//UPS-NEXT/pri-intl-us-ag/0/0508-08:00/0508-02:38

Visit Amazon.com/returns
Return or replace your item

1645852776 9781645852773
1645852776
Gerhard Cardinal Müller --- Hardcover
True and False Reform: What it Means to Be Catholic   1

Qty.   Item

Your order of May 5, 2023 (Order ID 113-0506673-7040245)

amazon.com

g peo-
e able
life; in
v you,

about
8–19).
ce the
s vast
of the
man
cause
ts on

In order to emphasize the need for man to cooperate with God's omnipotence (*Allwirksamkeit*) for his salvation, St. Augustine offered encouragement to those who doubt themselves: "He who created us without our help will not save us without our consent."[28] In building a better world and preparing for the coming kingdom of God, the cooperation of the free will is required, which with grace "will do greater works than these" (John 14:12). For Jesus sends us the Holy Spirit from the Father. Even though "a great multitude that no one could count" appears before God (Rev 7:9), every single person does count before God, for his or her name is written in "the book of life" (Rev 20:12, 15; 21:27; Dan 12:1–2; Luke 10:20; Phil 4:2–3; Rev 20:12, 15; 21:27). And these words are addressed to God's people and to every single individual: "But now thus says the LORD, he who created you, O Jacob, he who formed you, O Israel: Do not fear, for I have redeemed you; I have called you by name, you are mine" (Isa 43:1).

In ancient cosmo-centrism, and in the modern sense of being lost in the infinite space-time of the universe (*horror vacui*), the individual human being flits past like a shadow of being or perishes from sheer boredom.[29] Blaise Pascal asked, "What is a man in the Infinite?" and stated first of all: "A Nothing in

---

[27] St. Thomas Aquinas, *ST* I-II, q. 113, a. 9.

[28] St. Augustine, *Sermo* 169.11.

[29] Pascal, *Pensées*, frag. 139.

comparison with the Infinite, an All in comparison with the Nothing, a mean between nothing and everything." The thinking human being searches in vain for the center of the cosmos, because he himself is the center. He finds his center not in the vast matter of the microcosm and macrocosm but in it and its Creator. "These extremes meet and reunite by force of distance, and find each other in God, and in God alone."[30]

In the Christian belief in God and image of man, the situation is reversed. It is man for whose sake everything else exists. Christ, the God-man in whom, through whom, and unto whom all things were created, became man for the sake of man (propter nos et propter nostram salute) and we are destined to "live for the praise of his glory" (Eph 1:12). God did not merely demiurgically initiate the course of the world and then leave its course to chance; nor did he deterministically exclude freedom because a personal interest in the trivialities of creation would be beneath his infinite majesty. Imputing to God a phobia of having any contact with the world on account of his supreme majesty is pre-cisely the approach taken by the wretched anthropomorphism with which the wise of this world have risen up against the Christian belief in God. Just why has "God made foolish the wisdom of the world? . . . [and] decided, through the foolishness of our proclamation, to save those who believe" (1 Cor 1:20–21)?

To protect absolute transcendence from any involvement in the world process is itself only a disguised anthropomorphism, springing from elitist presumption regarding mass man and confusing disgust at one's own corrupt-ibility with reverence for divine majesty (cf. 1 Cor 1:18–25).

Who would be so foolish as to hold his nose at "the fragrance that comes from knowing him [God]" (2 Cor 2:14–15) in Christ? For Christ, who was "theomorphic," became "anthropomorphic" (see Phil 2:6–7) in order to make us "christomorphic" (see Rom 8:29) as children of God. God becomes man so that men might become God, i.e., are deified in theopoiesis by God dwelling in us and we in him.[31]

The infinite greatness of the Creator of heaven and earth (Gen 1:1) is revealed precisely in the fact that he bends down to us fondly, in the way that a mother's love does not feel revulsion at her child when changing its diapers. "Can a woman forget her nursing-child, or show no compassion for the child of her womb? Even these may forget, yet I will not forget you" (Isa 49:15). What would be noticed less than a hair falling out? Yet God's providence cares for us in such a way that "even the hairs of your head are all [!] counted" (Luke

---

[30]   Pascal, *Pensées*, frag. 72.

[31]   St. Irenaeus, *Adversus haereses*, 3.18.7; 3.19.1; 4.33.4; St. Athanasius of Alexandria, *De Incarnati-one Verbi Dei* 54.

12:7). And citing the two pennies that would buy five sparrows in the currency of his day, Jesus calls on us not to be afraid, for "you are of more value than many sparrows" (Luke 12:7). God is not just interested in our life as a whole but also in every day and every hour. He is close to us as the source of life, but not like George Orwell's "Big Brother," who observes and terrorizes everyone with omnipresent surveillance cameras, intimidating and gagging them with the bludgeon of political correctness in the dictatorship of relativism. God sees into our hearts because he loves us. We are in him and he in us. Love does not control but builds up and sets free.

With the Creator of the universe, who is directly committed to me and has infinite love for me as a person, the nihilistic feeling of nothingness of contingency disappears, whereas without God it can change dialectically into arrogance or self-contempt.

In preparing them for the encounter with Christ in the Gospel and the sacraments of the Church, Paul had made it clear to the philosophizing Athenians that everyone should "search for God and perhaps grope for him and find him—though indeed he is not far from each one of us. For 'In him we live and move and have our being'" (Acts 17:27–28). Man's arrogance, from which springs the theoretical denial of God and the will to rule over his own kind, has a metaphysical root since he allowed himself at the beginning of creation, and thus at the root of our creaturely existence, to be seduced by the suggestion: "[Y]ou will be like God, knowing good and evil" (Gen 3:5).

But there is also a hidden atheism, which can even go hand in hand with religious practice and joining in with bustling church activity, but which in its heart denies God and "keeps him at arm's length." The Church-hater, like the Church functionary, finds it an imposition that God comes too close to him incarnationally and sacramentally in the Flesh and Blood of his Son. If even Catholics who are well versed in the faith reject the Incarnation as a banal truth couched in myth, or the Real Presence of Christ in the Eucharistic species that results from transubstantiation as embarrassing and unreasonable (for their "enlightened" reason to believe), then what lies at the root of this is not that they have theoretical difficulties with the metaphysics of substance or a natural-philosophical nature but rather a social distancing from God in the flesh of his Son, which is expressed in the tetchily indignant question: "How can this man give us his flesh to eat?" (John 6:52).

It was precisely when "his hour had come to depart from this world and go to the Father," and he wanted to show his own that "he loved them to the end" (John 13:1), that the "Lord and Teacher" (John 13:14) performed the servile task of foot-washing on his disciples. And the practical atheism that exists—even within the Church—will only be overcome when we, like Peter, give up resisting God's serving love and allow our feet to be washed by our Creator and Redeemer, our Judge and Perfecter (John 13:9).

Voltaire,[32] the "sacred cow" of all smug mockers of religion,[33] ridiculed the disproportionality between the infinite God and the necessity of the sacraments for salvation as taught by the Church, e.g., that a little water poured over the head at Baptism along with the tripartite baptismal formula is supposed to confer eternal life, or that Jesus himself, the Son of God, is supposed to meet us poor and least of men as the eternal judge of our deeds and omissions (Matt 25:31–46).

Voltaire, who was always ready to combat fanaticism, superstition, and clericalism—and who had denigrated the Catholic-nationalist defenders of Polish freedom (in the Bar Confederation of 1768) against the Russian occupation as a *"faction criminelle"* (criminal faction)[34]—wrote to his enlightened absolutist friend, Frederick II of Prussia, the person chiefly responsible for the three Silesian wars in the eighteenth century, "I have an insurmountable aversion to the way in which one concludes one's life in our Roman Catholic religion. It seems to me most ridiculous to be oiled when setting out for that other world, something like the way one lubricates the wheel axles of one's touring car when going on a long journey. This nonsense disgusts me."[35] This same "philosopher-king" on the Prussian throne, who was praised by his admirers as the greatest general of the eighteenth century, is said to have shouted in rage at his grenadiers fleeing certain death during the Battle of Kolin (1757), "Dogs, would you live forever?"[36]

Jesus, the Son of God, on the other hand, was not above touching people who were suffering from all kinds of illnesses and infirmities (Mark 1:32–34), so that his disciples also "anointed with oil many who were sick and cured them" (Mark 6:13). For they were, after all, the apostles of the Messiah (Mark 3:13–19; 6:13), the anointed of the Holy Spirit, who brought to the poor the Gospel of freedom, redemption from physical and spiritual suffering, and the promise of eternal life (Luke 4:18–19).

Since Jesus, the Son of God and our high priest, became like us in everything except sin (Heb 4:15), he can also sympathize in everything that

---

[32] Jean Orieux, *Voltaire ou la royauté de l'esprit*; dt: *Das Leben des Voltaire* (Frankfurt: Insel, 1978).

[33] Cf. Voltaire's concentrated criticism of divine Revelation and the Church in his *Dictionnaire philosophique* (1764) (Paris, 1994).

[34] Theodor Schieder, *Friedrich der Große. Ein Königtum der Widersprüche* (Frankfurt a.M., 1983,) 462.

[35] Quoted in German from "Voltaire," Wikipedia, https://de.wikipedia.org/wiki/Voltaire.

[36] Klaus-Jürgen Bremm, *Preussen bewegt die Welt. Der Siebenjährige Krieg* (Darmstadt, 2017), 142–54.

constitutes being human, right down to temptation to sin. Even in the trivialities of everyday life, God is close to us, in the daily getting up, eating, working and going to bed, the illnesses, the playing of children, the burdens of aging, and the responsibilities we take on in family, society, state, and Church. It is precisely the boundless trust in God that saves us from irresponsible idleness, as well as from an excessive solicitude for existence, as if everything depended on us. "For . . . your heavenly Father knows that you need all these things [food, drink, clothing]. But strive first for the kingdom of God and his righteousness, and all these things will be given to you as well" (Matt 6:32–33).

It is in this spirit that Christians ask their heavenly Father, "Give us each day our *daily* bread" (Luke 11:3, emphasis added).

And to all his disciples, the same Jesus who taught them the Lord's Prayer says, "If any want to become my followers, let them deny themselves and take up their cross *daily* and follow me" (Luke 9:23, emphasis added).

It is not just in the extraordinary deeds of good works or even martyrdom, and in life choices such as entering a religious order and marrying but also in everyday prayer and work that being conformed to Christ occurs, in which we become "perfect . . . as your heavenly Father is perfect" (Matt 5:48). When Jesus teaches us to say "Father" to God in the Lord's Prayer, this does not just relate the attribute "fatherly" to God; even more, it relates the Christian to the Triune God in the First Person of the Father. Since we have become children of God through Baptism, we say to God, "Abba, Father," through the Son in the Holy Spirit (Rom 8:15). In our daily prayer and suffering, we are not only comforted and cared for by God in a "fatherly" way; we also participate in the saving work of the Triune God and assist in building up his kingdom in this age and this world. Hence Paul can write to "the saints who are in Ephesus and are faithful in Christ Jesus" (Eph 1:1): "Therefore be imitators of God, as beloved children, and live in love, as Christ loved us and gave himself up for us, a fragrant offering and sacrifice to God" (Eph 5:1–2).

The personal relationship with God takes place in the innermost depths of the heart, which are accessible only to God, by means of the virtues the Holy Spirit infuses into the soul and also by the freely performed acts of faith, hope, and love. Corresponding to this in the outward dimension is the Church's mediation of salvation, grounded in the Incarnation, on her earthly pilgrimage: the apostles' preaching and Baptism (Acts 2:14, 37–38). Inner communion with God takes place in the pilgrim state only when believing and baptized Christians devote "themselves to the apostles' teaching and fellowship, to the breaking of bread and the prayers" (Acts 2:42). What matters is to believe with the Church and live with her in her liturgy and Christian ethics. Christianity is not a *Gesinnungsreligion* (religion of conviction) which, on a secondary level, should also express itself in religious myths and cults and prove itself in humanitarian actions. Because of the Incarnation, it is God himself who awakens salvific faith in the Church's preaching. It is God himself, too, who really distributes his grace to us in the sacraments of the Church and who personally entrusted the ministry of reconciliation to the apostles and their successors, which means that they act in the Person of Christ (2 Cor 1:10; 5:20).

Regarding the *precepts of the Church*, we read in the Catechism of the Catholic Church (CCC), 2041–2043:

> The precepts of the Church are set in the context of a moral life bound to and nourished by liturgical life. The obligatory character of these positive laws decreed by the pastoral authorities is meant to guarantee to the faithful the very necessary minimum in the spirit of prayer and moral effort, in the growth in love of God and neighbor:
>
> The first precept ("You shall attend Mass on Sundays and holy days of obligation and rest from servile labor") requires the faithful to to sanctify the day commemorating the Resurrection of the Lord as well as the principal liturgical feasts honoring the mysteries of the Lord, the Blessed Virgin Mary, and the saints; in the first place, by participating in the Eucharistic celebration, in which the Christian community is gathered, and by resting from those works and activities which could impede such a sanctification of these days.
>
> The second precept ("You shall confess your sins at least once a year") ensures preparation for the Eucharist by the reception of the sacrament of Reconciliation, which continues Baptism's work of conversion and forgiveness.
>
> The third precept ("You shall receive the sacrament of the Eucharist at least during the Easter season") guarantees as a minimum the reception of the Lord's Body and Blood in connection with the Paschal feasts, the origin and center of the Christian liturgy.
>
> The fourth precept ("You shall observe the days of fasting and abstinence established by the Church") ensures the times of ascesis and penance which prepare us for the liturgical feasts and help us acquire mastery over our instincts and freedom of heart.
>
> The fifth precept ("You shall help to provide for the needs of the Church") means that the faithful are obliged to assist with the material needs of the Church, each according to his own ability.
>
> The faithful also have the duty of providing for the material needs of the Church, each according to his abilities.

The Catholic lifestyle

At the end of the Sermon on the Mount, in which he instructs his disciples in the new righteousness, Jesus says, "Everyone then who hears these words of mine and acts on them will be like a wise man who built his house on rock" (Matt 7:24). This results in a new lifestyle, both for the individual disciple and for the whole community of Christ's disciples.

But Christians do not cut themselves off from society and distinguish themselves from their contemporaries in their language, food, clothing, national customs, or (non-)participation in the culture, without which a better quality of life is not possible. But by participating in political, social, and cultural life, "they surpass the laws in their way of life. They love all and yet are persecuted by all," as a second-century author describes the closeness and distance of Christians to their pagan and hostile environment.[37] Christians are at the same time citizens and strangers in this world, because their homeland is community of life with God who became flesh in his Word, died on the Cross, and rose from the dead. Faith leads to a new morality. It is their profession of faith and this new morality that distinguish Christians from the world. No one can be admitted to Baptism who, in their personal conduct or work, has been guilty of immoral and misanthropic attitudes or actions and not renounced these.[38]

The critical and constructive relationship of the Christian to the world was already formulated in the early days of Christian persecution: "What the soul is in the body, Christians are in the world. . . . The soul is imprisoned in the body, yet keeps together that very body; and Christians are confined in the world as in a prison, and yet they keep together the world."[39]

At work, in the spirit of Christ's love, Catholics are involved in everyday living with their family and public life, but in prayer they lift up their heads and fix their gaze on Christ.

The day should begin with our making the Sign of the Cross while praying: "In the name of the Father, and of the Son, and of the Holy Spirit," for this is how in Baptism we became children of God. In the morning, at noon, and in the evening, we recall God's Incarnation for us by praying the Angelus. We never sit down at table without thanking God for our daily bread. For Christians are always aware that they owe their existence and everything they have, believe, hope, and love to God. Thus food is not just animal-like fuel for the metabolism but rather a thanksgiving meal for the joy of life and community of life with God and with all the redeemed.

---

[37] Mathetes, *Epistle to Diognetus*, 5, https://www.newadvent.org/fathers/0101.htm.

[38] St. Hippolytus, *Traditio Apostolica*, 16, https://web.archive.org/web/20020923091527/http://www.bombaxo.com/hippolytus.html..

[39] Mathetes, *Epistle to Diognetus*, 6, https://www.newadvent.org/fathers/0101.htm.

In the Lord's Prayer, we ask for the coming of the kingdom of God, our daily bread, the forgiveness of sins, and deliverance from all evil. We close the day with an examination of conscience and give thanks by giving glory to God in everything: "Glory be to the Father, and to the Son, and to the Holy Spirit."[40]

The liturgy is faith proclaimed in the celebration of the mysteries and the sharing in grace. Those who consciously follow the liturgical year enter into the sacramental-making-present of God's historical self-communication, which culminated in the Cross and Resurrection from the death of his Son and the eschatological outpouring of the Spirit from the Father and the Son.[41] The Church, in her motherly concern for the faithful, also values the authentic forms of the Catholic sacramentals and those instituted by her, which are by no means remnants of pagan myths and rites.[42] In the prayers of the Rosary, the litanies, and the devotions (Stations of the Cross, etc.), we contemplate the mysteries of redemption from sin and exaltation in grace. In liturgical processions and pilgrimages to the Holy Land, to the tombs of the apostles and martyrs, and to the shrines of Our Lady or the saints, we commend ourselves in our diverse life situations through intercession and thanksgiving to God's grace, which remains incarnationally present in Christ.

The Christian "does not live by bread alone, but by every word that comes from the mouth of God" (Matt 4:4). The private reading of Scripture must be embedded in the hearing of the word of God in the community of the Church, which alone is and can be the full hearer of the word. For revelation is addressed to all humanity, of which, however, everyone should be an active and productive member according to his or her measure. A love for Sacred Scripture is a specific feature that does not distinguish Protestants from Catholics but should rather unite them.

No one has expressed this more beautifully than their common Father of the Church, St. Jerome: "Ignorance of Scripture is ignorance of Christ."[43]

---

[40] Adolf Adam, *Grundriss Liturgie* (Freiburg, 1985); Hermann Kirchdorf, *Grundgebete der Christen* (Munich, 1998); Georg Langgärtner, *Jesus Christus ist der Herr. Gebete, Hymnen, Meditationen aus den Liturgien des Ostens und des Westens* (Munich, 1978).

[41] Adolf Adam, *Das Kirchenjahr mitfeiern. Seine Geschichte und seine Bedeutung nach der Liturgie-erneuerung* (Freiburg, 1979); Adam, "Das Kirchenjahr," *Schlüssel zum Glauben. Betrachtungen* (Freiburg, 1990).

[42] Ludwig Andreas Veit, *Volksfrommes Brauchtum und Kirche im deutschen Mittelalter. Ein Durchblick* (Freiburg, 1936); Ludwig Andreas Veit and Ludwig Lenhart, *Kirche und Volksfrömmigkeit im Zeitalter des Barock* (Freiburg, 1956); Ludwig Mödl, *Den Alltag heiligen. Rituale, Segnungen, Sakramentalien. Die Bedeutung der Volksfrömmigkeit und praktische Vorschläge für die Seelsorge* (Stuttgart, 2008).

[43] St. Jerome, *Comm. In Is.* prol. (PL, 24:17); Vatican II, *Dei Verbum*, §25.

The reading of Scripture forms an integral part of the Eucharistic celebration.[44] On every Sunday and holy day, Catholics are exhorted to gather for the celebration of the Eucharist by Jesus's command to do this in memory of him (Luke 22:19), and by the precepts of the Church specifying when to do so. Here the Third Commandment, which enjoins the Old Testament people of God to keep the Sabbath, the day of rest after the six-day work of creation, is not set aside but rather fulfilled in Sunday.[45] As the day that commemorates Jesus's Resurrection, Sunday points to the new creation. Thus, Sunday is the anticipation of the eighth day of creation, which no longer has any setting of the sun and no longer needs any sun in the heavenly Jerusalem.[46] "And the city has no need of sun or moon to shine on it, for the glory of God is its light, and its lamp is the Lamb" (Rev 21:23). The linking of the Eucharist with Sunday is well attested to in the Bible and otherwise in early Christianity. "And on the day called Sunday, all who live in cities or in the country gather together to one place";[47] and so to this day, with the Liturgy of the Word and Liturgy of the Altar, the Eucharist is celebrated as a real memorial of Christ's Sacrifice on the Cross and as communion with him in the Lord's Supper.[48]

The Church lives from the Eucharist, and Church life takes place to the highest degree in the Eucharist. For "taking part in the Eucharistic Sacrifice . . . is the fount and apex of the whole Christian life."[49] The priest does not celebrate Mass just for the private edification of the faithful who are present; rather, with the whole Church, he offers spiritually and sacramentally the Sacrifice of Christ, from which comes the salvation offered for the whole world. In the Eucharistic Sacrifice, the inseparable unity of the common priesthood of all believers and the sacramental priesthood of the Church is revealed; and, at the same time, the whole priesthood of the Church reaches its unsurpassable pinnacle in the priesthood of Christ.[50] The Eucharistic Sacrifice must also be the source and center of all the activity of priests, who teach, guide, and

---

44 Second Vatican Council, *Sacrosanctum Concilium* (1963), §56.
45 Willy Rordorf, *Sabbat und Sonntag in der Alten Kirche* (Zürich, 1972).
46 Eu. Augustino, *De civitate Dei* 22,39.
47 St. Justin Martyr, *First Apology* 67.
48 Hermann Volk, *Sonntäglicher Gottesdienst, Theologische Grundlegungi* (Münster i.W., 1956); Adam, *Grundriss Liturgie*, 1985; Volk, *Die Eucharistiefeier—Quelle und Gipfel des Glaubens* (Freiburg, 1991).
49 Vatican II, *Lumen Gentium*, §11; cf. *Presbyterium Ordinis* (1965), §5.
50 Vatican II, *Lumen Gentium*, §10.

sanctify the people of God.[51] Therefore, the daily celebration of the Eucharist is also the source and wellspring of priestly spirituality:

> In the mystery of the Eucharistic Sacrifice, in which priests fulfill their greatest task, the work of our redemption is being constantly carried on; and hence the daily celebration of Mass is strongly urged, since even if there cannot be present a number of the faithful, it is still an act of Christ and the Church. Thus, when priests join in the act of Christ the priest, they offer themselves entirely to God, and when they are nourished with the Body of Christ, they profoundly share in the love of him who gives himself as food to the faithful. In like fashion, they are united with the intention and love of Christ when they administer the sacraments. This is true in a special way when, in the performance of their duty in the Sacrament of Penance, they show themselves altogether and always ready whenever the sacrament is reasonably sought by the faithful. In the recitation of the Divine Office, they offer the voice of the Church, which perseveres in prayer in the name of the whole human race, together with Christ, who "lives on still to make intercession on our behalf" (Heb 7:25).[52]

The liturgy stands between *martyria* (preaching and pastoral care) and *diakonia* (*caritas* and social ethics), and it links the two, because it culminates the Christian worship of God and the Church's service to the world.

> Nevertheless the liturgy is the summit toward which the activity of the Church is directed; at the same time it is the font from which all her power flows. For the aim and object of apostolic works is that all who are made sons of God by faith and Baptism should come together to praise God in the midst of his Church, to take part in the Sacrifice, and so to eat the Lord's Supper.
>
> The liturgy in its turn moves the faithful, filled with "the paschal sacraments," to be "one in holiness"; it prays that "they may hold fast in their lives to what they have grasped by their faith"; the renewal in the Eucharist of the covenant between the Lord and man draws the faithful into the compelling love of Christ and sets them on fire. From the liturgy, therefore, and especially from the Eucharist, as from a font, grace is poured forth upon us; and the sanctification of men

---

[51] Vatican II, *Lumen Gentium*, §28; *Presbyterorum Ordinis*, §§4–7.

[52] Vatican II, *Presbyterium Ordinis*, §13.

in Christ and the glorification of God, to which all other activities of the Church are directed as toward their end, is achieved in the most efficacious possible way.[53]

It is towards the Eucharist that the other sacraments are oriented, through which we are irrevocably incorporated into the Church, the body of Christ (Baptism and Confirmation); or through which the life of grace is restored or deepened in us (Penance and Anointing of the Sick); or through which the Church is built up and guided as a community (Marriage and the Sacrament of Holy Orders).

The request to our Father in heaven for *daily* bread has been fulfilled in still another way, one that allows us to look into the heart of Christian faith and Catholic life.

Jesus, in his Person, is himself the *Bread of Life* which has come down from heaven, which overcomes our hunger for existence and gives us eternal life. The Christological and Eucharistic discourse that Jesus himself held in the synagogue at Capernaum is the perfect self-interpretation of the incarnational-sacramental-ecclesial presence of God in the life of the Christian and of the whole Church. It is the unsurpassable characterization of the disciples' being and life:

> "Do not work for the food that perishes, but for the food that endures for eternal life, which the Son of Man will give you." . . . They said to him, "Sir, give us this bread always."
>
> Jesus said to them, "I am the bread of life. Whoever comes to me will never be hungry, and whoever believes in me will never be thirsty. . . . And this is the will of him who sent me, that I should lose nothing of all that he has given me, but raise it up on the last day. . . .
>
> "Not that anyone has seen the Father except the one who is from God; he has seen the Father [cf. John 1:18]. Very truly, I tell you, whoever believes has eternal life. I am the bread of life. . . . I am the living bread that came down from heaven. Whoever eats of this bread will live for ever; and the bread that I will give for the life of the world is my flesh." . . .
>
> "Those who eat my flesh and drink my blood have eternal life, and I will raise them up on the last day; for my flesh is true food and my blood is true drink. Those who eat my flesh and drink my blood abide in me, and I in them. Just as the living Father sent me, and I live because of the Father, so whoever eats me will live because of me. This is the bread that came down from heaven, not like that which your ancestors ate, and they died. But the one who eats this bread will live for ever." (John 6:27–58)

---

[53]   Vatican II, *Sacrosanctum Concilium*, §10.

And this is the reaction of the Church, in which Simon Peter makes his free and grace-filled choice for Jesus: "Lord, to whom can we go? You have the words of eternal life. We have come to believe and know that you are the Holy One of God" (John 6:68–69).

When asked about their lifestyle, Christians can only echo Paul's words to them, that "your life is hidden with Christ in God. When Christ who is your life is revealed, then you also will be revealed with him in glory" (Col 3:3–4).

The Eucharist: the center of Catholic life

The connection between Church and Eucharist is constitutive for the profession and living of the Catholic faith. Therefore, in principle, only those baptized who are in full ecclesial communion with the "one Church of Christ which . . . , constituted and organized in the world as a society, subsists in the Catholic Church, [and] which is governed by the Successor of Peter and the bishops in communion with him,"[54] can receive sacramental Communion in the Eucharist. Anyone who questions this Revelation-based truth in theory, or abrogates it in practice, thereby enters into open opposition to the Catholic faith.

By using only the precepts contained in divine Revelation as it is faithfully and fully preserved in the Catholic Church, I would like to show the connection between sacramental and ecclesial communion.

For we are living in times when the revealed teaching of the Church is subordinated to ecclesio-political goals. Today, every problem is personalized and thus neutralized. Instead of arguments being exchanged in open debate, individuals are discredited. Every problem is personalized and thereby neutralized. No matter if someone knows the whole of Sacred Scripture by heart, has studied all the Church Fathers, and is well qualified in modern philosophy and science, all it takes is for one journalist from the provinces, or a mediocre hobby theologian, to stigmatize him as "conservative," and then all his knowledge is cancelled out in the same way the finest wine is rendered unfit for consumption if some idiot mixes poison with it. Every newly appointed bishop is tested at his first press conference and then labeled as conservative or liberal, whatever that might be, depending on whether he is personally "for or against" women's ordination, "for or against" the blessing of homosexual couples, "for or against" priestly celibacy, and "for or against" Holy Communion for "remarried divorcees." Other topics are of little interest, and differentiated arguments don't count with the "evergreens." Thus, there is a shift from factual discussion to the imputation of personal ideological bias. Those who loosen the connection between ecclesial

---

54   Vatican II, *Lumen Gentium*, §8.

and sacramental *communio*, in order to purportedly make the faith easier for people today, then accuse their critics of having closed minds and rigidly clinging to dogmas that the secularized Christian can no longer understand.

There is an anti-dogmatic climate that also has a negative effect on the understanding of the sacraments. They are then no longer the signs instituted by Christ and celebrated in the Church that bring about invisible grace in the rightly disposed recipient. They morph into psychological and social props for inner mystical experiences with a "Christ" made—within our consciousness—in our own image and likeness. To be sure, the grace of the sacrament is not a reward for good moral behavior, but it is even less a justification for immoral behavior and a life that is contrary to God's commandments. Between grace and morality there is no either-or but rather an *et-et* (and-and), and so Vatican II states, "It is through the sacraments and the exercise of the virtues that the sacred nature and organic structure of the priestly community [of the Church] is brought into operation."[55]

The reason why many people today are "incapable of liturgy" (*liturgieun-fähig*), something Romano Guardini already noted at the *Katholikentag* in Mainz in 1948, lies in their viewing Christianity as a historical variant of the religious sense of some vague transcendence, instead of tracing the Church back to the fact of the Incarnation in her dogma and life. The nature, the manner of working, and the effect of the sacraments are only disclosed in the light of the Incarnation and the historical and real mediation of salvation in the Cross and Resurrection of Christ, God's Incarnate Word. Anyone proceeding from this principle immediately senses how totally un-Catholic the way of thinking is of those who say, "That may be right in dogmatics, but it's no good for pastoral work."

For in the Church's faith consciousness, dogma expresses the truth received in divine Revelation, which we have to accept with our intellect and free will in the divine and Catholic faith for the sake of our salvation.[56] This is something quite different from the theory of the philosophers who, loosely based on Karl Marx, have hitherto only interpreted the world in various ways, whereas the point now is to change it. Christ, the teacher of the truth that is God himself, who reveals himself to us to know and love, is the same as him who, as the Good Shepherd (*bonus pastor*) and "guardian [*episkopos*] of our souls" (1 Pet 2:25), gave up his life for us on the Cross. Therefore, there can be no double truth in Catholic dogma. For what is dogmatically false will

---

[55] Vatican II, *Lumen Gentium*, §11.
[56] Vatican II, *Dei Verbum*, §5.

have a damaging effect for the salvation of souls, if employed pastorally in accordance with erroneous principles.

Rarely has St. Paul's warning to Timothy, the prototype of the Catholic bishop, been more pertinent than today: "[P]roclaim the message; be persistent whether the time is favorable or unfavorable. . . . For the time is coming when people will not put up with sound doctrine, but having itching ears, they will accumulate for themselves teachers to suit their own desires" (2 Tim 4:2–3).

Precisely in an age of social media, digital communication, and totalitarian mainstreaming, it is not a matter of whether the pope and bishops come across well to the people but rather of whether, through their message, Christ comes across to the people as the truth and life of God. For this reason, the Church's unique and indivisible Magisterium bears the ultimate responsibility for ensuring that no ambiguous signs and unclear teachings emanate from the pope and the bishops which might confuse the faithful or give them a false sense of security. It is an occupational hazard for the pope and the bishops to be pilloried, by the opinion leaders and powerful of this world, as unworldly, hostile to life, or medieval. If the prophets were already persecuted, why then do the bishops, as the successors to the apostles, imagine that it is because they're getting their media policy wrong? People utter "all kinds of evil against you falsely" (Matt 5:11) for the sake of the true faith.

In an age of dogmatic relativism, which quickly turns into verbal and physical persecution of witnesses to the revealed truth, it takes a clarity of theological thinking, and the courage of the martyrs, to bear witness to the truth as Jesus did before Pilate. The Church's concern in discipleship is God's truth, not the power of the world.

But we want to testify to the Catholic faith and live it in such a way that we can journey together with Christians from other churches and ecclesial communities on the way to the full unity that Christ, the founder of the Church, wishes to exist.

When he instituted the Eucharist, Jesus did not answer in detail all the individual questions that would come up on later reflection. But all the Church's dogmatic elucidations are founded on the nature of this sacrament as it was instituted by Jesus. Whoever wishes to receive the sacramental Body and Blood of Christ must already have been incorporated through the profession of faith and sacramental Baptism into the body of Christ, the Church. There is therefore no Church-free mystical and individualistic community of feeling with Christ, who is always the head of his body, the Church, that bypasses Baptism and membership in the Church. "The cup of blessing . . . is it not a sharing in the blood of Christ? The bread that we break, is it not a sharing in the body of Christ? Because there is one bread, we who are many are one body, for we all partake of the one bread" (1 Cor 10:16–17). Whoever visibly belongs through faith and Baptism to the Church, and thereby also participates in the supernatural community of life with God because the Church is in Christ a sign and instrument of the most intimate union between man and God, must also be conformed to Christ in his religious and moral life, so as to receive Christ in sacramental communion unto his salvation and not unto his judgment (cf. 1 Cor 11:27). "You cannot partake of the table of the Lord and the table of demons" (1 Cor 10:21).

In his *First Apology* (ca. AD 150), the philosopher St. Justin Martyr already formulated the three conditions for the rightful and worthy reception of the Eucharist's spiritual nourishment. He said no one is allowed to partake of it "but the man who believes that the things which we teach are true, and who has been washed with the washing that is for the remission of sins, and unto regeneration, and who is so living as Christ has enjoined."[57] For this is not common bread that binds us together as in an agape or some random religious meal; it is the Flesh and Blood of Christ that the Logos assumed at the Incarnation. And we, too, are nourished by this sacred food and transformed into the body of Christ by being conformed to him and strengthened in our membership of the Church. We really receive Christ, the head of the Church, in the sacrament, and we are symbolically and really joined more and more to his ecclesial body, to the extent that the Church is a visible community through which we share in the invisible community of grace with God. A few decades earlier, St. Ignatius of Antioch spoke of Docetist Christians who stayed away from the celebration of the Eucharist or were excluded from it because they rejected the corporeal, Real Presence of Christ in the sacrament and because, in general, they wished to understand the salvific events of the Incarnation, Cross, and Resurrection of Jesus in a purely metaphorical way and not a realistic and corporeal way—thus robbing themselves of salvation. The only thing that helps against heretical beliefs and schisms is unity with the diocesan bishop and the visible Church in general:

> You should regard that Eucharist as valid which is celebrated either by the bishop or by someone he authorizes [presbyter]. Where the bishop is present, there let the congregation gather, just as where Jesus Christ is, there is the Catholic Church. Without the bishop's supervision, no baptisms or love feasts are permitted.[58]

---

[57] St. Justin Martyr, *First Apology* 66.
[58] St. Ignatius of Antioch, *Epistula ad Smyrnaeos* 8.1–2.

These pointers to the indissoluble connection between the sacraments and membership in the visible, sacramental, and episcopally ordered Church express the essential elements of the Catholic understanding of Church and Eucharist. Since St. Justin's time, it has been clear to every Catholic that only full communion with the ecclesial body of Christ in the profession of the faith, the sacraments, and the hierarchical constitution of the visible Church can be the prerequisite for the permissible and fruitful reception of the Body and Blood of Christ in Holy Communion. In addition, a Catholic must be in a state of sanctifying grace, i.e., the person must sincerely repent of any mortal sins committed since baptism and confess them combined with the resolve not to sin again and in this way be normatively freed through sacramental absolution from the guilt that radically separates him or her from God and the Church. Membership in the pilgrim Church is a prerequisite for salvation for every one of the baptized, albeit with this further proviso: "Whosoever, therefore, knowing that the Catholic Church was made necessary by Christ, would refuse to enter or to remain in it, could not be saved."[59] When popes and councils excommunicated heretics and schismatics, they excluded them from Eucharistic fellowship until the day that they repented and were reconciled with God and the Church. Conversely, popes who held false beliefs but regarded themselves as being orthodox believers for their part denied Catholics ecclesial fellowship by not granting them Eucharistic communion.

Up until the Leuenberg Concord signed between Protestant ecclesial communities in Europe (1973), even Lutherans and Reformed did not share any fellowship of pulpit and table, because they held fast to the early Church principle of community of sacrament and church.[60] But not all ecclesial communities derived from the Reformation joined this Christian fellowship, because the controversy over the Real Presence of Christ at the Lord's Supper had been settled by it in favor of a more Calvinistic view, and so a true unity of faith among Protestants on the question of the Lord's Supper had yet to be achieved—and still hasn't today.

In spite of significant progress in dialogue with various Protestant communities, the Catholic Church cannot depart from the essential doctrines about her own mission—and the sacraments mediated through it—without being disloyal to Christ. And it is not enough for non-Catholic Christians to selectively accept a number of the Church's teachings for themselves and reject others or regard them as unimportant. In the doctrine of the Eucharist, there is almost

---

59   Vatican II, *Lumen Gentium*, §14.
60   Elisabeth Schieffer, *Von Schauenburg nach Leuenberg. Entstehung und Bedeutung der Konkordie reformatorischer Kirchen in Europa* (Paderborn, 1983).

complete agreement with the Orthodox churches—i.e., the Real Presence, the sacrificial character of the Mass, and the ordained priests without whom there is no Eucharist—and partial agreement with several Protestant communities, especially the Lutherans. However, for both Orthodox and Catholic thinking, the mutual requirement of ecclesial community and reception of the Eucharist is indispensable. The sacraments are not merely signs for us of a justification of the sinner that has already come about in faith alone but rather signs *that effect* what they signify. Even if in some circumstances it is not possible to celebrate the sacraments of grace as visible and symbolic actions as well, God nevertheless gives those who open themselves completely to him in faith, hope, and love the grace of these sacraments. He does this for the person's salvation, not in order to relativize the visible sacramental mediation of salvation that is grounded in the Incarnation and in conformity with human nature.

People who now interpret their spiritual hunger for God and his grace using psychological instead of theological categories run the risk of confusing pagan magic and Christian sacrament. The Eucharist is "the medicine of immortality"[61] because of supernatural faith and grace, not a pharmaceutical remedy for psychodramatic experiences and traumas. The latter call for the natural treatments of medicine and therapy. Nor can it, as it were, physically restore lost ecclesial communion unless a supernatural unity has already been achieved by virtue of a shared profession of faith, sacraments, and visible unity with the pope and bishops.

The call not to be so scrupulous about this and leave it at the pious feelings and goodwill of those who simply come forward for Holy Communion and should not be excluded actually only appears to be displaying generosity, whereas, in reality, it reveals a disdain for the revealed faith entrusted to the Catholic Church. To simply replace a striving after an understanding of the Catholic faith with a pronouncement made by individual episcopal conferences, with the tacit approval of the pope, constitutes an undermining of itself by the Magisterium. For the latter's authority does not lie in administrative power; rather, it has

> the task of authentically interpreting the word of God, whether written or handed on. . . . This teaching office is not above the word of God, but serves it, teaching only what has been handed on, listening to it devoutly, guarding it scrupulously and explaining it faithfully in

---

[61] St. Ignatius of Antioch, *Epistola ad Ephesios* 20.2.

accord with a divine commission and with the help of the Holy Spirit, it draws from this one deposit of faith everything which it presents for belief as divinely revealed.[62]

God instituted only one teaching office in the Catholic Church. The idea that there could be a conflicting variety in matters of faith and the praxis of the sacraments—and that even episcopal conferences or individual bishops could possess a teaching office capable of interpreting revelation in a dogmatically binding manner without being linked to the pope and the entire body of bishops—not only displays a frightening lack of theological literacy but also represents nothing other than a monstrous attack on the revealed unity of the Church in Christ that has been given to us. The fact is that, for the universal Church and the whole body of bishops, the pope—and by analogy the bishop for the local church—is the principle and foundation of unity in faith and communion in the grace of the sacraments,[63] and not the reason for them to split into autocephalous national churches. The secular principle of the decentralization of political power can only be applied analogously to purely organizational aspects of governing the Church, but absolutely not to the truth that unites all the faithful in God when they devote themselves "to the apostles' teaching and fellowship, to the breaking of bread and the prayers" (Acts 2:42).

Nevertheless, in an extreme situation where it is a matter of immediate preparation for individual judgment and eternal life, i.e., in a case of mortal danger, the Church cannot refuse a non-Catholic baptized Christian pastoral assistance if the person seriously requests it. This can only occur when respect is shown for the person's religious convictions. For most non-Catholic Christians have not made themselves guilty of formal heresy or become an apostate of their own accord. Christians who belong to ecclesial communities derived from the Reformation do, in any case, have a real connection to the Catholic Church because of their baptism and many other Church-building elements.[64] It is not communion as such that is lacking but just full communion with the visible Church and all her means of grace. When a Christian asks a Catholic priest for sacramental forgiveness of sins, and also for Holy Communion as Viaticum, in a case of grave necessity that affects his eternal salvation and must not be confused with socio-psychological constraints, then that person may be given the sacraments of grace if he at least implicitly affirms the Church's belief regarding these two sacraments, because God bestows the grace of the

---

[62]   Vatican II, *Dei Verbum*, §10.
[63]   Vatican II, *Lumen Gentium*, §§18, 22.
[64]   Second Vatican Council, *Unitatis Redintegratio* (1964), §§3–4.

sacraments (*res sacramenti*) on him on the grounds of his faith, hope, and love. Any appearance of doctrinal indifference among Christians must be avoided. It is not permissible, for example, to arbitrarily stretch the concept of "grave necessity"[65] so that de facto sacramental communion of the Catholic Church comes about with communities that are not joined to her in full unity.[66] Church law is to be interpreted on the basis of revealed Faith and, where the *ius mere ecclesiasticum* (purely ecclesiastical law) is concerned, also corrected. And, by the same token, the faith cannot be de facto overruled by positive canons of ecclesiastical law. A disparity between the teaching and practice of the faith is impossible if we wish to remain Catholic. For the goal is not intercommunion between visible churches that remain separate but, rather, the visible unity of the Church, which is represented and realized in the unity of faith, sacraments, and the recognition of the office of teaching and governance exercised by the pope and the bishops.[67]

Although a marriage between a Catholic and another Christian poses a great challenge to the two spouses, their children, and their larger families, this can even offer an ecumenical opportunity for Christians to grow together on the way to Church unity; however, it is in itself on no account a case of "grave necessity" that would make the sacraments of the Catholic Church necessary for the non-Catholic members for the sake of their souls. If a Protestant becomes inwardly convinced of being able to affirm the whole of the Catholic faith and its ecclesial form in his or her conscience, then the right course of action is to seek full, visible communion with the Catholic Church. From experience in my own country of Germany, which has suffered confessional division among Christians for five hundred years, so that every Christian there has relatives of a different communion, I know that there are loyalties and attachments to one's own original communion that cannot be undone by simply being received into the Catholic Church. For some, it would mean sacrificing their economic existence too. Anyone wanting to pass judgment on their fellow Christians should ask themselves just how courageous they would be about their faith in a non-Catholic environment. But there is no call here for regulation by episcopal conferences and self-congratulation by ecclesial bureaucracies that allow themselves to be praised by the media for their ecumenical openness. A good pastor knows what advice given to a person's conscience he can take responsibility for in the *forum internum* (internal forum).

---

[65] *Code of Canon Law*, can. 844.

[66] Manfred Hauke, *Kommunionspendung an Protestanten?* (Augsburg, 2018).

[67] Second Vatican Council, *Unitatis Redintegratio* (1964), §4.

With respect to Orthodox churches, the questions are dogmatically and theologically quite different, because they share with us an understanding of the Church as a sacramental reality. Like us, they have valid sacraments, including a sacramental priesthood and the valid ordination of bishops, who are then true and legitimate successors of the apostles. Therefore, in a grave emergency, i.e., when the salvation of one's soul is at stake and one cannot reach a Catholic priest, it is permissible for a Catholic to ask an Orthodox priest for the Sacraments of Penance, Anointing of the Sick, and the Eucharist as Viaticum. A Catholic priest is also permitted to administer these sacraments to an Orthodox Christian under the same conditions. The other way round, the Orthodox are more cautious; this is because in sacramental teaching they have not invariably and consistently implemented the conclusions drawn by the Catholic Church in the fourth and fifth centuries from the fundamental decision taken against the Donatists. For them, this decision is problematic, as it ruled that even a heretical or schismatic priest, or one not living a morally impeccable life, can, if he is validly ordained, validly administer the sacraments if he celebrates them according to the mind of the Church.

In the case of the competence of episcopal conferences, one must not look just at legal competences as they have been positively laid down canonically between Rome and the local authorities.[68] Of greater importance is the insight that neither the bishops nor the pope have any competence to interfere with the substance of the sacraments,[69] or to tacitly initiate processes that establish errors and confusion in practice, thus endangering the salvation of souls.

It is also not possible to leave the wording of a doctrine unchanged but, by employing a changed fundamental hermeneutic, attribute a completely different or even contradictory meaning to it. For example, a differentiated theological explanation of the sacrificial nature of the Mass does not relativize it but rather shows it in a light that brings out more clearly the real unity of the Sacrifice of the Cross and the Sacrifice of the Altar, as well as their liturgical difference. Or when categories other than those of Aristotelian philosophy are also employed in order to explain the somatic Real Presence, then the awareness of the problem of the doctrine of Transubstantiation that has been achieved cannot be subverted by a less consistent theory of a professor of theology and his epigones. Ecumenism must aim to overcome the doctrinal

---

[68]   Achim Buckenmaier, *Lehramt der Bischofskonferenzen? Anregung für eine Revision* (Regensburg, 2016).

[69]   Council of Trent, *Doctrine and Canons on Communion* (DH 1728).

differences in the matter itself and not content itself with a scarcely sustainable compromise on formulation.[70]

If you make things easy for yourself by holding that academic theology is to blame for the divisions in Western Christendom, all this does is promote indifference in matters of faith. And that would be an ecclesiological nihilism into whose abyss "the church of the living God, the pillar and bulwark of the truth" (1 Tim 3:15), would be bound to fall.

---

[70] Lawrence Feingold, *The Eucharist: Mystery of Presence, Sacrifice, and Communion* (Steubenville, OH: Emmaus Academic, 2018).

Chapter 3

THE ORIGIN AND PROFILE OF THE CONCEPT OF "CATHOLIC"

The concept of "catholic": at the beginning of its history

St. Isidore of Seville (ca. AD 560–634), the last in the series of Latin Church Fathers, provides us with an etymological and factual explanation of the term "catholic" as a result of patristic developments:

> "Church" [*ecclesia*] is a Greek word that is translated into Latin as "convocation" [*convocatio*], because it calls [*vocare*] everyone to itself. "Catholic" [*catholicus*] is translated as "universal" [*universalis*], after the term *kath-holon*, that is, "with respect to the whole," for it is not restricted to some part of a territory, like a small association of heretics, but is spread widely throughout the entire world. And the apostle Paul assents to this when he says to the Romans, "I give thanks to my God for all of you, because your faith is spoken of in the whole world" [1:8].[1]

A good six hundred years of ecclesial and theological history already lie behind him.[2] In the Latin-speaking West of the Roman cultural sphere, a terminology that met the needs of the Church had first developed from North

---

[1]   St. Isidore of Seville, *Etymologiae* 8, 1, https://sfponline.org/Uploads/2002/st%20isidore %20in%20english.pdf.

[2]   Jean Daniélou, *Les origens du christianisme latin* (Paris, 1978); Karl S. Frank, *Grundzüge der Geschichte der Alten Kirche* (Darmstadt, 1984); Alister E. McGrath, *Christian Theology: An Introduction* (Oxford: Basil Blackwell, 1994); Johannes Hofmann, *Zentrale Aspekte der Alten Kirchengeschichte* (Würzburg, 2012).

Africa—with Tertullian, St. Cyprian, and St. Augustine—and is essentially still in use today. The Latin translation of the Bible (Vulgate) by the notable scholar St. Jerome (AD 347–420) also played an influential role. The Church counts him, together with St. Ambrose of Milan (AD 339–397), St. Augustine (AD 354–430), and Pope St. Gregory the Great (ca. AD 540–604), among the four great Latin Fathers of the Church. The four great oriental or Eastern Church Fathers, i.e., who wrote in Greek, are St. Athanasius of Alexandria (ca. AD 296–373), St. Basil the Great (ca. AD 330–379), St. Gregory of Nazianzus (ca. AD 329–390), and St. John Chrysostom (ca. AD 344–407).

Just as Isidore of Seville is called the last Latin Church Father, in the East John of Damascus (ca. AD 650–754) is accounted the last of the Greek Church Fathers. The authority of some of these great theologians is emphasized by the Church in recognizing them as Doctors of the Church. Among the Fathers and Doctors of the Church, the Second Vatican Council especially recommends St. Thomas Aquinas (1225–1274) as a model for the study of theology because of his incomparable clarity in presenting the *whole* of Catholic truth in the inner unity of faith and reason.[3] This is meant positively, not exclusively, and we should be happy to attend the school of the great masters of theological reflection and contemplation. It is well worth bearing in mind the admonition of St. Bernard of Clairvaux (ca. 1090–1153): "If anyone makes himself his own master in the spiritual life, he makes himself scholar to a fool."[4] A teacher of theology can only be someone who has previously been schooled by good theologians.

This is why Vatican II states:

> Dogmatic theology should be so arranged that these biblical themes are proposed first of all. Next there should be opened up to the students what the Fathers of the Eastern and Western Church have contributed to the faithful transmission and development of the individual truths of Revelation. The further history of dogma should also be presented, account being taken of its relation to the general history of the Church. Next, in order that they may illumine the mysteries of salvation as completely as possible, the students should learn to penetrate them more deeply with the help of speculation, *under the guidance of St. Thomas* [*S. Thoma magistro*], and to perceive their interconnections. They should be taught to recognize these same mysteries as present and working in liturgical actions and in the entire

---

3   Second Vatican Council, *Gravissimum Educationis* (1965), §10.
4   St. Bernard of Clairvaux, Epistle 87, 7.

life of the Church. They should learn to seek the solutions to human problems under the light of Revelation, to apply the eternal truths of Revelation to the changeable conditions of human affairs, and to communicate them in a way suited to men of our day.[5]

But the starting point was the New Testament written in Greek and the Hebrew Bible in the Greek translation of the Septuagint (LXX). The first post-biblical writings of the Apostolic Fathers and apologists in the second and third centuries were also predominantly written in Greek. The apologists defended the reasonableness of the revealed faith against populist prejudices of the pagan population, and against the philosophical objections of Greco-Roman philosophy (Celsus, Porphyry, and Julian the Apostate).[6]

Christ is the Logos in person, and thus the presence of God in the world as a reality in salvation history, and certainly not clothed in myth and poetry. In the Incarnation of the Logos, God was not afraid or ashamed to take on our flesh, even "in the likeness of sinful flesh" (Rom 8:3), and to die innocently the shameful death on the Cross for the forgiveness of our sins (Phil 2:7; 1 Cor 15:3–5). He rose from the dead so that we might be taken with an incorruptible body into eternal communion with the Triune God.[7] The critic of Christianity Porphyry (ca. AD 233–305) begins his vita on the influential thinker Plotinus (AD 205–279), the founder of Neoplatonism, with the sentence: "Plotinus, the philosopher our contemporary, seemed ashamed of being in the body."[8]

Knowing that God created man in his own image and likeness, and that we came from God's love, which is generous without ulterior motives, the psalmist, on the other hand, prays, "For it was you who formed my inward parts; you knit me together in my mother's womb. I praise you, for I am fearfully and wonderfully made" (Ps 139:13–14). The "Son" of God and "high priest" of the New Covenant," who took on our flesh and blood (Heb 1:2; 2:17), said when he came into the world, "a body you have prepared for me. . . . See, I have come to do your will" (Heb 10:5, 9). From this it follows that "it is by God's will that

---

5   Second Vatican Council, *Optatum Totius* (1965), §16, emphasis added.

6   Michael Fiedrowicz, *Apologie im frühen Christentum. Die Kontroverse um den christlichen Wahrheitsanspruch in den ersten Jahrhunderten* (Paderborn, 2006).

7   On Origen's paradigmatic dispute with the anti-Christian polemics of the Middle Platonist philosopher Celsus, whose arguments were taken up again almost unchanged by the eighteenth- and nineteenth-century critics of divine Revelation and religion (against the personality and freedom of God, the Incarnation, the miracles of Jesus as incompatible with the laws of nature, etc.), cf. Michael Fiedrowicz, *Einleitung zu Origenes, Contra Celsum* (= FC50/1) (Freiburg, 2011), 9–122.

8   Porphyry, *On the Life of Plotinus and the Arrangement of His Work*, in Plotinus, *The Enneads*, trans. Stephen MacKenna, https://www.gianfrancobertozzi.it/plotino/testi/PorfirioVitaPlotino.pdf.

we have been sanctified through the offering of the body of Jesus Christ once for all" (Heb 10:10).

And in the famous fourth-century hymn *Te Deum Laudamus* ("Thee, O God, We Praise"), the Church triumphs over all Platonic and Manichaean hostility to the body, calling out to Christ:

> Thou art the King of Glory: O Christ.
> Thou art the everlasting Son: of the Father.
> When thou tookest upon thee to deliver man: thou didst not abhor
> the Virgin's womb.
> (Tu ad liberandum suscepturus hominem,
> non horruisti Virginis uterum.)[9]

The most important of the apologists were St. Justin Martyr (the philosopher), Tertullian, Origen, Lactantius, and finally St. Augustine with his mighty work *De civitate Dei*. These are the beginnings of the Catholic Church.

In the New Testament, the word "catholic," in connection with faith and the Church, does not yet occur as such, although it is seen indirectly in Paul's letter to "all God's beloved in Rome, who are called to be saints" (Rom 1:7) and whose "faith is proclaimed throughout the world" (Rom 1:8), i.e., universally or *catholic* (see also Matt 28:18–20). In defining the term "catholic," the Church Fathers later often refer to this passage (Rom 1:8), because it expresses—*ante litteram*—the world-spanning dimension of the proclamation of the Gospel of Christ. In profane Greek, *kata holos* ("about the whole") means among the philosophers that which corresponds to the "whole" and which constitutes the universal principles of being.[10]

According to St. Isidore of Seville, "catholic" is to be translated into Latin literally as "universal," and means that the whole of the world is summed up in unity (Christ as head of the body) and multiplicity (the members of his body) and finds in these the principle of its unity.[11] Catholic, as a statement about the credo of a Christian, is what a person is who believes *and* lives (praxis) in an ortho-dox (i.e., right [*orthós*] way), and who gives God the glory (*doxa*) in Christian worship.[12] For the Christian liturgy and lifestyle are a glorification of God in his works of creation, redemption, and reconciliation.

---

[9]   Adolf Adam, ed., *Te Deum laudamus. Große Gebete der Kirche* (lat.-dt.) (Freiburg, 2001).

[10]   Wolfgang Beinert, *Art. Katholisch, Katholizität*: HWPh 4, 787–789; H. Moureau, *Art. Catholicité*: DThC II, 2, 1999–2012.

[11]   St. Isidore of Seville, *Etymologiae* 7.4.4; 7.1,1; 10.153.

[12]   Joachim Drumm, *Doxologie und Dogma. Die Bedeutung der Doxologie für die Wiedergewinnung theologischer Rede in der evangelischen Theologie* (Paderborn, 1991).

The factual meaning of "catholic" is that Christians are catholic when they are in agreement with the Church in their faith, especially with the bishops united with the pope, and do not belong to the small groups of heretics and schismatics who are restricted to a certain region. For unlike the heretics and schismatics, the orthodox Catholic Church is spread over the whole earth in accordance with St. Paul's praise for the Romans, whose "faith is proclaimed throughout the world [en holo to kosmo; in universo mundo]" (Rom 1:8; see Matt 28:18–20).

St. Augustine (AD 354–430), the most influential provider of ideas to the Western Church and theology, points out that the content of what is "catholic" is constituted not merely by the formal determination of the Church's universal spread but rather also by the observance of the divine precepts, participation in all the Church's sacraments, and dissociation from all false teachings. In the face of their particularism, the truth of the Catholic faith is demonstrated by the witness of God's truth in his revelation, which is proclaimed by the Church in a catholic way, i.e., throughout the world.[13]

And when we consider the Ordo (College) of Bishops in the apostolic succession, we recognize in Peter and his successors, the Bishops of Rome, the surest and most powerful criterion of what defines catholic. For it was to Peter, as the representative of the whole Church (cui totius ecclesiae figuram gerenti) that the Lord himself said, "[O]n this rock I will build my church" (Matt 16:18). And Augustine enumerates all the successors of St. Peter as Bishops of Rome, beginning with St. Linus (r. ca. AD 67–79), St. Anacletus (r. ca. AD 79–90), and St. Clement I (r. ca. AD 90–93), who are also mentioned by name in the Roman Canon, down to the popes of his own time: St. Damasus I (r. AD 366–384), St. Siricius (r. AD 384–399), and St. Anastasius I (r. AD 399–402), who counted Ss. Augustine, Jerome, and Paulinus of Nola among his friends.[14]

The use of the term "catholic" as a concept of faith in confession and theological reflection was begun by St. Ignatius of Antioch († ca. AD 110). With his seven letters—to the Ephesians, Magnesians, Trallians, Romans, Philadelphians, Smyrnaeans, and Bishop St. Polycarp—along with the First Letter of St. Clement (ca. AD 93–97)[15] and the letter of St. Polycarp of Smyrna, he acts as a bridge between the late New Testament writings and the Christian literature of the second century.

In the expression "Catholic Church," the two components of subject and predicate are firmly linked. "Catholic" denotes an essential quality (attribute)

---

[13] St. Augustine, Epistula 93.7.38.

[14] St. Augustine, Epistula 53.1.2.

[15] St. Clement, Epistula Clementis ad Coronthios (= FC 15) (Freiburg, 1994), 7–61.

of the Church of Christ, thus highlighting her identity in relation to God and his revelation in Christ. It is also the characteristic that distinguishes her from other teachings and Christian communities, even if these claim to be themselves the true Church of Christ. On the occasion of the martyrdom of St. Polycarp of Smyrna (February 22, AD 156), who had "in our own times been an apostolic and prophetic teacher, and bishop of the Catholic Church which is in Smyrna,"[16] his community wrote "to all the congregations of the Holy and Catholic Church in every place"[17] of "our Lord Jesus Christ, the Savior of our souls, the Governor of our bodies, and *the Shepherd of the Catholic Church* throughout the world."[18]

Forty years earlier, his fellow bishop St. Ignatius of Antioch had already used the term for the first time to reference this universal (*catholic* in Greek) community of faith founded by Christ and led by the Spirit of God:

> Wherever the bishop shall appear, there let the multitude [of the people] also be; even as, wherever Jesus Christ is, there is the Catholic Church.[19]

In the *Muratorian Fragment* (ca. AD 180–200), which contains the oldest list of the New Testament canon, the Catholic Church is described as the authentic Church against the Gnostics. Their claim to be the true Church is denied by the Catholic Church, the *ecclesia catholica*.

Tertullian already used the term "catholic" as a substantive adjective to refer to the Church: "the *catholica*."[20] She alone is the true Church of Christ, which sacramentally mediates salvation. In the *Martyrdom of Pionius*, which describes a "priest of the Catholic Church"[21] during the persecution of Christians under Roman Emperor Decius (r. AD 249–252), St. Pionius and each of his companions answer the pagan judge's question "What is your name?" with "Christian." To the additional question "Of which church?" they reply, "Of the Catholic."[22]

Augustine regularly speaks of the *Catholica* in contrast to the heretics, who, like the Donatists (the *Pars Donati*), cannot be the true Church because they only exist in a limited region (in Roman Africa) and because they lack

---

[16] *Martyrdom of Polycarp* 16.

[17] *Martyrdom of Polycarp* introduction.

[18] *Martyrdom of Polycarp* 19, emphasis added; cf. 1 Pet 2:25.

[19] St. Ignatius of Antioch, *Epistula ad Smyrnaeos* 8.1–2.

[20] Tertullian, *Praescriptione* 26.9.

[21] *Martyrium Pionii* 2.

[22] *Martyrium Pionii* 9.

the characteristic of (diachronic and synchronic) universality. The Council of Nicaea (AD 325) requires heretics and schismatics who wish to return to the Catholic and apostolic Church and be readmitted to full communion to subscribe to *Catholic teaching* in everything.[23]

There is no Christ without the Catholic Church, and the Catholic Church concretely represents Christ on earth. The visible Church is the *Christus praesens*. And this is illustrated in the bishop who, with the presbyterate and the deacons, represents the authority of Christ in the Church. The bishop is also the criterion which assures that the Church's teaching accords with the truth and that her sacraments of Baptism and the Eucharist, along with all her pastoral activity, are valid:

> Let no man do anything connected with the Church without the bishop. Let that be deemed a proper Eucharist, which is [administered] either by the bishop, or by one to whom he has entrusted it. Wherever the bishop shall appear, there let the multitude [of the people] also be; even as, *wherever Jesus Christ is, there is the Catholic Church.*[24]

In the nineteenth century, the most significant theologian apart from St. John Henry Newman and Matthias Joseph Scheeben (1835–188), namely, Johann Adam Möhler (1796–1838),[25] was to offer a definition of Catholic Church that was developed entirely from the spirit of the Church Fathers and which also had an influence on Vatican II:

> By the Church on earth, Catholics understand the visible community of believers, founded by Christ, in which—by means of an enduring apostleship established by him and appointed to conduct all nations, in the course of ages, back to God—the works wrought by him during his earthly life, for the redemption and sanctification of mankind, are, under the guidance of his Spirit, continued to the end of the world.
>
> Thus, to a *visible society of men*, is this great, important, and mysterious work entrusted. The ultimate reason of the visibility of the Church is to be found in the *Incarnation* of the Divine Word. . . . Thus, the visible Church . . . is the Son of God himself, everlastingly manifesting himself among men in a human form, perpetually renovated,

---

23 Cf. Council of Nicaea, can. 8; 9; 19 (COD 9, f., 15).

24 St. Ignatius of Antioch, *Epistula ad Smyrnaeos* 8.1–2, emphasis added.

25 The great Karl Barth assesses his significance: "In the German area, he was certainly the greatest to have been produced by the Roman Catholic Church in modern times." Quoted from Eberhard Busch, *Karl Barths Lebenslauf* (Munich, 1986), 428.

and eternally young—the permanent incarnation of the same, as in Holy Writ even the faithful are called "the body of Christ." Hence it is evident that the Church, though composed of men, is yet not purely human. Nay, as in Christ, the divinity and the humanity are to be clearly distinguished, though both are bound in unity; so is he in undivided entireness perpetuated in the Church. Hence these two parts change their predicates. If the divine—the living Christ and his Spirit—constitute undoubtedly that which is infallible, and eternally inerrable in the Church, so also the human is infallible and inerrable in the same way, because the divine without the human has no existence for us: yet the human is not inerrable in itself, but only as the organ, and as the manifestation of the divine.[26]

The term "catholic" applies to the Christological foundation of the Church, as well as to the episcopal constitution that is inextricably linked to this. It refers to the quantitative spread of the Church throughout the whole world and the quality of her teaching, which is vouchsafed by orthodoxy. The same idea of catholicity is found in the *Martyrdom of Polycarp* (ca. AD 156), which uses the term in this sense no less than four times and understands it in terms of universality and the true Church, as distinguished from schismatic and heretical communities. In the course of time, catholicity becomes a means of contrasting the Church with those who fall away from the true faith (apostasy), those who distort it through false doctrine (heresy), and those who destroy the unity of the Church or fall away from its communion (schism).

St. Cyprian of Carthage directed his treatise *On the Unity of the Catholic Church* against the Christians who fell away from the faith and unity of the Church during the two persecutions under Roman Emperor Decius and also against schismatic tendencies, showing in his writing that the unity of the Church is grounded in the mystery of the Trinity. And from this, he says, it follows that

> whoever is separated from the Church and is joined to an adulteress, is separated from the promises of the Church; nor can he who forsakes the Church of Christ attain to the rewards of Christ. . . . He can no longer have God for his Father, who has not the Church for his mother. If anyone could escape who was outside the Ark of Noah, then he also may escape who shall be outside of the Church. . . . He

---

[26] *Symbolik*, no. 36 (Geiselmann, 387–389); *Symbolism*, no. 36, https://archive.org/details/symbolismorexpoomh/page/n5/mode/2up?re.

who breaks the peace and the concord of Christ, does so in opposition to Christ; he who gathers elsewhere than in the Church, scatters the Church of Christ.[27]

This expresses the (instrumental) necessity of the Church for salvation and the principle is born: extra ecclesiam nulla salus (outside the Catholic Church community and the Catholic Creed there is no salvation).[28] This does not, however, mean "that there is no grace outside the Church,"[29] for those who do not visibly belong to it through no fault of their own.[30] This is not a matter of abstract speculation about the possibilities of salvation for non-Catholic Christians—the usual meaning since the sixteenth century—or for the non-baptized but rather a question of binding Christians to the visible community given to them by God with its means of grace.

Although the relationship of the primacy of the Roman Church to the unity of the episcopate, i.e., as the ecclesia principalis unde unitas sacerdotalis exorta est, has not yet been captured conceptually with final clarity, the Cathedra Petri (Chair of Peter) nevertheless embodies the principle of the one origin of the priesthood,[31] in which all the bishops have their share while still preserving the totality.[32] The Catholic Church is the mystery of the unity of the members with Christ as the head of the body:

> Does he who does not hold this unity of the Church think that he holds the Faith? Does he who strives against and resists the Church trust that he is in the Church when, moreover, the blessed apostle Paul teaches the same thing, and sets forth the sacrament of unity, saying, "There is one body and one spirit, one hope of your calling, one Lord, one faith, one Baptism, one God?" [Eph 4:4–6]. And this

---

[27] St. Cyprian, De unitate Ecclesiae 6; cf. Origen, In Jesu nave 3.5.

[28] St. Cyprian, Epistula 73.21: "Extra ecclesiam salus non est."

[29] A statement made by the Jansenist Pasquier Quesnel, which was condemned by Pope Clement XI in the constitution Unigenitus Dei Filius on September 8, 1713 (DH 2429). Cf. the rejection of particular salvific will already made by Pope Innocent X in the constitution Cum occasione of May 31, 1653, with respect to Bishop Cornelius Jansen of Ypres, who is the originator of Jansenism (DH 2006).

[30] Cf. the statement by Pasquier Quesnel that no grace is granted outside the Church (DH 2429), which was likewise condemned in the constitution Unigenitus Dei Filii (1713), and also Vatican II's Dogmatic Constitution on the Church Lumen Gentium.

[31] St. Cyprian, Epistula 59.14.

[32] St. Cyprian, De unitate Ecclesiae 5.

unity we ought firmly to hold and assert, especially those of us that
are bishops who preside in the Church, that we may also prove the
episcopate itself to be one and undivided.[33]

Bishop St. Fulgentius of Ruspe († AD 533), who served in the province
of Byzacena in North Africa and was even able to impress the anti-Catholic
Arian Vandal King Thrasamund with his erudition, differentiates, in the tradition of Augustine via Prosper of Aquitaine († AD 463), what he says about
the necessity of the Church for salvation. For Catholics, mere formal Church
membership is no guarantee of entry into heaven; for all others, the possibility
of conversion remains until death. In his summary of the Catholic doctrines
for a layman named Peter, he declares:

> For just as without community with the Catholic Church Baptism
> and works of mercy have no value except perhaps that of being pun-
> ished more leniently, but not that of being numbered among the
> children of God, so, in spite of belonging to the Catholic Church,
> one cannot attain eternal life through Baptism alone if after Baptism
> one leads a bad life.[34]

From this comes rule 37 in chapter 40:

> Hold fast with firm and unshakeable faith that not all who have
> received the Sacrament of Baptism in the Catholic Church will attain
> eternal life, but only those who after Baptism lead a right life, abstain-
> ing from the vices and allurements of the flesh.[35]

The Church is a *congregatio permixta* in which the good, like it or not, have
to put up with the bad—and there are all sorts among the clergy, monks, and
laity—provided that they do not shake the foundations of the Church through
heresy and schism.[36] The necessity of good works for salvation, however, has
nothing to do with self-justification from good works or even the works of
the law without faith, hope, and love. For in chapter 31, rule 28, of his work,
St. Fulgentius impresses on Catholics who, in empty self-confidence, want to
boast to God of their life's achievements: "Hold fast with firm and unshakeable

---

[33] St. Cyprian, *De unitate Ecclesiae* 4–5; *Epistula* 55.21.
[34] St. Fulgentius, *De fide ad Petrum* 42; cf. *De fide ad Petrum* 78 (ch. 37), regula 34.
[35] St. Fulgentius, *De fide ad Petrum* 81.
[36] Cf. St. Fulgentius, *De fide ad Petrum* 84 (ch. 43, rule 40).

faith that here no man can repent whom God does not enlighten and convert by his grace, which is bestowed without merit."[37]

Faith is meritorious because man freely consents to God's self-revealing truth in supernatural love, insofar as he is moved by grace to immediacy to God. For only a spiritually endowed creature is immediate to God, even though this personal relationship requires mediation through Christ, the God-man.[38] It is a question of the genuine and true transmission of the Gospel in the legitimate Church standing in the Apostolic Tradition. Only through the Church do we know whether the teachings claimed by these or those groups to be the word of God really do come from God, or are of their own invention. It is not enough to be subjectively convinced of the truth of private enlightenment and revelation; the faith of the Church has its foundation in the objective teaching of the apostles (Acts 2:42) and "the church of the living God" (1 Tim 3:15). For the revelation in Christ is present in the apostolic witness in a completed form. Therefore, in the historical growth of the Church's faith consciousness, what comes about is merely a deeper understanding, not a substantive change or an increase in content.[39] It was not done to place the authority of the Church above the word of God but precisely to increase the certainty of its being passed on faithfully in the Church, rather than abandoned to the subjective interpretation of Scripture by heretics or the semi-Christian speculations of Gnosticism and Manichaeism, to whom St. Augustine spoke the famous words: "I should not believe the Gospel except as moved by the authority of the Catholic Church [Ego vero Evangelio non crederem, nisi me catholicae ecclesiae commoveret auctoritas]."[40]

It is remarkable that the term "catholic," which found its way into the Creed as a predicate of the Church, was first coined in Antioch of all places. Antioch, the third largest city in the Roman Empire, was the Church's first missionary center after Jerusalem and the location of the activities of Peter and Paul and Barnabas: "it was in Antioch that the disciples were first called 'Christians'" (Acts 11:26). So the disciples are Christianoi because they believe in "Jesus Christ, the Son of God" (Mark 1:1) and publicly confess him: "[B]ecause if you confess with your lips that Jesus is Lord and believe in your heart that God raised him from the dead, you will be saved. For one believes with the heart and so is justified, and one confesses with the mouth and so is saved" (Rom 10:9 10). But the disciples are also called Christians because they are anointed in Christ, the Lord's Anointed (Messiah), with the Holy Spirit in

---

[37]   St. Fulgentius, De fide ad Petrum 72.

[38]   St. Thomas Aquinas, ST II-II, q. 2, a. 9.

[39]   Vatican II, Dei Verbum, §8.

[40]   St. Augustine, Contra epistulam Manichaei quam vocant fundamenti 5.6.

Baptism and Confirmation (Acts 8:15–16) through the water of rebirth and renewal by the Holy Spirit (Tit 3:5).

After all the disputes with the heretics and schismatics in the formulation of dogma on the theology of the Trinity, Christology, grace, and the sacraments at the end of the fourth century, Bishop St. Pacian of Barcelona († AD 392)[41] succeeded in conceptualizing catholicity as the criterion for being a true Christian and for the true Church:

> Christian is my name, but Catholic my surname
> [Christianus mihi nomen est, catholicus vero cognomen].[42]

It is clear that henceforth anyone explaining the Creed will portray the predicate "catholic" in reference to the Church of the Triune God with its two components of universality and orthodoxy. The catecheses that St. Cyril of Jerusalem gave to baptismal candidates in the Church of the Holy Sepulchre in his episcopal city (ca. AD 348) are famous. We are well-informed about the episcopal catecheses before and after Baptism in the Jerusalem liturgy by the consecrated virgin Egeria, who provides an account of her pilgrimage through the Holy Land in AD 381–384.[43] Cyril explains the words of the Creed regarding the Catholic Church thus:

> It is called Catholic then because it extends over all the world, from one end of the earth to the other; and because it teaches universally and completely one and all the doctrines which ought to come to men's knowledge, concerning things both visible and invisible, heavenly and earthly; and because it brings into subjection to godliness the whole race of mankind, governors and governed, learned and unlearned; and because it universally treats and heals the whole class of sins, which are committed by soul or body, and possesses in itself every form of virtue which is named, both in deeds and words, and in every kind of spiritual gifts.[44]

Starting from the concept of "*ecclesia*" as an "assembly of people," Cyril adds that even the heretics have their meetings and therefore see themselves as a church. This is why in the Creed the Church is further defined by the adjectives "holy" and "catholic." The assemblies of the heretical churches are to be avoided.

---

[41] Eckhard Reichert, Art. *Pacianus: Lexikon der antiken christlichen Literatur* (Freiburg, 1998), 472.

[42] St. Pacian of Barcelona, *Epistula* 1.7.

[43] Egeria, *Itinerarium*, 45–47 (= FC 20), 294–305.

[44] St. Cyril of Jerusalem, *Catecheses* 18.23.

Then he exhorts his baptismal candidates, "And if ever you are sojourning in cities, inquire . . . not merely where the Church is, but where is the Catholic Church. For this is the peculiar name of this Holy Church, the mother of us all, which is the spouse of our Lord Jesus Christ, the only-begotten Son of God."[45]

The concept of catholicity thus formed remained unchallenged until the time of the great upheaval of the Protestant Reformation of the sixteenth century. As a sum of Tradition, the catholicity of the Church can be said to manifest itself as follows:

1. in her *universal spread* in accordance with God's universal salvific will (Rom 1:8; 1 Tim 2:4; Tit 2:11) and Jesus's commission for world mission (Matt 28:19–20); and

2. in her *orthodoxy*, because she is "the church of the living God, the pillar and bulwark of the truth" (1 Tim 3:15) and cannot be destroyed by external persecutions and internal decay (indestructibility). She is infallible in presenting the revealed faith received from the apostles and faithfully interpreted in Tradition (infallibility).

3. In addition, there is the doctrine of the *epistemological principles of Catholic theology*:
    a. Sacred Scripture (*Sacra Scriptura*);
    b. the Apostolic Tradition (*Traditio Apostolica*); and
    c. the sense of faith of believing Catholics (*sensus fidei fidelium*). This finds its definitive and defining expression in the Church's Magisterium (*magisterium ecclesiasticum*). It receives its legitimacy on the basis of the apostolic succession of the College of Bishops, with the pope as the principle of its unity in faith and ecclesial communion (*successio apostolica et Petrina*).

Even the schism between the Christian West and East that took place in 1054, after a long process of estrangement and several interruptions of communion, did not abolish the principle of the Church's catholicity—with the aforementioned essential characteristics—but merely opened up its culmination in the doctrinal and jurisdictional primacy of the pope as a matter requiring consideration. The Catholic Church—by no means only the Latin-Western Church that is in communion with the pope, holds fast to its claim of orthodoxy. She understands the primacy of the Bishop of Rome as an institution of

---

[45] St. Cyril of Jerusalem, *Catecheses* 18.26.

divine right that is contained in the revealed faith, a primacy which thus must not be relativized as an accidental product of history and hence an institution of (mutable) canon law (*ius mere ecclesiasticum*).[46] Even if the dogma of papal doctrinal and jurisdictional primacy did develop conceptually over the course of history, the history of Christian doctrinal development is by no means an accidental construct.

The churches of the Eastern patriarchates that are separated from the Holy See collectively call themselves the Orthodox Church. But by holding fast to their claim to be in substantive and formal continuity with the churches of the Fathers, they are one with us in confessing the Niceno-Constantinopolitan Creed of the Church which the work of the Triune God has brought forth as "the one, holy, catholic, and apostolic Church."[47]

The heritage of common catholicity lies in successfully resisting all heresies against belief in the Holy Trinity ("one God in three Persons") and the doctrine of the hypostatic union (the unity of God and man) in the Person of the eternal Son of God, who is true God with the Father and the Holy Spirit and who assumed our human nature from Mary ("one divine Person in two natures"). Mary is the God-Bearer, the Mother of God, not because she was the female-maternal co-principle (alongside a male-paternal one) in the eternal procession of the Son from the Father, through which the Son is true God, but rather because he who was born of her as a man is the divine Person of the Son who took on flesh from her. Therefore, the predicates (*idiomata*) of being human can be applied to the divine Person of Jesus, and it is correct to say that God was born and suffered (*communicatio idiomatum*).

Although the symbol of the faith *Quicumque*, which dates back to the fifth century and is—probably falsely—attributed to St. Athanasius, has practically only gained any importance in the West, it is nevertheless of universal significance in that it understands the confession of the mysteries of the Trinity and Christ as the epitome of the Catholic faith:

> Whoever wishes to be saved must, before all else, hold the Catholic Faith. . . . This, then, is Catholic Faith: We worship one God in the Trinity and the Trinity in the unity; . . . But it is necessary for everlasting salvation also to believe faithfully the Incarnation of our Lord Jesus Christ. . . . This is the Catholic Faith; unless each one has believed it faithfully and firmly, he will not be saved.[48]

---

[46] Karl Rahner, *Über den Begriff des "Ius divinum" im katholischen Verständnis*: SW 10, 605–625.

[47] DH 150.

[48] DH 75–76.

Even the scholar Boethius († ca. AD 524–526), the last Roman, who became so significant for medieval theology, limited himself in his work *On the Catholic Faith* to these two central mysteries. For him, as he writes in his theological tractate *The Trinity Is One God Not Three Gods*, these are also the crucial criteria for calling oneself "Catholic":

> There are many who claim as theirs the dignity of the Christian religion; but that form of faith is valid and only valid which, both on account of the universal character of the rules and doctrines affirming its authority, and because the worship in which they are expressed has spread throughout the world, is called catholic or universal.[49]

But, in addition to the universal spread of the Church in the service of the universal salvific will, and to her calling to hold fast to revealed truth as handed down in their teaching by the apostles in the rule of faith (*regula fidei*) or in the Creed (*symbolum fidei catholicae*) [orthodoxy], there is a third determinant of the conceptual content of "catholic," namely, Catholic hermeneutics or theological epistemology.[50]

When it came to heretics who were guilty of a false understanding or lack of intellectual grasp of the revealed truths about God, Christ, grace, and the sacraments, it is obvious the dispute initially revolved round to the content of divine Revelation. It was only in the course of the spiritual struggles that the question arose of formal authority and the competent agencies legitimized by divine authority to present a dogmatic decision to the Church in a binding way and one that was relevant to salvation.

Against the Gnostics, who appealed only to the secret teachings of the apostles known to an esoteric circle, or who saw themselves as empowered in their abstract speculations by higher spiritual forces, St. Irenaeus, the Bishop of Lyons—who came from Asia Minor in the Greek East but was very familiar with the Roman Church—develops the clear principles of Catholic epistemology in his *The Demonstration of the Apostolic Preaching* and *Against Heresies* (ca. AD 180). Revelation took place in the history of salvation in the historically real people of Israel. According to Christian understanding, it became fully historically present in the Incarnation of God in Jesus Christ, and in his Cross and Resurrection, and remains effective in the Church in the

---

49 Boethius, *De Trinitate*, 1, http://www.documentacatholicaomnia
    .eu/03d/0480-0524,_Boethius,_The_Theological_Tractates,_EN.pdf.

50 Johannes Beumer, *Die theologische Methode*: HDG I, 6 (Freiburg, 1972); Georg Söll, *Dogma und Dogmenentwicklung*: HDG I, 5 (Freiburg, 1971).

Holy Spirit until the consummation of mankind and the whole cosmos on the Last Day and for all eternity.

A doctrine or its declaration can only be orthodox if it conforms to three principles in its composite and inner relative structure. Sacred Scripture is the source and basis, and thus the fundamental and supreme communication of the word of God in the mouth of man (1 Thess 2:13). Connected with this is the oral Tradition of apostolic teaching and practice. The liturgy is the prayed Apostolic Tradition and thus its heart. The rule of faith manifests itself in the rule of prayer and vice versa: lex orandi, lex credendi.[51] That is why the liturgy is a privileged *locus theologicus* (topic of theology).[52] Added as a formal criterion guaranteeing the correct interpretation of the word of God in the faith of the Church is the authority of the legitimate bishops, i.e., who have genuine apostolic succession and are also in communion with the pope. Although Irenaeus does not yet use the term "catholic" as a technical term, he nevertheless proceeds from the theological (not merely empirical-statistical) datum that the Church is spread over the whole (*kat-holes*) inhabited world to the very edges of the earth.

Since he cannot enumerate all the episcopal successors since the time of the apostles, Irenaeus simply uses the apostolic succession of the bishops of the "Church founded and organized at Rome by the two most glorious apostles, Peter and Paul" to illustrate "the tradition originating with the apostles and the faith preached for men (Rom 1:8)." "For it is a matter of necessity that every Church should agree with this Church, on account of its preeminent authority (*propter potiorem principalitatem*)."[53] And when summing up the principles of Scripture, Tradition, and succession, the martyr-bishop of Lyons concludes:

> And by this succession, the ecclesiastical Tradition from the apostles, and the preaching of the truth, have come down to us. And this is most abundant proof that there is one and the same vivifying Faith, which has been preserved in the Church from the apostles until now, and handed down in truth.[54]

This framework of criteria is formulated by the monk and Church Father St. Vincent of Lérins († ca. AD 445) in his classic treatise on the catholicity of the faith and the Church, the *Commonitorium* (AD 434), a defense of the

---

[51] Cf. Pseudo-Celestine, *Indiculus*, ch. 8 (DH 246).

[52] Gerhard Cardinal Müller, *Dogma e liturgia: Una nuova giovinezza per la Chiesa*, ed. Vincenzo Nuara, Verona, 2019, 23–35.

[53] St. Irenaeus, *Adversus haereses* 3.3.2.

[54] St. Irenaeus, *Adversus haereses* 3.3.3.

age and universality of the Catholic faith against the unholy innovations of all heretics:

> In the Catholic Church itself, all possible care must be taken, that we hold that Faith which has been believed everywhere, always, by all [quod ubique, quod semper, quod ab omnibus creditum est]. . . . This rule we shall observe if we follow universality, antiquity, consent. We shall follow universality if we confess that one Faith to be true, which the whole Church throughout the world confesses; antiquity, if we in no wise depart from those interpretations which it is manifest were notoriously held by our holy ancestors and fathers; consent, in like manner, if in antiquity itself we adhere to the consentient definitions and determinations of all, or at the least of almost all priests and doctors [bishops and teachers].[55]

It should be noted that the criterion of age here is not a nostalgic reference to "the good old days" but rather refers to the Tradition of faith from the apostles, as manifested in the rules of faith and creeds. In this, the Roman Church and its bishop have a special guiding function in the fight against heretics.[56] There is also no change in the substance of revealed truth but simply a development in the deeper appropriation and understanding of it (profectus fidei non permutatio in eodem scilicet dogmate, eodem sensu eademque sententia).[57] This is also how the Second Vatican Council understands the development of doctrine in the Catholic Church in accordance with the mutually dependent Sacred (Apostolic) Tradition, Sacred Scripture and the Church's Magisterium of the pope and the bishops united with him.[58]

This author does not admire the heretics, as is the case in modern times, as critical and provocative (unorthodox) thinkers against ossified traditions and thoughtless habits, or as brave fighters for freedom against the Church's authority. Rather, he despises them as falsifiers of the truth. In the Church, the revealed truths of the faith must not be understood from the point of view of the genius of individual teachers and school leaders. Instead, these truths must be measured against the teaching of the Church in accordance with the authority of the councils and popes:

---

55 St. Vincent of Lérins, *Commonitorium* 2.6.
56 St. Vincent of Lérins, *Commonitorium* 6.3ff.
57 St. Vincent of Lérins, *Commonitorium* 23.2–3.
58 Vatican II, *Dei Verbum*, §§7–10.

This being the case, he is the true and genuine Catholic who loves the truth of God, who loves the Church, who loves the body of Christ, who esteems divine religion and the Catholic Faith above everything, above the authority, above the regard, above the genius, . . . and continuing steadfast and established in the Faith, resolves that he will believe that, and that only, which he is sure the Catholic Church has held universally and from ancient time.[59]

In addition to the criteria regarding the content of what is "catholic," the criterion of the formal authority of the Church's Magisterium had emerged ever more clearly in the course of the debates on the correct version of the mysteries of the Trinity, the Incarnation, the objective efficacy of the sacraments, justification and grace in the confession of faith, and theological reflection. But what is the origin of the ultimate authority of the bishops and the pope in the binding and salvation-relevant presentation of the content of the faith and its authentic or infallible interpretation? Those who view the development of the early Church exclusively in empirical-phenomenological terms, will only be able to point to the sociological function of the leaders of a community. But anyone who believes that the Church is a work of God, who wants to communicate himself through her proclamation to mankind in his *Word* and *Spirit* as salvation and truth, will recognize the origin of the teaching and pastoral office of the bishops in the will of Jesus for his Church and in his sharing of his messianic consecration and mission with the apostles.[60]

The apostles and their successors in the episcopate are authorized by Jesus as the witnesses and proclaimers of the Gospel of God. This includes the authority to judge or condemn a doctrine in the Holy Spirit according to the degree to which it conforms with divine Revelation and its full content being presented in Sacred Scripture and Apostolic Tradition. This is the "sound doctrine [*sana doctrina*]" (2 Tim 4:3) to which Timothy, as a fellow apostle and successor to the apostle Paul, must hold fast against false teachers (heretics).

Following the example of when the apostles met in Jerusalem to decide whether the Gentiles who had come to faith in Christ must first be circumcised before they were baptized and had to adopt the Jewish law, "bishops came together" (Greek: *synod*; Latin: *concilium*) to defend the faith against false doctrines, as well as to present it to the Church in all its truth as a confession. These were at first regional gatherings of bishops, such as at the Synod of

---

59 St. Vincent of Lérins, *Commonitorium* 10.1.

60 Cf. Second Vatican Council, *Lumen Gentium* (1964), §§18–27; Antonine Roulhac de Rochebrune, *Le munus sanctificandi des évêques selon Lumen Gentium*, §26, Rome, 1996.

Antioch (AD 268), called to condemn the heresy of Paul of Samosata that Christ was a mere man and not God who really became man.

When the Alexandrian presbyter Arius (ca. AD 260–327), with his thesis that the Son of God was not equal to the Father in divine essence, but that Christ was only the first creature and mediator of the rest of creation, the Roman Emperor Constantine summoned the bishops in the territory of his entire empire (the *ecumene*) to Nicaea to clarify the Catholic belief that God truly became man in his Son, Jesus Christ. This is why it is called an ecumenical council. The Emperor took the initiative for this Church assembly, but the teaching authority belongs to Christ's bishops. Just as the Lord had charged the apostles as a whole with the proclamation of the Gospel throughout the world, so all are together responsible for ensuring that all his followers learn the full teaching of Christ (Matt 28:19). Beyond the geographical and temporal limitations of the old Roman Empire, the teaching authority of all bishops, with the pope as the principle of their unity, extends to the whole world, and the dogmatic decisions taken are valid to the ends of the earth.

The concept of the Church's teaching authority also includes the special position of the Bishop of Rome as the Successor of St. Peter. His teaching and jurisdictional primacy, and his relationship to the whole College of Bishops of which he is the head, was clarified definitively by the Ecumenical Councils of Vatican I and Vatican II at the end of a doctrinal development that goes back to the foundation of the Church by Christ.[61]

A representative summary of the definitions of "catholic" from patristic and scholastic sources can be found in the explanation of the Apostles' Creed by St. Thomas Aquinas, the *Doctor communis* (common Doctor).[62] He sees himself, as he says in the prologue to his *Summa theologiae*, as "the doctor of Catholic truth," which means nothing other than "the Christian religion" in the fullness of its truth and in the unity of divine reason with its visible form: in the form of the doctrine of the faith, in the liturgy and the sacraments for the glorification of God and the salvation of men, and finally in the Church as the visible community of salvation led by the bishops and the pope. We do *not* believe, as can be finely distinguished in Latin, *in* the Church, because faith is an exclusive relationship of trust and devotion to God (credo *in* unum Deum), who in his triune life is pure truth and love.[63] We believe the Church in that she is God's saving work and instrument of salvation: *credimus sanctam*

---

[61]   Gerhard Kardinal Müller, *Der Papst. Sendung und Auftrag* (Freiburg, 2017); Eng.: *The Pope: His Mission and His Task* (Washington, DC: The Catholic University of America Press, 2021).

[62]   St. Thomas Aquinas, *Expositio in Symbolum Apostolorum*, a. 9.

[63]   St. Thomas Aquinas, *ST* II-II, q. 2, a. 2; Rufinus of Aquileia, *Commentarius in Symbolum Apostolorum*, 36 (PL 21:373 AB).

ecclesiam. The Church is God's house and people. "Rising from the dead he sent his life-giving Spirit upon his disciples and through him has established his body which is the Church as the universal sacrament of salvation [ut universale salutis sacramentum constituit]."[64] The Church, however, is a mystery of faith because, in her visible social form, we cannot recognize her inner being and divine mission without the aid of the Holy Spirit. But the sins of her members, as well as the failure of her official representatives to face the cultural and political challenges of their epoch, can do great damage to the Church's credibility. Although she is holy in Christ and serves the sanctification of the people, "the Church, embracing in her bosom sinners, at the same time holy and always in need of being purified, always follows the way of penance and renewal."[65]

The Church is the *one* body of Christ with the *many* believers as its members. Christ is the head and the Holy Spirit is the soul of the Church. When we speak of the holy Church, this means nothing other than the assembly of the faithful (*congregatio fidelium*). Later, addressed to the reform movement at the Diet of Augsburg (1530), the Church is also defined as "the congregation of saints, in which the Gospel is rightly [*recte* (purely)] taught and the sacraments are rightly [*recte* (according to the Gospel)] administered."[66] In this particular respect, there is no contradiction between the Catholic and the Reformed-Protestant concept of "church." In the *Apostolic Symbolum* (Apostles' Creed) already, the Church is defined as the "communion of saints" (Acts 20:32), i.e., of the sanctified and of Christians who share in the sacred. It is also classical Catholic doctrine that man's sanctification takes place in the Church through the means of grace of preaching and the sacraments. The only thing missing at this point is a precise indication of the role of ordained office holders in the ministry of the word and the administration of the sacraments. What is interesting now is how St. Thomas explains the four conditions that go to make the true Church of Christ.

There is only one Church, because there is only the one and indivisible body of Christ. Those who separate themselves from her or are excluded from her jeopardize their eternal salvation, because they are then outside her sacramental mediation of salvation. From the unity of the Church, rooted as it is in—and representing—the unity of the Father with the Son (John 17:20–23; 1 John 1:3), grows the unity of the faithful in faith, hope, and love.

The Church is holy because her members live from the bath of regeneration and the anointing with the Holy Spirit of Christ, the Lord's Anointed, and

---

64   Vatican II, *Lumen Gentium*, §48.

65   Vatican II, *Lumen Gentium*, §8.

66   *Confessio Augustana* (Augsburg Confession), art. 7.

because the Triune God has made his dwelling in them. And wherever God is, people live from his sanctifying presence. The Church is catholic-universal because she makes God known through the Gospel, not only among the Jews but among all peoples throughout the earth. The Church consists of three parts: the faithful on their earthly pilgrimage, the saints already perfected in heaven, and the souls still in need of purification in Purgatory.

The Church is also catholic because she does not tolerate any membership restrictions based on legitimate diversity, including race and income. For neither the situation in salvation history (Jews or Gentiles), nor the socio-political status (masters or slaves), nor the distinction of the sexes (male and female) can annul or even impair the unity in Christ (Gal 3:28). The Church is also catholic-universal because, as well as not being spatially limited, she is not temporally limited either. She begins with Abel and continues until the end of the world, and then lives on in the perfected kingdom of God as the community of the blessed.

Finally, the Church is apostolic because her primary and real supporting foundation is Christ himself (1 Cor 3:11). The secondary foundation is the Twelve Apostles as people chosen and commissioned by Christ (Rev 21:14), and then "the apostles' teaching" (Acts 2:42). Among the apostles, however, St. Peter represents the summit and apex, the "head" (*vertex*), i.e., the visible and everlasting principle and foundation of the Church's unity in faith and in the communion of the bishops and all the faithful.[67] For this reason, the Church cannot be destroyed from within by heresies and schisms, nor from without by bloody persecutions or manipulative propaganda. The gates of Hades will fight against her but will not prevail (*non praevalebunt*) [Matt 16:18]. The Church remains free from error and infallible in her faith and teaching (*infallibilitas in credendo et docendo*). Nor can she be undermined by ideologies or relativized by hermeneutics that fundamentally deny the capacity for truth of human reason and the possibility of divine Revelation a priori, and thus reduced to a mere religion of humanity or civil religion. The Church is also promised indestructibility as a social body. Whether there are many or few who gather in the name of the Lord, Christ is always in their midst (Matt 18:18), and he remains with his Church until the end of time (Matt 28:20). And only the Church of Peter at Rome (*sola Ecclesia Petri*) has always stood firm in the faith and remained pure and free from all error. Nor can this come as any surprise since Jesus did say to Peter, "I have prayed for you that your own faith may not fail [ut non deficiat fides tua]" (Luke 22:32).

---

67 Vatican II, *Lumen Gentium*, §§18, 23.

How a Catholic sense of Tradition is formed:
a self-experiment

I was born on New Year's Eve 1947 and am now going to put myself in the position of a first-century Christian born in AD 47, the exact year of the eight-hundredth anniversary of the foundation of Rome (*ab urbe condita*). In his life story, it is possible to study the effects of the Christ event (ca. AD 30), the formation of the early Church (from AD 30–33), and Paul's conversion (AD 35) up to the turn of the second century.

Over a distance of nineteen hundred years, it might be possible to construct "parallel lives" in the style of the Greek writer Plutarch (AD 45–125) and in them biographically map the course of events in an individual lifetime.[68]

When my time-displaced contemporary was born in AD 47, there were already (Jewish) Christians in Rome who, in around AD 49, were affected by expulsions under Emperor Claudius (r. AD 41–54).[69] Let us identify this man with someone called Claudius Ephebus. At the age of forty-nine, he was with Valerius Bito and Fortunatus (from Corinth) as one of the three emissaries of the "Church of God sojourning at Rome"[70] who delivered the great letter of exhortation to the Church of Corinth (written ca. AD 96).[71] This letter is also called the "First Letter of Clement" after St. Clement, the third episcopal Successor of St. Peter in Rome. Both St. Irenaeus of Lyons[72] and then Eusebius of Caesarea in his *Church History* also credibly report[73] that this Bishop of Rome was the author of the letter in question. The fact that he is not named individually as the author but writes in the name of the Roman Church is not an argument against papal primacy and the monepiscopacy but rather one in favor of understanding that the primacy of the pope is embedded in the primacy of the Church of Rome, which is a "foundation" (in the ecclesiological sense) of Ss. Peter and Paul. Thus, the Roman primacy is exercised ideally in the collegiality of the bishops and the synodality of the Roman Church, represented by the Sacred College of Cardinals, the pope's very own (historically evolved) advisory body.

I have chosen the historical person Claudius Ephebus—displaced by nineteen hundred years—because our sense of the stretch of time in which our

---

[68]   Plutarch, *Griechische und römische Heldenleben*, Wiesbaden, 1996; Eng.: *Plutarch's Lives of the Noble Greeks and Romans*, commonly called *Parallel Lives* or *Plutarch's Lives*.

[69]   Suetonius, *De vita Caesarum, lib V. De Vita Claudii*, 25, 4: "Judaeos impulsore Chresto assidue tumultantis Roma expulit."

[70]   St. Clement, *Epistula Clementis ad Coronthios* praescr.

[71]   St. Clement, *Epistula Clementis ad Coronthios* 61.1.

[72]   St. Irenaeus, *Adversus haereses* 3.3.2.

[73]   Eusebius of Caesarea, *Historia ecclesiastica* 3.16.

lives are lived has much in common. My father was born in 1905 and, before he died, had experienced and suffered two World Wars and two inflations, including the inferno unleashed by the spiritually and morally bankrupt Nazi dictatorship, and, after that, the positive reconstruction period of the Federal Republic of Germany, which together gave him a keen awareness of the whole period from 1930–1990. The corresponding stretch of time in the first century is the phase between the origin and spread of Christianity from Jesus to the apostles and their successors in the episcopate, of whom we read in the Acts of the Apostles and Paul's pastoral Letters to Timothy and Titus. During this period, there were two cruel persecutions of the Christians in Rome under the emperors Nero (r. AD 54–68) and Domitian (r. AD 81–96). If I combine the traditions told to me orally by my father and grandfather with my own life experience, and recount them to my now six-to-ten-year-old grand-nephews, the memory of them in narrative mode will—if God allows them to live until the turn of the twenty-second century—add up to a continuum of tradition of around two hundred years.

Let us assume that the father of Claudius Ephebus was one of the Jews in the multi-ethnic city of Jerusalem, who were gathered for the feast of Pentecost when the Holy Spirit descended on them all. He might have been one of the "visitors from Rome" who were staying there (Acts 2:10) and who heard the sermon by St. Peter with which the history of the visible Church begins. For Peter with the eleven other apostles founded the Church's Tradition of the Gospel of the Cross and Resurrection of Christ, in that they were "from the beginning . . . eyewitnesses and servants of the word" (Luke 1:2):

> But Peter, standing with the eleven, raised his voice and addressed them: "Men of Judea and all who live in Jerusalem. . . .
>
> "You that are Israelites, listen to what I have to say: Jesus of Nazareth, a man attested to you by God with deeds of power, wonders, and signs that God did through him among you, as you yourselves know—this man, handed over to you according to the definite plan and foreknowledge of God, you crucified and killed by the hands of those outside the law. But God raised him up, having freed him from death, because it was impossible for him to be held in its power.
>
> "Fellow Israelites, I may say to you confidently of our ancestor David that he both died and was buried, and his tomb is with us to this day. Since he was a prophet, he knew that God had sworn with an oath to him that he would put one of his descendants on his throne. Foreseeing this, David spoke of the resurrection of the

Messiah, saying, 'He was not abandoned to Hades, nor did his flesh experience corruption.' This Jesus God raised up, and of that all of us are witnesses. Being therefore exalted at the right hand of God, and having received from the Father the promise of the Holy Spirit, he has poured out this that you both see and hear. . . . Therefore let the entire house of Israel know with certainty that God has made him both Lord and Messiah, this Jesus whom you crucified." (Acts 2:14–36)

The first Christians did not come to faith through theories devised after reading the New Testament but through the preaching of the apostles and the early Church's profession of Jesus, the Christ of God and Savior of the world. Certainly, the Holy Scriptures of the Old and New Testaments contain the word of God and are thus (through inspiration) "God's word" as a "human word" (1 Thess 2:13; 2 Tim 3:16). But with the enormous size of the Bible and all the different literary genres, as well as the various historical circumstances in which it came into being, it is not easy to discover those statements that are binding for the faith.

What is then the common thread in reading the Bible, and the decisive criterion for finding in it God's revelation for our salvation?

The confessional formulas regarding Jesus's identity with God allow us to understand the whole of Sacred Scripture, even without specialist study. They come from the original Apostolic Tradition and live on to this day: in our baptismal Creed, in the rules of faith (*Regula fidei seu veritatis*), and in the versions of the Creed (*symbolum fidei*). These do not contain any later additions but only explanations, because the whole of the word of God and all truths relevant to salvation are contained, at least implicitly, in Sacred Scripture.[74] This means that a Christian of the first, or tenth, or twenty-first century confesses at his or her baptism exactly the same faith as St. Peter, who said to Jesus for the apostles and the Church of all times: "You are the Messiah [Christ], the Son of the living God" (Matt 16:16). In this all the truths of revelation are contained and bound together.

So the father of our Roman messenger to Corinth may have been one of the "three thousand persons" (Acts 2:41) who came to faith that day and followed the call: "be baptized every one of you in the name of Jesus Christ so that your sins may be forgiven; and you will receive the gift of the Holy Spirit" (Acts 2:38).[75] The newly baptized, who had now become members of Christ's

---

[74] St. Thomas Aquinas, *ST* II-II, q. 1, a. 9.

[75] Lars Hartmann, *Auf den Namen des Herrn. Die Taufe in den neutestamentlichen Schriften* (= SBSt 148) (Stuttgart, 1992).

Church, "devoted themselves to the apostles' teaching and fellowship, to the breaking of bread and the prayers" (Acts 2:42).

Believing in Jesus, the Messiah of Israel and Savior of the whole world, the newly baptized Roman returned from Jerusalem to his homeland. He eagerly participated in the life of the rapidly developing Christian community in Rome. When he married a beautiful Roman woman, he knew about marriage being grounded in the order of creation but also that the vows exchanged by the baptized were given "only in the Lord" (1 Cor 7:39). The young couple knew God's word in Jesus's definitive interpretation:

> But from the beginning of creation, "God made them male and
> female." "For this reason a man shall leave his father and mother and
> be joined to his wife, and the two shall become one flesh." So they are
> no longer two, but one flesh. Therefore what God has joined together,
> let no one separate. (Mark 10:6–9)

Whoever wrote the Letter to the Ephesians was certainly familiar with the Letter to the Romans and was certainly thinking of the hour of the wedding when one gives the bride and groom a few practical tips to take with them; but, instead of a few tips, he discusses the Christological foundation of the marriage between man and woman: "Husbands, love your wives, just as Christ loved the church and gave himself up for her, in order to make her holy by cleansing her with the washing of water by the word" (Eph 5:25–26).

So one of our couple's children may have been born in AD 47 and, like me nineteen hundred years later, have grown into the Christian faith, been baptized and confirmed, and then have participated in the Holy Eucharist.

If Claudius Ephebus, now fifty years old in AD 97, is going to lead the ecclesiastical and theological dispute with the rebellious Corinthians as a representative of the Roman congregation, he will certainly already have a thorough general education and theological training behind him. He was possibly ordained a presbyter in his thirties, around AD 80, and thus belonged to the overseers (*hegoumenoi*) of the Church.[76] These *hegoumenoi*, i.e., the presbyters or ministerial priests, are, as has to be pointed out to the Christians, referencing the Letter to the Hebrews, which was possibly written before *1 Clement*:[77]

> [Obey] your leaders, those who spoke the word of God to you; con-
> sider the outcome of their way of life, and imitate their faith. . . . Obey

---

[76] St. Clement, *Epistula Clementis ad Corinthios* 1.3.
[77] St. Clement, *Epistula Clementis ad Corinthios* 17.1; 36.2–5.

your leaders and submit to them, for they are keeping watch over your souls [like shepherds] and will give an account. Let them do this with joy and not with sighing—for that would be harmful to you. (Heb 13:7, 17)

For the ministerial priesthood—in the two emerging degrees of bishop and presbyter—goes back to the apostles, whose sending is grounded in Jesus's sending by the Father (John 20:21; see also Matt 28:18). And it was the apostles who instructed that, after their deaths, the presbyters they had appointed should in turn appoint successors to serve "the flock of Christ, in a humble, peaceable, and disinterested spirit."[78]

In the *Didache*, a work dating from around AD 100, it is the "bishops and deacons" (cf. Phil 1:1) who have taken over the ministry of the "apostles, prophets, and teachers,"[79] who are "your high priests."[80] For "offerings are to be presented and service performed" according to the ordo, as there are, according to the will of the Lord, different liturgical orders for the high priest, priests, Levites, and laity.[81] For God the Father is our "Creator and Guardian [Bishop],"[82] and the Son of God and our Lord is "the shepherd and guardian of your souls" (1 Pet 2:25). Jesus Christ is "the High Priest of all our offerings,"[83] "the High Priest and Guardian of our souls."[84]

The oldest Church order that has come down to us is the *Traditio Apostolica*. It originates from the Roman Church around AD 200. It contains in nuce all the later rites that go back to a biblical root, as when Paul presents the Lord's Supper in the Letter to the Corinthians and passes it on as primitive apostolic practice and direct revelation from the Lord (1 Cor 11:23).[85] The *Traditio Apostolica*, which was written by St. Hippolytus, attests to the sacramental order of bishops, priests, and deacons ordained by the laying on of hands and prayer in the Holy Spirit. The bishop is called the shepherd of God's holy flock,

---

[78] St. Clement, *Epistula Clementis ad Corinthios* 44.3.

[79] *Didache* 11.3; 15.1; Eph 4:11.

[80] *Didache* 13.3.

[81] St. Clement, *Epistula Clementis ad Corinthios* 40.5.

[82] St. Clement, *Epistula Clementis ad Corinthios* 59.3.

[83] St. Clement, *Epistula Clementis ad Corinthios* 36.1.4.

[84] St. Clement, *Epistula Clementis ad Corinthios* 61.3.

[85] So already, in spite of early Protestant reservations regarding the Mass as a Sacrifice, the Protestant New Testament scholar Hans Lietzmann, *Die Entstehung der christlichen Liturgie nach den ältesten Quellen* (1926) (Darmstadt, 1963), 8–9, Lietzmann, *Messe und Herrenmahl. Eine Studie zur Geschichte der Liturgie* (Berlin, 1955), 117–86.

who "will wear your [God's] high priesthood without reproach, serving night and day, incessantly . . . offering the gifts of your holy church."[86]

This does not mark a return to the Old Testament temple cult, which is abolished in Christ, let alone a borrowing from the pagan cults of the gods, which would imply a complete destruction of the Christian belief in the Triune God and the Incarnation of Christ.

The bishop stands for the true high priest, Christ (in the Old Latin Bible translation, *pontifex*). At his consecration, the bishop receives the guiding Spirit (*spiritus principalis*) and the sure charism of truth (*charisma veritatis certum*).[87] The consecrating bishop prays over the bishop to be consecrated:

> Grant to this thy servant, whom thou hast chosen to be bishop, . . . by the Spirit of high priesthood to have authority to remit sins according to thy commandment, to assign the lots, i.e., appoint the *clergy* according to thy precept,[88] to loose every bond according to the authority which thou gavest to thy apostles, and to please thee in meekness and purity of heart, offering to thee an odor of sweet savor. Through thy Servant Jesus Christ our Lord, through whom be to thee glory, might, honour, with [the] Holy Spirit in [the] holy Church, both now and always and world without end.[89]

I myself was ordained to the priesthood on February 11, 1978, by the eminent theologian Hermann Cardinal Volk (1903–1988), whose age compared to mine was analogous to that of the apostles to the "suitable candidates" they appointed, "having first proved them by the Spirit . . . to be bishops and deacons of those who should afterwards believe."[90] On the first missionary journey (ca. AD 47), Paul and Barnabas, in their apostolic authority, had already "appointed presbyters for them in each church, with prayer and fasting they entrusted them to the Lord in whom they had come to believe" (Acts 14:23). As faithful stewards of the apostolic inheritance, the first co-workers and successors of the apostles were to appoint bishops/presbyters "with the laying on of hands" and (consecratory) prayer (1 Tim 4:14; 2 Tim 1:6) for the churches in which they would serve as presbyters "who labour in preaching and teaching" (1 Tim 5:17).

---

[86] St. Hippolytus, *Traditio Apostolica*, 3.
[87] St. Irenaeus, *Adversus haereses* 4.26.2.
[88] Judas's share (*kleros; sors*) of the apostolate was to go to St. Matthias after his election (Acts 1:25–26).
[89] St. Hippolytus, *Traditio Apostolica*, 3.
[90] St. Clement, *Epistula Clementis ad Corinthios* 42.4.

At the ordination of the bishops/presbyters in Rome, the sermon might also have resembled Paul's farewell address to the presbyters of Miletus, whom he had gathered in Ephesus: "Keep watch over yourselves and over all the flock, of which the Holy Spirit has made you overseers, to shepherd the church of God that he obtained with the blood of his own Son" (Acts 20:28). The "apostles and presbyters" (Acts 15:6, 23) at the Council of Jerusalem (AD 48) jointly made the decision that the Gentiles—without first having to become Jews through circumcision—could become full members of the Church of the New Covenant through faith in Christ and Baptism in his name.

So the bearers of the letter from the Roman Church had to make it clear to the rebellious Corinthians that "our sin will not be small, if we eject from the episcopate those who have blamelessly and holily fulfilled its duties."[91] "Rome" represents the unity of the Church in reminding the Corinthians that they had once before attracted negative attention with factionalism and church divisions[92] when they appealed to Cephas (i.e., Peter), Paul, and Apollos against each other and when Paul was forced to counter: "Is Christ then divided?" (1 Cor 1:13).

Today, historical persons and events are fully present to me through the oral tradition of my parents' generation and through my study of the written sources; and, from 1957 onwards, I am experientially aware of all the developments in the Church up to the present time, as a result of both my own experience and reflection, including the Second Vatican Council and its controversial reception, eight pontificates, and related upheavals in the Church and also those in society. In just such a way, the first and second generations of Christians, from the apostles to the Apostolic Fathers—Ss. Clement of Rome, Ignatius of Antioch, Polycarp of Smyrna, and Papias of Hierapolis, and also the Letter of Barnabas and the Shepherd of Hermas—may similarly have captured the continuity of the Apostolic Tradition and developed it in fidelity to the origin of Christ's Church.[93]

Just as my parents' generation—bishops, priests, laity—had to prove themselves and stand up for their Christian faith in the struggle against Hitler's Reich or Communist East Germany, the Church in Rome in the first century endured much over a period of thirty years, with the severest Christian persecutions under the Emperors Nero and Domitian.[94]

---

[91] St. Clement, *Epistula Clementis ad Corinthios* 44.4.

[92] St. Clement, *Epistula Clementis ad Corinthos* 47.1–4.

[93] Wilhelm Pratscher, ed. *Die Apostolischen Väter. Eine Einleitung* (Göttingen, 2009).

[94] Karl Suso Frank, *Lehrbuch der Geschichte der Alten Kirche* (Paderborn, 1996); Ernst Dassmann, *Kirchengeschichte* (Stuttgart, 1991), ff.

The soil of the Church in Rome is soaked with the blood of countless martyrs. And this does not mean just the geological soil but rather the apostolic soil upon which the Church stands. For that is her apostolic authority and teaching, the witness of word and life that Peter and Paul sealed with their martyrs' blood.[95] Thus, especially with the death of the apostles Peter and Paul, the Roman primacy has the dual dimension of bearing apostolic witness to Christ with both word and blood.

Christian martyrdom cannot be reduced, in a way of thinking that remains inner-worldly, simply to being true to one's own convictions unto death, or to a final act of selflessness for the sake of the life of others, or for the ideas of a political-ideological party. "Martyrs for the movement or the party," or suicide bombers who are blindly celebrated as martyrs by like-minded people, are misguided despisers of the life given them by God and, despite the use of the (equivocal) identical word, are the opposite of martyrs for Christ. The martyrdom of the word and the blood takes place, following in the footsteps of God's Son, as a glorification of the Father (cf. John 13:1; 15:8; 17:5; 21:19). After entrusting him with the universal pastoral office for the Catholic Church, Jesus said to Peter:

> "Very truly, I tell you, when you were younger, you used to fasten your own belt and to go wherever you wished. But when you grow old, you will stretch out your hands, and someone else will fasten a belt around you and take you where you do not wish to go." (He said this to indicate the kind of death by which he would glorify God.) After this he said to him, "Follow me." (John 21:18–19; cf. John 13:36ff.)

Although the intention of the *First Letter of Clement* is limited to the restoration of divine order in Corinth, the author implicitly shows himself well-acquainted with the writings of the Old Testament and the Apostolic Tradition, and especially with the Pauline epistles. For Paul had not only addressed his most important letter to the Romans, but he also "lived there [in Rome] for two whole years . . . , proclaiming the kingdom of God and teaching about the Lord Jesus Christ with all boldness and without hindrance" (Acts 28:30–31). Every Christian in Rome had heard from him the original Christological confession both in writing and orally: "because if you confess with your lips that *Jesus is Lord* and believe in your heart that *God raised him from the dead*, you will be saved" (Rom 10:9, emphasis added).

---

95 St. Clement, *Epistula Clementis ad Corinthios* 5.4; 47.1–4.

But the purpose of Clement's many references to the Old Testament and apostolic writings was not to give the letter a literary shine. He merely wanted to put the mission of the Church into the context of the revealed mysteries of creation, the covenant with the whole history of salvation, and the eschatological redemption in Christ at the end of time. "God and the Lord Jesus Christ and the Holy Spirit," who will save his elect in faith, hope, and love "through Jesus Christ,"[96] has granted us the fullness of grace and peace.[97]

God gains nothing and loses nothing when, out of the "holy will" of his infinite love, he creates man "the most excellent [of his creatures], and . . . the express likeness of his own image."[98] In truth, creation is anthropocentrically conceived in God's eternal ideas as Christocentrically mediated towards God and thus, in its entirety, theocentrically directed towards "the praise of his glorious grace" (Eph 1:6). In the letter written to the same congregation in Corinth from Ephesus in AD 54, Paul had pointed out this inner direction of the flow of man through Christ towards God as the basic understanding of the whole mystery of salvation: when sin and death have lost their power and all things are subjected to Christ, "then the Son himself will also be subjected to the one who put all things in subjection under him, so that God may be all in all" (1 Cor 15:28).

The early Christian consciousness, as it took shape conceptually in the Apostolic Tradition, is therefore anything but a primitive core construct with ever new layers superimposed on it over the centuries, only for the end result to be broken down again into its component parts under the critical gaze of literary scholars and archaeologists of the history of dogma. Such a deconstruction would show the whole thing to be nothing more than the dramatizing composition of a fiction, which could then, in an arbitrary "paradigm shift," be served up according to taste as a different menu.

For the Church's Creed is one and indivisible because, it contains and reflects the one and the same historical self-revelation of God the Father, and the Son, and the Holy Spirit. The later magisterial definitions regarding the Trinity, the mystery of Christ, and redemption and grace (i.e., theological anthropology) add nothing in terms of content. The first-century Christian knows neither more nor less about salvation-mediating faith and has neither more nor less access to sacramentally-mediated grace than any Christian in any century after him.

If a Catholic in today could take a leap back to the Rome of the first Christian century, he would find himself using the same Creed, the same liturgy, and the same moral order of life, and would joyfully extol the miracle of being

---

[96] St. Clement, *Epistula Clementis ad Corinthios* 58.2.
[97] St. Clement, *Epistula Clementis ad Corinthios* prol.
[98] St. Clement, *Epistula Clementis ad Corinthios* 33.4.

at home in the same Catholic Church. If he were to belong to the Latin rite, the difference in the stage of dogmatic and liturgical development would be no greater for him than the merely phenomenological difference that today exists compared to the Eastern-Rite Catholic Churches. For just as we today are children of God through accepting the faith, and through Baptism have been incorporated into the Church of Christ as living members of his body, so, too, nineteen hundred years ago in the first century, in obedience to the Lord's commandment (Matt 28:19), our brothers and sisters were baptized in the name of the Father, and of the Son, and of the Holy Spirit by immersion in water or by pouring water over them.[99]

And the Eucharist—quite apart from the fact that we believe nothing about it as a real memorial of Christ's Sacrifice and the Real Presence other than what is testified in Sacred Scripture—was already structured according to the same pattern as it is today in all Catholic rites. It begins with the Liturgy of the Word—just as *on Sunday* the Risen Lord in his own Person explained the meaning of his Passion to the Emmaus disciples beginning with Moses and the prophets (Luke 24:27). And the liturgy continues to follow his example when "he took bread, blessed and broke it, and gave it to them," by which they recognized him (Luke 24:30–31). Thus they are united to Jesus Christ through the "word of Christ," which they are to "let dwell in them richly," and, with the "psalms, hymns and spiritual songs" that they already know from Jewish worship, they are to sing with gratitude to God (Col 3:16).

When the Church, following Christ's command, celebrates his Eucharistic memorial and offers the prayer of thanksgiving with the priest's words over the bread and wine—"This is my body that is for you" and "This cup is the new covenant in my blood"—she proclaims the Lord's death until he comes (cf. 1 Cor 11:23–26; Luke 22:14–20; Mark 14:22–25; Matt 26:26–29). We are at the Lord's table and share in the sacramental Body and Blood of Christ so that the many who are baptized become one body with him (1 Cor 10:14–22).[100]

Only someone baptized in the name of the Lord can rightfully and worthily partake of the Eucharist,[101] someone "who believes that the things which we teach are true, and who has been washed with the washing that is for the remission of sins, and unto regeneration, and who is so living as Christ has enjoined."[102]

Nineteen hundred years ago, in AD 121, I would have been seventy-three, so the martyr and philosopher Justin could have been an academic student

---

[99] *Didache* 7.1–4.

[100] *Didache* 9.4.

[101] *Didache* 9.5.

[102] St. Justin Martyr, *First Apology* 66.

of mine when, in his *First Apology* of Christianity (ca. AD 150), he wrote a description of the tradition of the community of Rome that divides the Eucharistic liturgy of the Church—around the one altar as a symbol of unity[103]—into the phases of proclamation of the word, offertory, canon with Christ's consecratory words of institution, and the distribution of Holy Communion:

> But we, after we have thus washed him who has been convinced and has assented to our teaching, bring him to the place where those who are called brethren are assembled, in order that we may offer hearty prayers in common for ourselves and for the baptized [illuminated] person, and for all others in every place, that we may be counted worthy, now that we have learned the truth, by our works also to be found good citizens and keepers of the commandments, so that we may be saved with an everlasting salvation. Having ended the prayers, we salute one another with a kiss. There is then brought to the president of the brethren bread and a cup of wine mixed with water; and he taking them, gives praise and glory to the Father of the universe, through the name of the Son and of the Holy Ghost, and offers thanks at considerable length for our being counted worthy to receive these things at his hands. And when he has concluded the prayers and thanksgivings, all the people present express their assent by saying, "Amen." This word "amen" answers in the Hebrew language to γένοιτο [so be it]. And when the president has given thanks, and all the people have expressed their assent, those who are called by us deacons give to each of those present to partake of the bread and wine mixed with water over which the thanksgiving was pronounced, and to those who are absent they carry away a portion.[104]
>
> And this food is called among us Eucharist. . . . For not as common bread and common drink do we receive these; but in like manner as Jesus Christ our Savior, having been made flesh by the word of God, had [offered] both [his] flesh and blood for our salvation, so likewise have we been taught that the food which is blessed by the prayer of his word, and from which our blood and flesh by transmutation are nourished, is the Flesh and Blood of that Jesus who was made flesh. For the apostles, in the memoirs composed by them, which are called gospels, have thus delivered unto us what was enjoined upon them; that Jesus took bread, and when he had given

---

[103] Stefan Heid, *Altar und Kirche. Prinzipien christlicher Liturgie* (Regensburg, 2019).
[104] St. Justin Martyr, *First Apology* 65.

thanks, said, "This do in remembrance of me" [Luke 22:19], this is my body"; and that, after the same manner, having taken the cup and given thanks, he said, "This is my blood"; and gave it to them alone.[105]

Let us return to our writers and conveyers of the Roman Church's letter to the Church in Corinth, who could well still have been living as leading personalities in Rome in around AD 120. In their youth, if they were born analogously to me in the forties of their century, they would certainly also have met Ss. Peter and Paul in Rome,[106] who, by their apostolic preaching and martyrdom (AD 64–67), established the Petrine and Pauline apostolicity of the Church of Rome and her episcopal succession. St. Irenaeus, the disciple of St. Polycarp of Smyrna, was residing in Rome at the time of the Roman Bishop St. Eleutherius (ca. AD 170) and paraphrased the special responsibility of the Church of St. Peter for the unity of the apostolic Church in faith and universal communion as follows: "For it is a matter of necessity that every Church should agree with this Church, on account of its preeminent authority [*potiorem principalitatem*]," for the Tradition "which comes down to our time by means of the successions of the bishops" has always been preserved by the faithful all around.[107]

Paul had sent his famous letter from Corinth to the Romans in AD 56–57, i.e., about forty years before the Church of Rome intervened with a letter admonishing the breakdown in community relations at Corinth. By then, Rome was no longer an unknown quantity on the geographical map of the Church. If, only two decades after the emergence of the early Church of Jerusalem, he can write to the Romans: "Your faith is proclaimed throughout the world" (Rom 1:8), then it is easy to understand why Paul, the apostle to the nations, should use the authority of the apostleship he received from Christ to set forth to them in great detail and depth the whole mystery of Christ, in order "to bring about the obedience of faith among all the Gentiles for the sake of his name" (Rom 1:5).

It is perhaps no coincidence that Paul, precisely in the Letter to the Romans as opposed to other addressees, expresses the mystery of Christ's salvation in legal categories. However, it would be wrong not to go beyond legal terminology and transcend it into the mystery of salvation. The latter does not establish an external relationship to God but rather a real participation in the relationship of the Son in the Holy Spirit to the Father (Rom 5:5; 8:14–17). Nor, however, must the Letter to the Romans be narrowed down to Luther's

---

[105] St. Justin Martyr, *First Apology* 66.

[106] Joachim Gnilka, *Paulus von Tarsus. Apostel und Zuge* (Freiburg, 1997); Gnilka, *Wie das Christentum entstand*, vol. 2, *Paulus von Tarsus* (Freiburg, 2004).

[107] St. Irenaeus, *Adversus haereses* 3.3.2.

question about the personal gracious God, which arose from the incommunicable personal distress he felt as an individual in his soul.

But the Gospel is proclaimed in order to establish God's universal and eschatological rule throughout the whole world, not merely as some sort of therapy in a psycho-drama. The Letter to the Romans deals with the antithetical nature of the existence of all human beings: either under sin or under the righteousness of God. "This is the very center of the so-called Pauline doctrine of justification. You see, the Pauline doctrine of justification, which is thoroughly eschatologically determined, actually only shares the *name* in common with Luther's doctrine of justification. In the matter itself and the manner of looking at it, something completely different is involved."[108]

Those who believe in Christ, place their hope in him, and love God and their neighbor have each already been saved from the night and death of sin into the light and life of being children of God. However, it is not a matter of the greatest possible number of individuals saved but rather of the objective salvation of the whole of humanity, of which the individual is, of course, undoubtedly a part with his or her personal immediacy to God and inability to be represented by anyone else (*Unvertretbarkeit*). From the outset, it was a pointless exercise in the Catholic-Protestant controversy to set up a contrast between forensic and effective justification and regard them as mutually exclusive alternatives, and then to speculate from this that an irreconcilable antithesis existed between Christians. In reality, St. Paul's Letter to the Romans unites all Christians in their common profession of Christ as the sole author of our salvation.[109]

"The gospel of God . . . [and] the gospel concerning his Son" (Rom 1:1–3), in Paul's version of it, was ever-present to the leaders of the Roman Church in a written and oral Tradition going back to its preaching by both apostles (Acts 28:16–31), combined with its Petrine version in 1 Peter (1 Pet 1:1; 5:1) and the Gospel of Mark, which most probably came into being in Rome.[110] Mark was a companion of the apostle Paul (Acts 12:12, 26) and is identified with Peter's interpreter (1 Pet 5:13), who, according to St. Papias of Hierapolis and St. Clement of Alexandria, is also said to have written the first and oldest Gospel in Rome.[111] No serious doubts exist that Rome was the location of

---

[108] Erik Peterson, *Der Brief an die Römer* (= *Ausgewählte Schriften 6*), ed. B. Nichtweiss (Würzburg, 1997), 78.

[109] Peterson, *Der Brief an die Römer*, 85; 95.

[110] Joachim Gnilka, *Petrus und Rom. Das Petrusbild in den ersten zwei Jahrhunderten* (Freiburg, 2002); Christian Gnilka, Stefan Heid, and Rainer Riesner, *Blutzeuge. Tod und Grab des Petrus in Rom* (Regensburg, 2015); Ernst Dassmann et al., *Roma Patristica* (FS Erwin Gatz) (Regensburg, 2003).

[111] Eusebius of Caesarea, *Historia ecclesiastica* 2.15; 3.39; 6.14.

their martyrdom, and even more so of their apostolic activity, in the case of Peter (1 Pet 5:13), the first, and of Paul, the last addressee and witness of the Easter appearances (1 Cor 15:3, 8). For this is attested by eyewitnesses, such as Clement of Rome,[112] or indirect witnesses, such as St. Ignatius of Antioch, who is familiar with Clement's *Letter to the Corinthians*.[113] Nearly all of St. Ignatius's letters are addressed to communities in the East, while the only addressee in the West is the Church of Rome, where he is taken to bloody martyrdom.

The addressee of the highly significant *Letter to the Romans* by St. Ignatius was "the Church . . . which also presides in the place of the region of the Romans . . . and which presides over love [i.e., the Church]"[114] and lives in the Tradition of the authority and teaching of the apostles Peter and Paul, the first and last witnesses of the Easter appearances of Jesus (1 Cor 15:5, 8).[115] The community constantly heard the Old and New Testament Scriptures during their worship and held them in high esteem as the source and norm of preaching and catechesis.

Hence, it is hard to understand the attempt to appeal to St. Paul's Letter to the Romans in the sixteenth century to prove that the Roman Church, of all churches, had fallen away from the Gospel, or to drive a wedge between the Apostolic and the post-Apostolic Tradition with the later hypothesis of early Catholicism.[116]

In the old confessional dispute over whether there was an irreparable break in the development of the early Church, between the intention of Jesus and a Catholic Church drifting into paganism or falling back into Judaism, the issue was not one of knowledge or ignorance of the historical source material but one of the basic hermeneutics of divine Revelation and its historical explication. In this context, it should be pointed out what the Catholic and the Old Protestant positions have in common. Both start from the facticity of divine Revelation.[117] Their paths diverged on the question of its transmission, i.e.,

---

[112] St. Clement, *Epistula Clementis ad Corinthios* 5.4–6.1.

[113] St. Ignatius of Antioch, *Epistula ad Romanos* 4.3.

[114] St. Ignatius of Antioch in the extremely formal salutation of the letter to the Church of God and Jesus Christ at Rome. Cf. Joseph Fischer, *Die Apostolischen Väter* (Darmstadt, 1993); W. Bauer and H. Paulsen, *Die Briefe des Ignatius von Antiochia und der Polycarpbrief* (Tübingen, 1985).

[115] Otto Knoch, *Die 'Testamente' des Petrus und Paulus. Die Sicherung der apostolischen Überlieferung in der spätneutestamentlichen Zeit* (= SBS 62) (Stuttgart, 1973).

[116] Cf. Karl Staab, *Pauluskommentare aus der Griechischen Kirche* (Münster, 1984); Heinrich Denifle, *Die abendländischen Schriftausleger bis Luther über Justitia Dei (Röm 1:17) und Justificatio* (Mainz, 1905).

[117] Cf. Karl Lehmann and Wolfhart Pannenberg, *Verbindliches Zeugnis I. Kanon-Schrift-Tradition* (Freiburg, 1992).

whether or not this takes place through the self-evidence of the word of God in Scripture, which is revealed to the hearer with the help of the inner witness of the Holy Spirit.[118] Catholic theology does not substitute the Magisterium for the Holy Spirit but assumes that, in the living nexus between Sacred Scripture, Apostolic Tradition, and the Church's Magisterium, the word of God becomes inwardly clear to us in faith—likewise through the Holy Spirit, as the Reformers, too, adopted from the Catholic Tradition. Thus, there are only two intermediary elements missing in the Old Protestant view, whereas liberal theology rejects the idea of starting from a supernatural revelation altogether.

In the eleventh and twelfth of his lectures on the essence of Christianity entitled *What Is Christianity*, Adolf von Harnack, reducing divine Revelation to a religion of inwardness, presented "The Christian religion in its development into Catholicism."[119]

He argued that the purely spiritual gospel had later become a sacramental institution of salvation. The biblical essential of the immediacy of each individual Christian to God had fallen into the hands of a priestly caste, who usurped the consciences with enforced dogma and the threat of hell, and deprived critical thinkers of their right to think for themselves. It was typical of the Catholic Church that, in order not to lose power over consciences, it was forced to oppose progress and science in everything and, instead of following the modern worldview, preferred to remain stuck in the Middle Ages. Harnack takes over categories from confessional systematic theology in order to denounce the development of dogmatic doctrine and the sacramentality of the Church in antiquity and the Middle Ages as contradictions to the pure gospel of Jesus.

What is important here is how the sacramental priesthood and the Eucharist as a Sacrifice are interpreted against the backlight of the justification through works that Luther denounced.[120] The doctrine of the Mass as a Sacrifice of the Church has, in fact, nothing whatsoever to do with the pagan sacrifices to propitiate the angry gods.[121] Bishop and presbyter are also called priests (*hiereus; sacerdos*) because they sacramentally represent Christ the high priest, who, in his Sacrifice on the Cross, makes himself present as Priest and Offering. The bishop, who has the *primatum sacerdotii* (primacy of the

---

[118] Friedrich Beisser, *Claritas scripturae bei Martin Luther* (Göttingen, 1966); Achim Buckenmaier, "*Schrift und Tradition*" *seit dem Vatikanum II* (Paderborn, 1996); Beisser, *Der gerettete Anfang. Schrift und Tradition in Israel und der Kirche* (Bad Tölz, 2002).

[119] Adolf von Harnack, *Das Wesen des Christentums* (1899) (Munich, 1964), 117–32.

[120] Gerhard Ludwig Müller, "*Ihr sollt ein Segen sein.*" *12 Briefe über das Priestertum* (Freiburg, 2018).

[121] Gerhard Ludwig Müller, *Die Messe. Quelle christlichen Lebens* (Augsburg, 2002); Müller, *Das Geheimnis der Eucharistie–Das Opfer der Kirche*; George Augustin, ed., *Eucharistie. Verstehen-Leben-Feiern* (FS Kurt Koch) (Mainz, 2020), 123–65.

priesthood), offers the Eucharistic Sacrifice together with the presbyters as the overseer (*hegoumenon*) of the Church (Heb 13:7).[122] Writing at the same time, Tertullian also calls the bishop, as the first minister of Baptism to be summoned, the *summus sacerdos* (high priest) and points out that enmity towards the episcopate is the mother of all schisms.[123] But, by being included in the "We" of the Sacrifice, all the faithful also share in the priesthood of Jesus. After the consecration, the bishop and presbyters say, "Having in memory, therefore, his death and Resurrection, we offer to thee the bread and the cup, yielding thee thanks, because thou hast counted us worthy to stand before thee and to minister to thee."[124] Thus the common priesthood of all the faithful and the office of the bishop/presbyter as teacher, shepherd, and liturgist of the Church are not mutually exclusive but belong inwardly together (1 Pet 2:5, 9; 1 Pet 5:1–4).[125] Among the many patristic and scholastic witnesses of the Catholic Tradition, it suffices to quote St. Augustine alone in order to prove the historical and systematic coherence of the Catholic concept of the oneness of the unique Sacrifice of the Cross, and its multiple liturgical celebrations: "To this supreme and true Sacrifice all false sacrifices [of the past] have given place."[126]

The anthropological premise is the unity of the body and soul of a human being who, as a creature, necessarily offers the sacrifice of the heart to God, his Creator, with his body and expresses it personally and socially with external liturgical gestures and signs as well as in acts of charity. For we are told "to present your bodies as a living sacrifice, holy and acceptable to God" (Rom 12:1). Those who belong to Christ through faith and Baptism have followed the call to "[c]ome to him, a living stone" (1 Pet 2:4), and are exhorted by the apostle: "[L]ike living stones, let yourselves be built into a spiritual house, to be a holy priesthood, to offer spiritual sacrifices acceptable to God through Jesus Christ" (1 Pet 2:5). There is no question here of an individualism that bursts the bounds of the Church, and in which everyone is egomaniacally "his own priest" beyond the sacramental communion of the Church. On the contrary, the Christological ground and ecclesiological framework of the common priesthood of the whole Church are clearly delineated.

Jesus Christ, as the only high priest of the New and everlasting Covenant according to the order of Melchizedek (Heb 5:7–10; 6:20; 7:15–17;), is the only mediator between God and man (1 Tim 2:5), because he himself is God and

---

[122] St. Hippolytus, *Traditio Apostolica*, 3; 4.

[123] Tertullian, *De baptismo* 17.

[124] St. Hippolytus, *Traditio Apostolica*, 4.

[125] Vatican II, *Lumen Gentium*, §10.

[126] St. Augustine, *De civitate Dei* 10.20, http://www.documentacatholicaomnia .eu/03d/0354-0430,_Augustinus,_De_Civitate_Dei_Contra_Paganos,_EN.pdf.

man (Heb 1:3; 2:16). As God, he receives with the Father the Sacrifice that he offers to the Father as man and as head of the Church. He is the addressee of the Sacrifice offered once and for all on the Cross and, at the same time, the volitional subject of the sacrificial offering of his Body. "And it is by that will that we have been sanctified through the offering of the body of Jesus Christ once for all" (Heb 10:10). Hence Augustine can now show the connection between the historically unique Sacrifice on the Cross and its being made present in the Church's many celebrations of the Mass.[127]

> Thus he is both the Priest who offers and the Sacrifice offered [per hoc et sacerdos est, ipse offerens, ipse et oblatio]. And he designed that there should be a daily sign [rei sacramentum] of this in the Sacrifice of the Church, which, being his body, learns to offer herself through him.[128]

Taking into account the objection of classical and liberal Protestant theology to the Catholic principle of Tradition, Vatican II clarified the concept of "living Tradition" from its origin in apostolic preaching to the current proclamation of the Gospel in the Church, which is the body and the visible form of *Christus praesens*:[129]

> And so the apostolic preaching, which is expressed in a special way in the inspired books, was to be preserved by an unending succession of preachers until the end of time. Therefore the apostles, handing on what they themselves had received, warn the faithful to hold fast to the traditions which they have learned either by word of mouth or by letter (cf. 2 Thess 2:15), and to fight in defense of the Faith handed on once and for all (cf. Jude 1:3). Now what was handed on by the apostles includes everything which contributes toward the holiness of life and increase in faith of the peoples of God; and so the Church, in her teaching, life, and worship, perpetuates and hands on to all generations all that she herself is, all that she believes.
>
> This Tradition which comes from the apostles develops in the Church with the help of the Holy Spirit. For there is a growth in the understanding of the realities and the words which have been handed down. This happens through the contemplation and study

---

[127] Gerhard Kardinal Müller, *Das Geheimnis der Eucharistie-das Opfer der Kirche*; George Augustin, ed., *Eucharistie* (FS Kurt Koch) (Mainz, 2020), 123–65.

[128] St. Augustine, *De civitate Dei* 10.20.

[129] Achim Buckenmaier, *"Schrift und Tradition" seit dem Vatikanum II. Vorgeschichte und Rezeption* (Paderborn, 1996).

made by believers, who treasure these things in their hearts (cf. Luke 2:19, 51) through a penetrating understanding of the spiritual realities which they experience, and through the preaching of those who have received through episcopal succession the sure gift of truth. For as the centuries succeed one another, the Church constantly moves forward toward the fullness of divine truth until the words of God reach their complete fulfillment in her.

The words of the holy Fathers witness to the presence of this living Tradition, whose wealth is poured into the practice and life of the believing and praying Church. Through the same Tradition the Church's full canon of the sacred books is known, and the sacred writings themselves are more profoundly understood and unceasingly made active in her; and thus God, who spoke of old, uninterruptedly converses with the bride of his beloved Son; and the Holy Spirit, through whom the living voice of the Gospel resounds in the Church, and through her, in the world, leads unto all truth those who believe and makes the word of Christ dwell abundantly in them (cf. Col 3:16).[130]

Beginning with my baptism as a baby on January 8, 1948, to the present day, the feast of Pentecost 2021—Origen already calls infant baptism an Apostolic Tradition ca. AD 245[131]—I have seen with my own eyes, reflected in my mind, and felt in my heart how the living process of the Tradition of the Gospel of Christ takes place in the life of the Church. Consequently, I can also feel a lively empathy with the tremendous trajectory that the ecclesial, cultural, and intellectual history of Christianity—with its inseverable roots in biblical Judaism—has followed over the course of an unbroken four-thousand-year development. In all the changes over time, with both brilliant high points and catastrophic upheavals, the faith community has preserved its identity in its belief in the Triune God of love. It has held fast to the teaching of the apostles, the fellowship of the Church, the means of grace of the seven sacraments, and the prayers (Acts 2:42). It knows that in the Lord's Prayer, and with the whole treasury of prayers of the Church and the Bible, we are allowed in the "spirit of adoption" to say "Abba! Father!" to God through his Son, Jesus Christ (Rom 8:15).

The Christian faith must not be confused with the vision of a perfect world and an ideal Church that is clung to stubbornly, despite all the injuries and disappointments, or trampled bitterly in the dust.

---

[130] Vatican II, *Dei Verbum*, §8.

[131] Origenes, *Commentarii in epistulam ad Romanos* 5.9 (= FC 2/3), 164.

Instead, faith as a gift of God is, on the one hand, the *light* in whose fullness we understand the world as his creation but also as being weighed down by sin and in need of redemption. And, on the other hand, faith is the *strength* with which we cope with the challenges of life so that we do not perish as a result of the wickedness of the world, the futility of everything finite, and the betrayal of love. The Church is holy because of God, but her credibility is also permanently jeopardized by human beings. That is why we as Catholics do not wish to boast about our historical achievements, when our failures over the course of ecclesiastical history are pointed out to us.[132] We cannot boast of our achievements before the world: "Let the one who boasts, boast in the Lord" (1 Cor 1:31):

> The Church . . . at the same time holy and always in need of being purified, always follows the way of penance and renewal. The Church, "like a stranger in a foreign land, presses forward amid the persecutions of the world and the consolations of God,"[133] announcing the Cross and death of the Lord until he comes" (1 Cor 11:26). By the power of the Risen Lord, she is given strength that she might, in patience and in love, overcome her sorrows and her challenges, both within herself and from without, and that she might reveal to the world, faithfully though darkly, the mystery of her Lord until, in the end, it will be manifested in full light.[134]

Scripture, Tradition, and the Church as a community of believers with its Magisterium are not given to us in order to archaeologically excavate earlier conceptual constructions and social constellations, with the aim of conjuring up a subjective memory image in our imagination. Rather, they are media through which the Risen Lord makes himself really present to his disciples so that they may share in him and become blessed through their faith. The faithful do not now recognize the risen Jesus, as the apostles once did at the Easter apparitions, in the transfigured form in which he is seated at the right hand of the Father. But they do recognize him—like the Emmaus disciples—through the medium of the Church's preaching and sacramental signs, which present his human nature in a way that can be experienced via the senses.

---

[132] Walter Brandmüller, *Licht und Schatten. Kirchengeschichte zwischen Glaube, Fakten und Legenden* (Augsburg, 2007); Arnold Angenendt, *Toleranz und Gewalt. Das Christentum zwischen Bibel und Schwert* (Münster i.W.), 207; Manfred Lütz, *Der Skandal der Skandale. Die geheime Geschichte des Christentums* (Freiburg, 2018).

[133] St. Augustine, *De civitate Dei* 18.51.2.

[134] Vatican II, *Lumen Gentium*, §8.

In the high priestly prayer before he was glorified in his death and Resurrection, the Son prayed to the Father for the apostles, and all those who would become his disciples in response to their preaching:

> Father, the hour has come; glorify your Son so that the Son may glorify you, since you have given him authority over all people, to give eternal life to all whom you have given him. And this is eternal life, that they may know you, the only true God, and Jesus Christ whom you have sent. . . . As you have sent me into the world, so I have sent them into the world. And for their sakes I sanctify myself, so that they also may be sanctified in truth. I ask not only on behalf of these, but also on behalf of those who will believe in me through their word. (John 17:1–3, 18–20)

"Catholic": seen through the eyes of faith; *sentire cum ecclesia*

> For where the Church is, there is the Spirit of God; and where the Spirit of God is, there is the Church, and every kind of grace; but the Spirit is truth.[135]

Only with the "eyes of faith"[136] can one recognize the true nature of the Church in her visible form and develop a sense of the greatness of her mission: "Now we have received not the spirit of the world, but the Spirit that is from God, so that we may understand the gifts bestowed on us by God" (1 Cor 2:12). The Church is not a human construct or a plaything that a little boy can take apart if he wants to but the unshakeable "church of the living God, the pillar and bulwark of the truth" (1 Tim 3:15).

The essence of politics is the struggle for power over the heads and bank accounts of the citizens, and in constitutional democracies often only pushed with difficulty onto the path of pursuing the common good. That is why the "politicians" see in the Catholic Church either a useful organization which, with its charitable and educational institutions as well as its moral authority, either benefits society or—if they are political ideologues—harms it. For God, through his Church, challenges society's total claim on man. The Church is the globally acting advocate of the dignity and freedom in which God constituted

---

[135] St. Irenaeus, *Adversus haereses* 3.24.1.

[136] Pierre Rousselot, «Les yeux de la foi»: *Recherches de Science Religieuse* (1910), 241–259, 444–475; Eng.: *The Eyes of Faith*, trans. Joseph Donceel, intro. John M. McDermott (New York: Fordham University Press, 1990).

the nature of man. Since the Enlightenment and French Revolution (1789), the issue has often been only superficially human rights and a democratic political system, whereas behind the scenes it was about the totalitarian rule of an ideology of self-redemption over the whole of humanity. That is why so many heads have had to roll in what have been, from the Jacobins to the Stalinists, and in a literal and bloody sense, reigns of terror. The guillotine is the symbol of murderers and liars (cf. John 8:44), but the Cross of Christ is the uplifted sign of life and truth (John 14:6).

The Church of God, when it conforms to the will of God, stands for the supremacy of truth over power. The community of believers understands its mission as the continuation of the sending by the Father of Christ, who, after his Resurrection from the dead, said to his apostles: "As the Father has sent me, so I send you. . . . Receive the Holy Spirit. If you forgive the sins of any, they are forgiven them; if you retain the sins of any, they are retained" (John 20:21–23).

The Church is not a political entity with a limited secular purpose; she has a spiritual mission that is integral to the entire salvation of mankind and the world. The boundaries are drawn once and for all with Jesus's ruling: "Therefore render to Caesar the things that are Caesar's, and to God the things that are God's" (Matt 22:21, ESV). If the Church as a social corporation and the individual Christians as citizens of the state contribute to the common good (*bonum commune*) of society, and if, on the other hand, every constitutional state guarantees religious freedom and welcomes the commitment of religion to the temporal good, then this is not a relativization of Jesus's words but merely an explanatory footnote to them.[137]

The Church is not subject to the secular law of political power; she serves the higher power of the merciful God, "who desires everyone to be saved and to come to the knowledge of the truth" (1 Tim 2:4). The Risen Lord, to whom all power in heaven and on earth has been given, invested the apostles and the Church with the authority (*ex-ousia*) to make disciples of all nations, "baptizing them in the name of the Father and of the Son and of the Holy Spirit, and teaching them to obey everything that I have commanded you" (Matt 28:19–20).

The Church does not use political and propagandistic means without first purifying them through the filter of her ethics. A good end never justifies a bad means. Nor does the Church allow herself to be instrumentalized by politicians, the self-appointed benefactors of humanity from the ancient Euergetes to the philanthropic foundations promoting an "open society."

---

[137] Jocelyn Maclure and Charles Taylor, *Laïcité et liberté* (Montreal: Les Éditions du Boréal, 2010); Eng.: *Secularism and Freedom of Conscience* (Cambridge, MA: Harvard University Press, 2011).

When states encroach on and violate or override fundamental human rights, the Church must put the powerful in their place. Bishops, as good shepherds, must even risk life and liberty, taking an example from the way St. Ambrose stood up to Emperor Theodosius, St. Thomas Becket to King Henry II of England, and Blessed Cardinal Stefan Wyszynski to the Polish Communists. The Church does not engage in politics, for Christ's kingdom is not of this world. Rather, she serves human beings in their personal, social, and cultural lives. She proclaims the Good News that man is not God to man, in a world that consumes itself in hatred and greed, but that God is man to man in his kingdom, in which man is built up by love and wins himself in the sacrifice of self-giving. Not *"homo homini Deus"* but *"Deus homini homo"*[138] is the motto that holds the future. For it is not the man who wants to be like God (*eritis sicut Deus* [Gen 3:5]) that can redeem us but only the eternal Son of God who became man for us. With the Incarnation, God himself rewrote our history, turning it into a history of hope that embraces all people past, present, and future: "Jesus Christ is the same yesterday and today and for ever" (Heb 13:8).

In Pilate's praetorium, the confrontation took place between God's rule and the world's rule at a uniquely critical moment in time. The kingdom of God does not spread with the splendor of earthly power and the terrifying potential of weapons. But Jesus is the true ruler over all creation—"the Lord our God the Almighty reigns" (Rev 19:6)—the Pantocrator, as he is depicted in the apse of many a church. And so he responds to the challenge of Pilate, the figure symbolizing the man of violence, and the weary skeptic: "You say that I am a king. For this I was born, and for this I came into the world, to testify to the truth. Everyone who belongs to the truth listens to my voice" (John 18:37). Friedrich Nietzsche, on the other hand, called Pilate the solitary figure in the New Testament "worthy of honor" and consequently foundered on him:

> Pilate, the Roman viceroy. To regard a Jewish imbroglio *seriously*—that was quite beyond him. One Jew more or less—what did it matter? ... The noble scorn of a Roman, before whom the word "truth" was shamelessly mishandled, enriched the New Testament with the only saying *that has any value*—and that is at once its criticism and its *destruction*: "What is truth?"[139]

---

[138] Yuval Noah Harari, *Homo Deus: A Brief History of Tomorrow* (London: Harvill Secker, 2016).

[139] Friedrich Nietzsche, *Der Antichrist. Fluch auf das Christentum 46: Sämtliche Werke 6*, ed. G. Colli and M. Montinari (Munich, 1980), 225, emphases added. Eng.: *The Antichrist*, trans. H. L. Mencken (New York: Alfred A. Knopf, 1918), 135 https://www.gutenberg.org/files/19322/19322-h/19322-h.htm.

There may have been historical reasons for the development of "Papal States" or "state churches," but these are nevertheless—dogmatically speaking—serious malformations which have made life difficult for such unhappy births.[140] Politicizing bishops who juggle power in order to hasten the kingdom of God, or politicians who try to use religious pathos to decide their selfish battles for power, are a tragic contradiction in terms. Since the shock of the French Revolution and the permanent hostility to the Church on the part of political liberalism, nationalism, and socialism, the leadership of the Church has vacillated between conformity and partisanship for the restorationists and progressivists, the Blackshirts and the Red Brigades.

Within the Church, a struggle for self-secularization rages between modernism and anti-modernism and goes by various names. In view of the unfortunate tradition of all our imperial prince and court bishops, our lobby prelates, the left- or right-leaning political "Catholicisms," one can only implore God to give us bishops who will fight manfully and courageously for the freedom of the Church—the *libertas ecclesiae*. And the cardinals of the Roman Church should never entertain the ideas of Cardinal Richelieu (1585–1642)—after whom a French battleship (!) was named—and his successor Cardinal Jules Mazarin (1602–1661) but should instead model themselves on the great figures of the Catholic Reform: St. Charles Borromeo (1538–1584) and St. Robert Bellarmine (1542–1621), the Cardinal Primate of Hungary Péter Pázmany (1570–1636), and the Papal Legate to Poland and the Grand Principality of Moscow Antonio Possevino (1534–1611), or Cardinal Gregorio Barbarigo (1625–1697), the great reform Bishop of Padua.[141] The pope is not the successor of the Roman emperors but of St. Peter, who was "a witness of the sufferings of Christ" (1 Pet 5:1) until his martyrdom in the circus of the pagan Emperor Nero.

And the bishops are successors not of Herod and Pilate, of Roman tribunes and Germanic tribal leaders, but rather of the "holy apostles and prophets" (Eph 3:5), who devote themselves "to prayer and to serving the word" (Acts 6:4) in accordance with the Lord's promise: "I will give you shepherds after my own heart, who will feed you with knowledge and understanding" (Jer 3:15). Diplomacy and politics can achieve short-term tactical successes, but they can never secure for the Church the freedom and respect among the powerful that she needs to proclaim the greatest human right, namely to love God above all else.

---

[140] The present Vatican City State is not a Papal State in the historical sense; rather, it is recognized under international law as a territory under the sovereign authority of the Holy See. The purpose of this is to ensure the independence of the Pontiff towards the states and has no ecclesiological significance, since it is the pope—not the Vatican—who leads the Church as her universal pastor instituted by Christ (John 21:15–17).

[141] Claudio Bellinati, *Gregorio Barbarigo. Un vescovo eroico*, Padua, ²2009.

How credible is the Church if she ignores her martyr-bishops, from Mindszenty to Zen, during their lifetime and canonizes them after their death?[142]

The bishops are instructed to "[k]eep watch over yourselves and over all the flock, of which the Holy Spirit has made you overseers, to shepherd the church of God" (Acts 20:28). They have no political mandate other than to show the political ideologues the limits of worldly power, which must stop at the conscience and fundamental rights of man. As early as AD 96, the Church of Rome wrote to the Church at Corinth:

> The apostles have preached the Gospel to us from the Lord Jesus Christ; Jesus Christ [has done so] from God. Christ therefore was sent forth by God, and the apostles by Christ. Both these appointments, then, were made in an orderly way, according to the will of God. Having therefore received their orders, and being fully assured by the Resurrection of our Lord Jesus Christ, and established in the word of God, with full assurance of the Holy Ghost, they went forth proclaiming that the kingdom of God was at hand. And thus preaching through countries and cities, they appointed the first fruits [of their labors], having first proved them by the Spirit, to be bishops and deacons of those who should afterwards believe.[143]

With regard to bishops, the Second Vatican Council says, "The bishop is to be considered as the high priest of his flock, from whom the life in Christ of his faithful is in some way derived and dependent."[144]

"A bishop marked with the fullness of the Sacrament of Orders, is 'the steward of the grace of the supreme priesthood,' especially in the Eucharist, which he offers or causes to be offered, and by which the Church continually lives and grows."[145] The bishops and all the baptized, as "members of the body" (1 Cor 12:12), of which Christ "*is* the head of the body, the church" (Col 1:18, emphasis added), must therefore never use pragmatic grounds to make the Church's existence plausible to the skeptics who cannot discern any higher meaning in this world, nor ever justify it before the world with utilitarian arguments, let alone make the Church take sides in the power game between ideologues on the left and right. The "holy Catholic Church" which we profess

---

142 Joseph Cardinal Zen, *For Love of My People I Will Not Remain Silent: On the Situation of the Church in China* (San Francisco: Ignatius Press, 2019).

143 St. Clement, *Epistula Clementis ad Corinthios* 42.1–4.

144 Second Vatican Council, *Sacrosanctum Concilium* (1963), §41.

145 Vatican II, *Lumen Gentium*, §26.

in the Creed is a "mystery of salvation"[146] whose depth of meaning is only revealed to us in the light of the universal (i.e., *catholic*) salvific will of the Triune God:[147]

> In former generations, this mystery was not made known to human-kind, as it has now been revealed to his holy apostles and prophets by the Spirit: that is, the Gentiles have become fellow-heirs, members of the same body, and sharers in the promise in Christ Jesus through the gospel. (Eph 3:5–6)

The manifold wisdom of God is now to be made known to all people "through the church . . . in accordance with the eternal purpose that he has carried out in Christ Jesus our Lord" (Eph 3:10–11; 1 Tim 2:4–6).

"Thus, the Church has been seen as 'a people made one with the unity of the Father, the Son and the Holy Spirit.'"[148] God realized his eternal salvific will in history by sending Jesus Christ into the world in the Incarnation of the Son of God and, ultimately (i.e., eschatologically), sending his Spirit into our hearts (Rom 5:5) to make human beings partakers of his divine life (2 Pet 1:4). The human person can find perfection in his nature, which in its ground of being is reason and freedom, only when he arrives in the love from which he came. And that is God as the origin, meaning, and goal of all creation. Even in the most banal flirtation, there is still a blurred trace left of the natural desire for the great love that seeks eternity:

> Natural desire cannot be frustrated; for nature does nothing in vain. Every rational being strives to exist perpetually, not only as a spec-imen of the species, but as an individual. While animals strive only for bodily self-preservation, man, as an intellect, strives knowingly and willingly for the felicity which, though beyond his capacity, can, through grace, attain to the vision of God.[149]

To dam a river is not to cause its source to dry up. A spiritual nature is in itself already a going-beyond-the-basis of its physical conditions and can necessarily only find satisfaction in the absolute Spirit. Anyone who zoolog-ically redefines man's nature back to that of an unreasoning animal—reason being intrinsically different from practical "intelligence"—can on no account

---

[146] Vatican II, *Lumen Gentium*, §1.

[147] Cf. Vatican II, *Lumen Gentium*, §5.

[148] Vatican II, *Lumen Gentium*, §4, with a quotation from St. Cyprian, *De dominica oratione* 23.

[149] St. Thomas Aquinas, SCG II, ch. 55; cf. IV, ch. 50.

downgrade man's nature as "spirit in the world"[150] to just a biological organism but can at most degenerate his character into that of a harmless cuddly animal or a "dirty pig." In George Orwell's *Animal Farm*, when the animals first take over the farm, the maxim is "Four legs good, two legs bad," but once the pigs usurp the leadership and start walking upright, this is changed to "Four legs good, two legs better." Consequently, the motto "All animals are equal" acquires the addition "but some animals are more equal than others."

The mass-murdering monsters of the twentieth century were experienced by their victims as "ravening wolves" and "bloodthirsty sharks."[151] But man's transcendence beyond the value-free instinctual character of sub-spiritual nature renders him responsible in his conscience for the good and evil he has done to, inflicted on, or withheld from his neighbor. Added to this is the need to care for the animate and inanimate environment.[152] Since the dynamism of reason finds peace only in the knowledge of the truth, and since the will strives for loving communion with the beloved, bliss cannot be found in the possession of transient material goods and finite spiritual values but only in a life lived in the Eternal Truth and Imperishable Good that is God himself. That is why man is naturally related to God in spirit and freedom—even if he resists God and thus frustrates himself; "but for me it is good to be near God; I have made the Lord God my refuge" (Ps 73:28):

> The eternal Father, by a free and hidden plan of His own wisdom and goodness, created the whole world. His plan was to raise men to a participation of the divine life. Fallen in Adam, God the Father did not leave men to themselves, but ceaselessly offered helps to salvation, in view of Christ, the Redeemer "who is the image of the invisible God, the firstborn of every creature" (Col 1:15). All the elect, before time began, the Father "foreknew and pre-destined to become conformed to the image of His Son, that he should be the firstborn among many brethren" (Rom 8:29). He planned to assemble in the holy Church all those who would believe in Christ. Already from the beginning of the world the foreshadowing of the Church took place. It was prepared in a remarkable way throughout the history of the people of Israel and by means of the Old Covenant. In the present era of time the Church was constituted and, by the outpouring of

---

[150] Karl Rahner, *Geist in Welt* (= SW 2) (Freiburg, 1996).

[151] Hans-Peter Schwarz, *Das Gesicht des Jahrhunderts. Monster, Retter, Mediokritäten* (Berlin, 1998), 221–339.

[152] Jósef Tischner, *Der Streit um die Existenz des Menschen* (Berlin, 2010); Volker Gerhardt, *Humanität. Über den Geist der Menschheit* (Munich, 2019).

the Spirit, was made manifest. At the end of time she will gloriously achieve completion, when, as is read in the Fathers, all the just, from Adam and "from Abel, the just one, to the last of the elect," will be gathered together with the Father in the universal Church [*in ecclesia universali*].[153]

The human being is finite and mortal in his contingent existence and cognitive possibilities, but, in the grounds of his being, he is oriented towards the infinity of truth and the eternity of love, and therefore exists within the tension of a finite-infinite nature.

This universal relatedness of every human person to God is indicated in God's universal salvific will, which was definitively realized historically in Jesus of Nazareth from Galilee. Hence, everything depends on faith in Jesus the Christ, the Son of God and the universal Savior of the world, and on living with him in the universal community of his disciples.

In Antioch, the disciples were for the first time called "Christians" (Acts 11:26). For they believed in "Jesus Christ, the Son of God" (Mark 1:1), the promised Messiah of the Jews (Jer 33:17; 2 Sam 7:13). Of him it is said, "The Spirit of the Lord is upon me, because he has anointed me to bring good news to the poor" (Luke 4:18; cf. Isa 61:1).

Simon Peter—for whom Jesus had prayed before his Passion and death on the Cross that his faith might not fail, and to whom he said in the Upper Room, "[W]hen once you have turned back, strengthen your brothers" (Luke 22:32)—acts as a spokesman for the young Church when he publicly professes his faith in *Jesus*: "There is salvation in no one else, for there is no other *name* under heaven given among mortals by which we must be saved" (Acts 4:12). The community of all who are baptized in the name of Jesus is also called the *Church of God*. According to her earliest profession of faith, the Church belongs to Jesus the *Kyrios*, the Lord—*Dominus Iesus est* (Rom 10:9; 1 Cor 12:3; Phil 2:11).

Because the Gospel of God and the Lord Jesus Christ is salvation for everyone who believes (cf. Rom 1:1, 4, 17), Paul writes to the Romans giving thanks to God that "your faith is proclaimed throughout the whole world [*holo to kosmo*]" (Rom 1:8). This missionary mandate of Jesus Christ, which encompasses the whole of humanity, imprints a special quality on his Church and determines her nature. It is uni-versal, i.e., *cat-holic*.

In the same Antioch where, according to Luke's Acts of the Apostles (ca. AD 80–90), Jesus's disciples were first called "Christians," their bishop, St. Ignatius, wrote a letter in about AD 110 to the "Church of Smyrna"

---

[153] Vatican II, *Lumen Gentium*, §2.

(today's Izmir), which is already known to us from the Revelation of John (ca. AD 95). It is in this letter that the universal community of Jesus's disciples is referred to for the first time as the "Catholic Church": "wherever Jesus Christ is, there is the Catholic Church."[154]

After a history of two thousand years, the Second Vatican Council, with the supreme magisterial authority of the Catholic Church, definitively reaffirmed the conceptual content of being a *Catholic* Christian, as distinguished from the baptized of all other Christian communions, members of other religions, and all people who seek the truth and strive after more justice in this world:

> They are fully incorporated in the society of the Church who, possessing the Spirit of Christ accept her entire system and all the means of salvation given to her, and are united with her as part of her visible bodily structure and through her with Christ, who rules her through the Supreme Pontiff and the bishops. The bonds which bind men to the Church in a visible way are profession of faith, the sacraments, and ecclesiastical government and communion.[155]

Membership in the pilgrim Church is necessary to attain eternal salvation for everyone who has accepted the Catholic faith *with inner freedom and conviction*. Membership in the Church is, however, only an instrumental prerequisite for salvation, not a guarantee of attaining eternal salvation. It is not enough to be called a Christian and to belong outwardly to the Catholic Church. The Catholic must also live in the spirit of following Christ, be directly connected to God's life in faith, hope, and love, and finally remain in the community of the visible Church, actively participating in her worship of God (i.e., liturgy) and her works of charity. Faith is a "gift from above." Thus, being a Christian is a divine election and calling. Its mystically-ethically-rooted spiritual state is union with Jesus in life and death: "I have been crucified with Christ; and it is no longer I who live, but it is Christ who lives in me. And the life I now live in the flesh I live by faith in the Son of God, who loved me and gave himself for me" (Gal 2:19–20).

But anyone who uses grace to exalt himself above others, or to make claims before God, makes himself unworthy of grace. The grace of election is only granted to give thanks to God and to serve the salvation of others—inside and beyond the visible bounds of the Church.[156] One cannot belong to the Church

---

[154] St. Ignatius of Antioch, *Epistula ad Smyrnaeos* 8.2.

[155] Vatican II, *Lumen Gentium*, §14.

[156] Cf. Vatican II, *Lumen Gentium*, §§8, 14–16.

like some kind of passive paying member of a human club. Some people belong to the Church without their hearts being in it. For them, Church membership is of little help in life and death: "For all of us must appear before the judgment seat of Christ, so that each may receive recompense for what has been done in the body, whether good or evil" (2 Cor 5:10).

And others who, through no fault of their own, have not found their way to the Church during their earthly life but have obeyed God's commandments in their conscience, belong to it inwardly and imperfectly, without knowing it.[157] It is not enough to know the teachings of the Church, to go to church, and be civically decent; the Catholic must also be intellectually and affectively present in the "church of the living God" (1 Tim 3:15; Matt 16:18). This requires a sense of the Church, a *sentire cum ecclesia*. It is the attitude of solidarity with the visible institutions and practices of the holy Church of God, especially with the hierarchy, the pope, the bishops and the priests who lead the visible Church on behalf of Christ and as successors to the apostles. This spiritual feeling for the visible Church in the holiness she has from God, and the spiritual narrowness and moral weakness that attaches to her members, prevents the "idealists"—as the Gnostics, Novatians, and Donatists once did—from imagining themselves in their dreams and utopias of a "Church of the pure" to be superior to the all-too-human and cynically camouflaged elements in the Church that go against Christianity and demonstratively turning their backs on her.

Churchliness as an attitude must also allow itself to be socialized, for man can only live the innermost convictions of his faith in the space of a culture and a formed piety. The faithful Catholic does not need a supportive milieu to enable external assimilation, but since faith is a matter of conviction and not habit, he does need the culture of a Christian lifestyle. For faith presupposes and perfects nature. It does not negate our everyday and higher cultural environment but humanizes it for us in the humanity and humaneness of Jesus.

"But when the goodness and loving-kindness [*phil-anthrología*] of God our Savior appeared, he saved us" (Tit 3:4); for the grace of God has come "bringing salvation to all, training us to renounce impiety and worldly passions, and in the present age to live lives that are self-controlled, upright, and godly" (Tit 2:11–12). Christians are the true humanists and philanthropists.

Belonging to the Catholic Church means living with her in her spirit and piety. A distanced wait-and-see attitude, as if one did not really belong, contradicts any identification with the concrete Church in her divine

---

[157] Cf. Vatican II, *Lumen Gentium*, §15; see §§14–16; St. Augustine, *De baptismo* 5.28.39.

mission and in her human lowliness, in which she must ask the Lord for forgiveness:[158] the *sentire cum ecclesia.*

In his *Spiritual Exercises* (1548), which St. Ignatius of Loyola (1491–1556)[159] wrote as a response to the Reformation challenge—but not without being colored by the times as well—he formulates a number of rules to be observed "to have the true sentiment which we ought to have in the Church Militant," i.e., the *sentire cum ecclesia* that we should have as the pilgrim people of God on earth:[160]

First Rule: all judgment laid aside, we ought to have our mind ready and prompt to obey, in all, the true spouse of Christ our Lord, which is our Holy Mother the Church hierarchical.

Second Rule: to praise confession to a priest, and the reception of the most Holy Sacrament of the Altar once in the year, and much more each month, and much better from week to week, with the conditions required and due.

Third Rule: to praise the hearing of Mass often, likewise hymns, psalms, and long prayers, in the church and out of it; likewise the hours set at the time fixed for each Divine Office and for all prayer and all canonical hours.

Fourth Rule: to praise much religious orders, virginity, and continence, and not so much marriage as any of these.

Fifth Rule: to praise vows of religion, of obedience, of poverty, of chastity, and of other perfections of supererogation. And it is to be noted that as the vow is about the things which approach to evangelical perfection, a vow ought not to be made in the things which withdraw from it, such as to be a merchant, or to be married, etc.

Sixth Rule: to praise relics of the saints, giving veneration to them and praying to the saints; and to praise stations, pilgrimages, indulgences, pardons, crusades, and candles lighted in the churches.

---

[158] Cf. Vatican II, *Lumen Gentium*, §8.

[159] Cf. Karl Rahner, *Ignatianischer Geist. Schriften zu den Exerzitien und zur Spiritualität des Ordensgründers* (= SW 13) (Freiburg, 2006).

[160] Cf. Vatican II, *Lumen Gentium*, §§48–51.

Seventh Rule: to praise constitutions about fasts and abstinence, as of Lent, Ember Days, Vigils, Friday and Saturday; likewise penances, not only interior, but also exterior.[161]

The Catholic profile: the same faith—in the entire Church— throughout the world

Against the heretical dissolution of the salvific reality of divine Revelation in the Gnostic myths and speculations, St. Irenaeus of Lyons, the "father of Catholic dogmatics," provides a summary of the "Faith accepted by the apostles and their disciples."[162] He presents belief in God the Father, the Son, and the Holy Spirit with the works of creation, redemption, and sanctification (i.e., *symbolum fidei*) as the rule of faith (*regula fidei*) of the one Church spread over the whole earth.[163] The rule of faith (regula fidei seu veritatis) emerges from the baptismal catechesis (Luke 1:4; Gal 6:6; Heb 6:1–17) and the baptismal confession,[164] and is condensed into the Apostles' Creed. Then he declares the unity of the Church, which is founded in the one and same faith and makes it known throughout the world. This leaves no room for special doctrines or special roles for national churches and realities of life today:

> As I have already observed, the Church, having received this preach-
> ing and this Faith, although scattered throughout the whole world,
> yet, as if occupying but one house, carefully preserves it. . . . For,
> although the languages of the world are dissimilar, yet the import of
> the Tradition [*paradosis*; *Traditio Apostolica*] is one and the same. For
> the Churches which have been planted in Germany do not believe or
> hand down anything different, nor do those in Spain, nor those in
> Gaul, nor those in the East, nor those in Egypt, nor those in Libya,
> nor those which have been established in the central regions of the
> world. . . . Nor will any one of the rulers in the Churches, however
> highly gifted he may be in point of eloquence,[165] teach doctrines
> different from these (for no one is greater than the Master [Matt

---

[161] St. Ignatius of Loyola, *Exercitia spiritualia*, 352–359; *Gründungstexte der Gesellschaft Jesu*, vol. 2 (Würzburg, 1998), 262. Quoted here from *The Spiritual Exercises of St. Ignatius of Loyola*, trans. Elder Mullan, S.J. (New York: P. J. Kenedy and Sons, 1914), http://www .documentacatholicaomnia.eu/03d/1491-1556,_Ignatius_Loyola,_Spiritual_Exercises,_EN.pdf.

[162] St. Irenaeus, *Adversus haereses* 1.10.1.

[163] Cf. also the profound formulation of the rule of faith in Origen, *De principiis* 1, praef. 4–5.

[164] St. Hippolytus, *Traditio Apostolica*, 15–21.

[165] Cf. St. Justin Martyr, *First Apology* 65.

10:24]); nor, on the other hand, will he who is deficient in power of expression inflict injury on the Tradition. For the Faith being ever one and the same, neither does one who is able at great length to discourse regarding it, make any addition to it, nor does one, who can say but little diminish it.

It does not follow because men are endowed with greater and less degrees of intelligence, that they should therefore change the subject-matter [of the Faith] itself, and should conceive of some other God besides him who is the Framer, Maker, and Preserver of this universe, (as if He were not sufficient for them), or of another Christ, or another Only-begotten [Son of the Father].[166]

And now St. Irenaeus comes to the task of theological reflection in the service of preaching and catechesis:

But the fact referred to simply implies this, that one may [more accurately than another] bring out the meaning of those things which have been spoken in parables, and accommodate them to the general scheme of the Faith; and explain [with special clearness] the operation and dispensation of God connected with human salvation; . . . and set forth *why* it is that one and the same God has made some things temporal and some eternal, some heavenly and others earthly; . . . and search out *for what reason* God has included every man in unbelief, that he may have mercy upon all (Rom 11:32); and gratefully describe on what account the Word of God became flesh (John 1:14) and suffered. . . . The different knowledge of faith, however, does not consist in lying about the Creator . . . beyond a pleroma, then a nation of thirty and finally of countless eons, as do the teachers of these people [Marcion, Basilides, Valentine] who are truly abandoned of all divine insight. Instead, as I said, the whole Church [i.e., in the apostolic succession of the apostles][167] has one and the same Faith throughout the world.[168] . . .

Now all these [heretics], . . . since they are blind to the truth, and deviate from the [right] way, will walk in various roads; and therefore the footsteps of their doctrine are scattered here and there without agreement or connection. But the path of those belonging to the

---

166 St. Irenaeus, *Adversus haereses* 1.10.2–3.

167 Cf. St. Irenaeus, *Adversus haereses* 3.3.1–2.

168 St. Irenaeus, *Adversus haereses* 1.10.3, emphasis added.

Church circumscribes the whole world, as possessing the sure Tradition from the apostles, and gives unto us to see that the Faith of all is one and the same, since all receive one and the same God the Father, and believe in the same dispensation regarding the Incarnation of the Son of God, and are cognizant of the same gift of the Spirit, and are conversant with the same commandments, and preserve the same form of ecclesiastical constitution, and expect the same advent of the Lord, and await the same salvation of the complete man, that is, of the soul and body. And undoubtedly the preaching of the Church is true and steadfast, in which one and the same way of salvation is shown throughout the whole world [eadem salutis via in universo mundo ostenditur].[169]

"The church of the living God" is not, however, an end in itself but as "the pillar and bulwark of the truth" (1 Tim 3:15) serves only the one purpose of God, "who desires everyone to be saved and to come to the knowledge of the truth" (1 Tim 2:4). "The Church is the Church only when it exists for others,"[170] and this means she has to confront every single person with the one decisive question: "Why am I on earth?"

Catholic catechisms are textbooks for baptismal candidates preparing to receive the divine virtues of faith, hope, and love, or for the baptized who want to make sure of "investigating everything carefully from the very first" (Luke 1:3); i.e., convince themselves of the reliability of the doctrine in which they have been instructed. Practically all these catechisms start with the question "Why am I on earth," and give something like the following answer: "We are here on earth in order to know and to love God, to do good according to his will, and to go someday to heaven."[171]

In the midst of the enormous conflicts over justification and faith, and sin and forgiveness, two representatives of the Reformation and Catholic casts of mind, respectively, which were conventionally regarded as irreconcilable, succeeded in expressing why we are on earth in a way that was theologically both compatible and complementary.[172]

---

[169] St. Irenaeus, *Adversus haereses* 5.20.1.

[170] Dietrich Bonhoeffer, *Widerstand und Ergebung. Briefe und Aufzeichnungen aus der Haft* (= DBW 8) (Munich, 1998).

[171] *Youcat: Youth Catechism of the Catholic Church* (San Francisco: Ignatius Press, 2011), no. 1.

[172] Cf. the ecumenically very helpful comparative study by Friedrich Richter, *Martin Luther und Ignatius von Loyola. Repräsentanten zweier Geisteswelten* (Stuttgart, 1954).

In Martin Luther's *Small Catechism* (1529), the first article of the common creed is couched in movingly personal terms:

> I believe that God has made me and all creatures; that he has given me my body and soul, eyes, ears, and all my members, my reason and all my senses, and still takes care of them. . . . All this he does only out of fatherly, divine goodness and mercy, without any merit or worthiness in me. For all this it is my duty to thank and praise, serve and obey him.[173]

And a few years later, St. Ignatius of Loyola begins his famous *Spiritual Exercises* (1548), written for the purpose of overcoming oneself and ordering one's life, with the "Principle and Foundation" (no. 23) by which man's creaturely existence stands or falls:

> Man is created to praise, reverence, and serve God our Lord, and by this means to save his soul. And the other things on the face of the earth are created for man and that they may help him in prosecuting the end for which he is created. From this it follows that man is to use them as much as they help him on to his end, and ought to rid himself of them so far as they hinder him as to it.[174]

The question of the faith-relevant (i.e., dogmatic) significance of the predicate "catholic" that the First Council of Constantinople (AD 381) attributes to the Church, along with the characteristics "one, holy, and apostolic,"[175] is not raised for the purpose of apologetic delimitation but rather in order to offer a positive explanation of it. What statements does the Catholic faith contain about the revealed mysteries of salvation? From what way of looking at God does Catholic theology's view of the world and mankind result? How is the life of a follower of Christ lived in the Catholic Church? How does one become a Catholic Christian at all? What are the sources, principles, forms, and contents of a Catholic life? Is there a specifically Catholic mentality and view of man and the cosmos? What are the specific characteristics that distinguish the Catholic faith from other religious persuasions? What connects Catholic men and women with Christians of other Christian churches and ecclesial communities, and with people of goodwill who at least believe in the absolute superiority of being over nothingness?

---

[173] Martin Luther, *Weimarer Ausgabe* 30/1, 368; Eng.: *Luther's Small Catechism*, p. 3, http://www.st-ansgars-montreal.ca/WhatIs/Small_Catechism.pdf.

[174] Erich Przywara, *Deus semper maior. Theologie der Exerzitien I* (Freiburg, 1938), 47–138.

[175] DH 150.

Is there a bridge leading from the existential questions as to the meaning of life and death, evil and suffering, to the Church's faith in Jesus Christ, the Son of God and Redeemer of all?[176]

After long aberrations on the wrong track in the spirit of Manichaeism and a libertarian lifestyle, Augustine was freed by God's grace from his doubts and finally converted to the truth. One day, in a corner of the garden, he heard a child chanting from a neighboring house: "Take up and read!"

And the saint describes his spiritual turmoil as follows:

So checking the torrent of my tears, I arose; interpreting it to be no other than a command from God to open the book, and read the first chapter I should find. For I had heard of [St.] Antony [of the Desert], that coming in during the reading of the Gospel, he received the admonition, as if what was being read was spoken to him: "Go, sell all that thou hast, and give to the poor, and thou shalt have treasure in heaven, and come and follow me." And by such an oracle he was forthwith converted unto thee. Eagerly then I returned to the place where Alypius was sitting; for there had I laid the volume of the apostle when I arose thence. I seized, opened, and in silence read that section on which my eyes first fell: "Not in rioting and drunkenness, not in chambering and wantonness, not in strife and envying; but put ye on the Lord Jesus Christ, and make not provision for the flesh, in concupiscence" (Rom 13:12–14). No further would I read; nor needed I: for instantly at the end of this sentence, by a light as it were of serenity infused into my heart, all the darkness of doubt vanished away.[177]

And there is the touching scene of St. Augustine's conversation in Ostia near Rome with his mother Monica, who, sensing her imminent death, told her son why she had persevered all these years: "One thing there was for which I desired to linger for a while in this life, that I might see thee a Catholic Christian before I died [Unum erat, propter quod in hac vita aliquantum immorari cupiebam, ut te christianum catholicum viderem, priusquam morerer]."[178]

---

[176] Second Vatican Council, *Gaudium et Spes* (1965), §10.

[177] St. Augustine, *Confessions*, 8.12.29, in *The Confessions of Saint Augustine*, trans. Edward B. Pusey, D.D. (Oak Harbor, WA: Logos Research Systems, 1999), http://www.documentacatholicaomnia .eu/03d/0354-0430,_Augustinus,_Confessionum_Libri_Tredecim-Pusey_Transaltion,_EN.pdf.

[178] St. Augustine, *Confessions* 9.10.

The innermost core of the Catholic faith

The whole of Christianity consists in a threefold understanding given to us "according to ... the proclamation of Jesus Christ" on the basis of the historical revelation of the mystery of God's universal salvific will "to all the Gentiles ... to bring about the obedience of faith" (Rom 16:25–26).

This consists in the mysteries of the Trinity, the Incarnation, and the deification of man (i.e., being made a child of God).

Inverting the relationship between reality and symbol, Nietzsche derived the historical reality of salvation from inner mythological and depth-psychological states of mind, which would not exist without the prior existence of the mysteries in the Church's profession of faith:

> The concept of "the Son of God" does not connote a concrete person in history, an isolated and definite individual, but an "eternal" fact, a psychological symbol set free from the concept of time. The same thing is true, and in the highest sense, of the *God* of this typical symbolist, of the "kingdom of God," and of the "sonship of God." Nothing could be more un-Christian than the *crude ecclesiastical* notions of God as a *person*, of a "kingdom of God" that is to come, of a "kingdom of heaven" beyond, and of a "son of God" as the *second person* of the Trinity.[179]

One wonders where Zarathustra's "remain true to the earth"[180] has gotten to here, when what is historical and contingent is dissolved into timeless speculation and phantasmagoria pregnant with symbols.

Time, however, is not like the shy deer that flees from the sunny clearing into the darkness of the forest when it senses danger; rather, it is like the cup that wants to be filled with fine wine. What Nietzsche fears, the Church hails as the beginning of freedom: "But when the fullness of time had come, God sent his Son, born of a woman, born under the law, in order to redeem those who were under the law, so that we might receive adoption as children" (Gal 4:4–5). St. Paul adds elsewhere:

> Now to God who is able to strengthen you according to my gospel and the proclamation of Jesus Christ, according to the revelation of

---

[179] Friedrich Nietzsche, *Der Antichrist. Fluch auf das Christenthum 34: Sämtliche Werke 6*, ed. C. G. Colli and M. Montinari (Munich, 1980), 206; Eng.: *The Antichrist*, 014.

[180] *Also sprach Zarathustra I, 3*, Sämtliche Werke 4, loc. cit. 15; Eng.: *Thus Spoke Zarathustra: A Book for All and None*, ed. Adrian del Caro and Robert B. Pippin, Cambridge Texts in the History of Philosophy (Cambridge, MA: Cambridge University Press, 2006), I, prol., 3.

the mystery that was kept secret for long ages but is now disclosed, and through the prophetic writings is made known to all the Gentiles, according to the command of the eternal God, to bring about the obedience of faith . . . be the glory for ever! (Rom 16:25–26)

The Greek term *mysterion* (Latin: *sacramentum*) in biblical and ecclesiastical usage does not mean information from the beyond or the magical background of the cosmos, known only to a small circle (a *secretum* or something inscrutable). "Mystery" in the biblical sense means God's eternal plan of salvation, which is communicated to us in the here of the world, and the now of history, and concretely to my person through and in Jesus Christ. The Person, message, and fate of Jesus right up to the Cross and Resurrection are the ways in which the mystery of God's love is communicated to mankind. With regard to God's becoming man in Jesus Christ, his Son—the *logos ensarkosis*, the *verbum incarnatum*—the evangelist explains most clearly at the end of his prologue what mystery means in the Christian faith: "No one has ever seen God. It is God the only Son, who is close to the Father's heart, who has made him known [ekeinos exegesato, ipse enarravit]" (John 1:18).

The mystery of the Most Holy Trinity

"Go therefore and make disciples of all nations, baptizing them in the *name of the Father and of the Son and of the Holy Spirit*" (Matt 28:19, emphasis added).

The one God, whose existence as its cause we can infer with certainty by means of reason from the effects of creation (Rom 1:19–20), has communicated himself to us in his innermost life as the fullness of grace and truth. God's existence is his essence (Exod 3:14).[181] And his life is love (1 John 4:8, 16). Therefore, we believe in the one God in three Persons. What is meant here by the term "Person" is not the individual existence of three human beings, who are, of course, not one individual being but merely numerically multiple realizations of universal human nature, which does not exist in reality as an individual substance but only in our minds as an idea, as an abstraction of what all human beings have in common. When we speak of the three Persons in God's incomprehensible mystery, though, this is based solely on the self-revelation of the Father, the Son, and the Holy Spirit, who are the one and only God, but are the bearers of the reciprocity of their relationship. Baptized in the name of the Father and of the Son and of the Holy Spirit, we have become children and friends of God and, in Christ, heirs of eternal life (Rom 8:14–17). We no longer

---

[181] Gerhard Kardinal Müller, *Der Glaube an Gott im säkularen Zeitalter* (Freiburg, 2020).

simply stand face to face with the transcendent God; now we are included in the inner life of the divine Persons in their relationship to each other. In the Holy Spirit and through the Son, we say "Father" to God. The Triune God lives in us and we live in God the Father through the Son in the Holy Spirit. God is not only a transcendent vis-à-vis but an immanent indwelling of the human being, wherein the love that is God is our life in fullness.

In accordance with this knowledge derived from God's self-revelation, human existence is theocentric: "And because you are children, God has sent the Spirit of his Son into our hearts, crying, 'Abba! Father!'" (Gal 4:6). In the light of the supernatural faith infused into us by the Holy Spirit, we see the entire existence (*Sein*) of the world and man in its relationship to God—*sub ratione Dei*. The riddle of man is solved and the knot of history untied when we understand that God is the origin and meaning of all creation.

From the Triune God proceeds his work of creation, redemption, and perfection. There is only one God whose goodness is reflected in the likeness of all that is good and true in creation. Evil is not created and has no God as its author but is the product of misdirected freedom. For this reason, Christian belief in creation excludes all metaphysical and moral dualism. Redemption takes place as God's saving work for the sake of mankind within historical reality. And the Christian hopes for the resurrection of the dead and the blissful life in the fellowship of the Triune God.

God's being and life in the mystery of triune love rules out the possibility in man—the creature, child, and friend of God—of any metaphysical and moral nihilism.

The mystery of the Trinity is not some kind of special insider knowledge for theologians but the revelation of the mystery of God's love in the Father, Son, and Holy Spirit. In this name we are baptized and in it we receive salvation:

> Therefore, since we are justified by *faith*, we have peace with God through our Lord Jesus Christ . . . and we boast in our *hope* of sharing the glory of God . . . because *God's love* has been poured into our hearts through the Holy Spirit that has been given to us. (Rom 5:1–5, emphasis added)

When, through Jesus Christ in the Holy Spirit, we are allowed to say to God, "Abba! Father!" (Rom 8:15; Gal 4:6), then in so doing we renew the divine virtues infused into our hearts through which we are directly and personally included in the triune mystery of love.

And every day a Christian can pray in humility and with confidence: "Lord, I believe in you: increase my faith. I trust in you: strengthen my trust. I love you: let me love you more and more."

And we worship the one and Triune God. For, like St. Irenaeus of Lyons, we know that "For the glory of God is a living man; and the life of man consists in beholding God [gloria Dei, vivens homo, vita autem hominis visio Dei]."[182] A Christian joyfully joins St. Francis's prayer "The Praises of God and the Blessing":

> You are the holy Lord God who does wonderful things.
> You are strong. You are great. You are the most high.
> You are the almighty king. You holy Father,
> King of heaven and earth.
> You are three and one, the Lord God of gods;
> You are the good, all good, the highest good,
> Lord God living and true.
> You are love, charity; you are wisdom, you are humility,
> You are patience. You are beauty, you are meekness,
> You are security, you are rest,
> You are gladness and joy, you are our hope,
> You are justice,
> You are moderation, you are all our riches to sufficiency.
> You are beauty, you are meekness,
> You are the protector, you are our custodian
> and defender,
> You are strength, you are refreshment, you are our hope,
> You are our faith, you are our charity,
> You are all our sweetness, you are our eternal life:
> Great and wonderful Lord, Almighty God,
> Merciful Savior. You are holy, Lord our God. You are the only God,
> the one who works miracles.
> You are the strong, you are the great, you are the highest,
> you are almighty,
> you are holy, the Father and King of heaven and earth.
> You are the Triune One and the one, God, the Lord.
> You are the Good, the highest good,
> the living and true God.
> You are the goodness, the love, you are the wisdom, you are the

---

[182] St. Irenaeus, *Adversus haereses* 4.20.7.

humility, you are the patience.
You are the security, the peace,
the joy and the gladness.
You are the justice and the measure.
You are all riches.
You are the mildness, you are our refuge and strength,
thou art our faith, our hope, and our love, our bliss.
You are infinite goodness, great and wonderful Lord,
God almighty, loving, merciful, and saving.

The mystery of the Incarnation of God in Christ[183]

But when the fullness of time had come, God sent his Son, born of a woman, born under the law, in order to redeem those who were under the law, so that we might receive adoption as children. (Gal 4:4–5)

The Eternal Word, who was with God and is God, took on our flesh and met us in Jesus of Nazareth (John 1:14). He is recognized by the Church as the only Son of the Father: "He is the only Son, who is close to the Father's heart, who has made him known" (John 1:18). "For God so loved the world that he gave his only Son, so that everyone who believes in him may not perish but may have eternal life" (John 3:16). In his earthly life, his preaching, and his realization of the kingdom of God, right up to his death on the Cross to redeem us from sin and death and his Resurrection from the dead, Jesus is the revelation and communication of the triune love of God in human nature, which the Son of God, the Second Person in the Trinity, assumed for our salvation.

Jesus is the remedy for all metaphysical dislocation and loss of moral orientation. He reveals in his own words that he is the mediator of salvation: *"I am the way, and the truth, and the life. No one comes to the Father except through me"* (John 14:6).

In the human nature of Christ, which is united to his divine nature through the Person of the divine Word, God himself is present as a man and in a human way in our historical world. As a man, Jesus is the way that leads from God to us and upon which we find our way back to God our Creator, Redeemer, and Perfecter. Against the Gnostic destruction of the mystery of the Incarnation, St. Irenaeus of Lyons asserts that the one who was born of Mary

---

[183]   Gerhard Ludwig Müller, *Christologie. Die Lehre von Jesus dem Christus* (= *Glaubenszugänge II*) (Paderborn, 1995), 3–297.

and suffered on the Cross is the same as the impassible God.[184] Concurring with all the Fathers, the Council of Chalcedon (AD 451) teaches that our Lord Jesus Christ is to be confessed as

> one and the same Son ..., the same perfect in divinity and perfect in humanity.... One and the same Lord Jesus Christ, the only begotten Son, must be acknowledged in two natures, without confusion or change, without division or separation. The distinction between the natures was never abolished by their union but rather the character proper to each of the two natures was preserved as they came together in the one Person and one hypostasis. He is not split or divided into two Persons, but he is one and the same only begotten Son, God the Word, the Lord Jesus Christ, as formerly the prophets and later Jesus Christ himself have taught us about him and has been handed down to us by the creed of the Fathers.[185]

In his divine nature Jesus is God's truth and life, which alone can offer adequate fulfillment to our minds and wills. The Son of God alone could be the mediator of creation in eternity and become the mediator of salvation in time. Inseparably linked to this mystery is "the mystery of the Church."[186] Hence, from the very beginning, the recognition of the Incarnation as a historical fact, as opposed to a speculative idea or existentialist metaphor, became the criterion that divided opinions:

> Beloved, do not believe every spirit, but test the spirits to see whether they are from God; for many false prophets have gone out into the world. By this you know the Spirit of God: every spirit that confesses that Jesus Christ has come in the flesh is from God, and every spirit that does not confess Jesus is not from God. And this is the spirit of the antichrist, of which you have heard that it is coming. (1 John 4:1–3)

In taking on the human body, Christ also took on the whole of human nature that exists in individual human beings, as the concrete persons for whom he laid down his life on the Cross and whom he thus made members of his body, which is called his Church. Between Christ and the faithful there exists an organic, life-giving relationship like that between the members of a

---

[184] St. Irenaeus, *Adversus haereses* 3.16.9.

[185] DH 301–302.

[186] Vatican II, *Lumen Gentium*, §1: the title of the first chapter.

body and their head or between the bridegroom and the bride, who as husband and wife "become one flesh" (Gen 2:24; Eph 5:30). Referring to this relationship, the apostle says, "This is a great mystery, and I am applying it to Christ and the church" (Eph 5:32).

By telling the baptized: "all of you are one in Christ Jesus" (Gal 3:28), Paul makes it clear that Christians are not only one in a moral sense but that in the diversity of his members they form a personal unity with Christ, the head of his body, which is the Church. With St. Augustine we have to say, "The whole Christ, one head and one body."[187] When God's rule and Christ's kingship are revealed at the end, the mystery of the nuptial union of Christ and the Church will also be fulfilled:

> "Let us rejoice and exult and give him the glory, for the marriage of the Lamb has come, and his bride has made herself ready; to her it has been granted to be clothed with fine linen, bright and pure"—for the fine linen is the righteous deeds of the saints.... "Blessed are those who are invited to the marriage supper of the Lamb." (Rev 19:7–9; cf. 22:17)

This is why Vatican II, in the Dogmatic Constitution on the Church, can unfold the mystery of the messianic people of God as follows:

> At all times and in every race God has given welcome to whosoever fears Him and does what is right (Acts 10:35). God, however, does not make men holy and save them merely as individuals, without bond or link between one another. Rather has it pleased Him to bring men together as one people, a people which acknowledges Him in truth and serves Him in holiness. He therefore chose the race of Israel as a people unto Himself. With it He set up a covenant. Step by step He taught and prepared this people, making known in its history both Himself and the decree of His will and making it holy unto Himself. All these things, however, were done by way of preparation and as a figure of that new and perfect covenant, which was to be ratified in Christ, and of that fuller Revelation which was to be given through the Word of God Himself made flesh. "Behold the days shall come saith the Lord, and I will make a new covenant with the house of Israel, and with the house of Judah.... I will give My law in their bowels, and I will write it in their heart, and I will be their God, and they shall be My people.... For all of them shall know Me, from

---

[187] St. Augustine, *Sermo* 341.1.

the least of them even to the greatest, saith the Lord" (Jer 31:31–34). Christ instituted this new covenant, the new testament, that is to say, in His blood (cf. 1 Cor 11:25), calling together a people made up of Jew and Gentile, making them one, not according to the flesh, but in the Spirit. This was to be the new people of God. For those who believe in Christ, who are reborn, not from a perishable, but from an imperishable seed through the word of the living God (cf. 1 Pet 1:23), not from the flesh but from water and the Holy Spirit (cf. John 3:5–6), are finally established as "a chosen race, a royal priesthood, a holy nation, a purchased people . . . who in times past were not a people, but are now the people of God" (1 Pet 2:9–10).

That messianic people has Christ for its head, "who was delivered up for our sins, and rose again for our justification" (Rom 4:25), and now, having won a name which is above all names, reigns in glory in heaven. The state of this people is that of the dignity and freedom of the sons of God, in whose hearts the Holy Spirit dwells as in His temple. Its law is the new commandment to love as Christ loved us (cf. John 13:34). Its end is the kingdom of God, which has been begun by God Himself on earth, and which is to be further extended until it is brought to perfection by Him at the end of time, when Christ, our life (cf. Col 3:4), shall appear and "creation itself will be delivered from its slavery to corruption into the freedom of the glory of the sons of God" (Rom 8:21). So it is that that messianic people, although it does not actually include all men, and at times may look like a small flock, is nonetheless a lasting and sure seed of unity, hope, and salvation for the whole human race. Established by Christ as a communion of life, charity, and truth, it is also used by Him as an instrument for the redemption of all and is sent forth into the whole world as the light of the world and the salt of the earth (cf. Matt 5:13–16).

Israel according to the flesh, which wandered as an exile in the desert, was already called the Church of God (Neh 13:1; cf. Num 20:4; Deut 23:1–8). So, likewise, the new Israel which while living in this present age goes in search of a future and abiding city (cf. Heb 13:14) is called the Church of Christ (cf. Matt 16:18). For He has bought it for Himself with His blood (cf. Acts 20:28), has filled it with His Spirit and provided it with those means which befit it as a visible and social union. God gathered together as one all those who in faith look upon Jesus as the author of salvation and the source of unity and peace, and established them as the Church that for each and all she may be the visible sacrament of this saving unity. While she transcends all limits of time and confines of race, the Church is destined to extend to all regions of the earth and so enters into the history of mankind. Moving forward through trial and tribulation, the Church is strengthened by the power of God's grace, which was promised to her by the Lord, so that in the weakness of the flesh she may not waver from perfect fidelity, but remain a Bride worthy of her Lord, and, moved by the Holy Spirit, may never cease to renew herself, until through the Cross she arrives at the light which knows no setting.[188]

The mystery of God's presence in the humanity of Jesus is not just objectively enshrined by us in the Creed and actually lived out in discipleship of Christ. It also points us subjectively onto the path of mystical union with Jesus, when we say in our innermost hearts, "I have been crucified with Christ; and it is no longer I who live, but it is Christ who lives in me. And the life I now live in the flesh I live by faith in the Son of God, who loved me and gave himself for me" (Gal 2:19–20).

St. Ignatius of Loyola places the prayer *Anima Christi* at the beginning of his *Spiritual Exercises*, wishing to say by doing so: "The Christian who through Baptism, Confirmation, and participation in the Sacrifice of the Altar is, in fact, objectively a member of the 'head and body of Christ,' should become subjectively aware of being animated by Christ and perfused by his Blood."[189]

Soul of Christ, sanctify me.
Body of Christ, save me.
Blood of Christ, inebriate me.
Water from the side of Christ, wash me.
Passion of Christ, strengthen me.
O Good Jesus, hear me.
Within thy wounds hide me.
Suffer me not to be separated from thee.
From the wicked enemy defend me.
In the hour of my death call me.
And bid me come unto thee,
That with all thy saints,
I may praise thee
Forever and ever.
Amen.

---

[188] Vatican II, *Lumen Gentium*, §9.

[189] Erich Przywara, *Deus semper maior. Theologie der Exerzitien I* (Freiburg, 1938), 3.

The mystery of the baptized as children of God

So God created humankind in his image, in the image of God he created them; male and female he created them. God blessed them, and God said to them, "Be fruitful and multiply, and fill the earth." (Gen 1:27–28)

We know that all things work together for good for those who love God, who are called according to his purpose. For those whom he fore-knew he also predestined to be conformed to the image [*symmorphous tes eikonos*] of his Son, in order that he might be the firstborn within a large family. And those whom he predestined he also called; and those whom he called he also justified; and those whom he justified he also glorified. (Rom 8:28–30)

Let the same mind be in you that was in Christ Jesus, who, though he was in the form of God [*morphe theou*], did not regard equality with God as something to be exploited, but emptied himself, taking the form of a slave [*morphe doulou*], being born in human likeness. (Phil 2:5–7)

"The truth is that only in the mystery of the Incarnate Word does the mystery of man take on light."[190] Those who are plagued by self-doubt and despair regarding the meaning of their lives should remember that God has "crowned them with glory and honour" (Ps 8:5). The cosmos, in its immeasurable expanse and life in the inexhaustible richness of its forms, only reveals the meaning of their existence when we understand that "man, who is the only creature on earth which God willed for itself, cannot fully find himself except through a sincere gift of himself."[191] The highest perfection in all nature is the person (persona est perfectissimum in tota natura).[192] Therefore, man's natural desire for truth and freedom cannot be definitively frustrated (by transience, death, the injustice of the world), because God will in the end be his beatitude and all his happiness.[193] Because man's intellectual nature is directed to the knowledge of God, he stands in the midst of the world.[194] And it belongs to man's status in the world that God communicates to the creature the "dignity of causality" in the second causes.[195]

---

[190] Vatican II, *Gaudium et Spes*, §22.

[191] Vatican II, *Gaudium et Spes*, §24.

[192] St. Thomas Aquinas, *ST* I, q. 29, a. 3.

[193] Boethius, *De consolatione philosophiae*, 2; St. Thomas Aquinas, *ST* I, a. 26, a.1.

[194] St. Thomas Aquinas, *SCG* III, ch. 111.

[195] St. Thomas Aquinas, *ST* I, q. 23, a. 8, ad 3.

The spiritually endowed creature cannot but be the master of its moral actions in free decisions of the will.[196]

Man is not in the world like a thing in a container; rather, he is the living being in which the material world is summated and which transcends itself intellectually towards the meaning of being and its principles. Man as a unique person in his spiritual-corporeal nature and life history is—metaphysically speaking—not on earth like a body in space. He integrates the spiritual and material culture and transcends them in a personal relationship to God, who is the Creator, origin, and end of the universe (anima quasi horizon et confinium corporeorum et incorporeorum, inquantum est substantia incorporea, corporis tamen forma).[197]

Man, then, cannot be reduced to the natural and historical conditions of his existence. In his person, which is carried by his spiritual-corporeal nature, he is the final purpose of creation and he exists for his own sake—but precisely as a person directed towards God, in whom alone man's longing for truth and love can be fulfilled. Man is the epitome of the world and its evolution. Of course, the person can only be perfected through grace. It was only possible to interpret modern anthropocentrism as emancipation because the radical nature of the change from ancient cosmocentrism to "Christian anthropocentrism"[198] was not understood. For the Christian faith sees the human being as the goal and center of cosmic development precisely because the human being is not a temporary phenomenon but contains within himself the meaning of all that exists, reflects on it, and relates it to the principles of being and knowledge, through which he—mediated through the world and the word of revelation—arrives at a knowledge of God. The solution to our environmental problems cannot be a return to the ancient cosmocentrism and the idolization of sub-personal powers such as flora and fauna, the dictatorship of fashion, or the absolutized state.

According to his nature and transcendent destiny, man is therefore not a settler on the margins of the cosmos, not a troublemaker in a healthy biosphere, not a destroyer of the environment who could only justify himself to his planet—as if the globe or the cosmos were a person—through collective self-abolition or a drastic reduction of his numbers.

With his mythical tale of the three wounds inflicted on modern man when he was driven, each time depressingly, from the center and relativized—through Copernicus's heliocentric system, Darwin's evolutionary biology, and Freud's depth psychology—the father of psychoanalysis, Freud, not only impressed the

---

[196] St. Thomas Aquinas, *ST* I, q. 22, a. 3, ad 5.
[197] St. Thomas Aquinas, *SCG* II, ch. 68.
[198] Johann Baptist Metz, *Christliche Anthropozentrik. Über die Denkform des Thomas von Aquin* (Munich, 1962).

educated but also turned the whole of humanity into a super-sanatorium.[199] But the fact that, in his corporeality, man is essentially part of the becoming and passing away of life does not contradict the other fact that his intellect (*Geist*) embraces the entire cosmos and can relate itself to the ground of being. It makes man the center that he is able to ask about the meaning of existence and within it his own destiny as a person. The intellect (*Geist*) cognizes and explains the world to itself; matter does not cognize itself and requires explanation. But there is no universal intellect in individuals, only the individual intellect of each person. That is why the whole of the world is reflected in the intellect of the individual person, and the individual's world begins with him or her at birth and ends at death. But since God is the goal of the creaturely intellect, infinite reason can also assimilate into itself all the events of the world, and the countless subjects of the cognized world and of moral decisions, and communicate itself to the individual human being as his or her goal. Thus man exists eternally through God.

This makes it clear that the world is there for the sake of man and not vice versa. As a species-being and as an individual, man has no need to apologize for his existence or to have a bad conscience talked into him on account of his use of earthly goods. He does not even have to apologize to the chosen few who abstract man from the world and, in so doing, merely elevate their own aesthetic of unspoiled, beautiful nature—undisturbed by man—to the criterion for judging who deserves to live and who does not. For God, every human being is welcome, from conception to death and for all eternity. Therefore, the killing of a human being in the womb or of the sick and dying is a grave crime against the sovereignty of the Creator because it subjects life to the criterion of utility. For a person's dignity and rights vis-à-vis anyone who wants to turn him or her (in a utilitarian manner) into a means to an end are grounded in man's being created in the image and likeness of God (Gen 1:26). The human being as a person is originally and universally related to God as his or her origin and goal. Man exists in an internally unified spiritual-corporeal nature. As a communicative and social being, he lives his life interacting with his personal world and within the temporal-spatial structure of the material world.

From revealed faith, the Christian knows that the goal of his search for the truth that reveals to us the mystery of being, as well as his desire for the unconditional security of his individual existence, can only both be attained and fulfilled in the knowledge of God and in loving communion with him. God's grace does not abrogate nature but rather elevates and perfects it in God.

---

[199] Sigmund Freud, *Vorlesungen zur Einführung in die Psychoanalyse* (1917), 3, 18. Vorl.: *Studienausgabe I*, ed. A. Mitscherlich (Frankfurt a.M., 2000), 283–84.

Faith does not begin where reason ends but leads reason beyond itself to its proper goal: the knowledge of God, who is the truth. Grace makes man like God, and, as the Fathers of the Church say, it "deifies" him. Since through faith in Christ and Baptism in his name, by which alone we are saved (Acts 4:12), we become sons and daughters of God, and we are permitted to say to God in the Holy Spirit, "Our Father" (Mark 11:25; Matt 6:9; Luke 11:2), and "Abba, Father" (Rom 8:15; Gal 4:6). Man dwells in God: "[s]ince in him we live and move and have our being" (Acts 17:28). And God is in us: "[t]hose who love me will keep my word, and my Father will love them, and we will come to them and make our home with them" (John 14:23).

God's greatness and glory, and man's creaturely freedom and moral autonomy, do not contradict or exclude one another. Since God neither gains nor loses anything through creation (cf. Acts 17:25), he can set a created freedom opposite him that affirmatively perfects itself in God, or negatively separates itself from God as the source of its happiness.

It is characteristic of the negation of God and his revelation—within the anti-Christian atheism that has existed since the seventeenth century (in the West)—that man is reduced to a transcendence-free inner-worldliness as a paradoxical condition of his liberation from God. If man is nothing more than a machine (de La Mettrie), no more than a more intelligent animal in the struggle for existence (Feuerbach), no more than a useful citizen for the state (Comte), no more than one proletarian more in the struggle for a classless society in the utopian future (Marx), no more than a soldier in the war waged by the stronger race for living space (Social Darwinism), nothing but a "featherless biped condemned to the awareness that he is doomed to die,"[200] no more than a robot in the rivalry of an exclusively profit-oriented capitalism, or no more than, for the time being, still an organically based intelligence that will be surpassed by a silicon-based artificial intelligence—if this is all man is, then he is at the mercy of his own kind, who idolize themselves and enslave him:

> Medicine and biology today seek to prove the Magna Carta of materialism, according to which the wiring of the brain and consciousness are determined solely by the chemistry of the genes and

---

[200] Umberto Eco, „Wenn der andere ins Spiel kommt, beginnt die Ethik," in Carlo M. Martini and Umberto Eco, *Woran glaubt, wer nicht glaubt* (Vienna, 1998), 82–93, at 92–93; Eng.: "Ethics Are Born in the Presence of the Other," in Martini and Eco, *Belief or Nonbelief?: A Confrontation* (New York: Arcade Publishing, 2000 and 2012).

the environment. Man, without a mind (*Geist*) that is independent of the substances, is then unfree in his actions, so to speak physically coded, a chemically regulated thing.[201]

Homo sapiens has turned into a god who creates the new human being— homo Deus.[202]

In the program of transhumanism with the abolition of the human being, the old insight is frighteningly confirmed: whoever wants to be like God and claims for himself the power to define what is "good and evil" (Gen 3:5) becomes to his neighbor the devil, who "was a murderer from the beginning . . . and the father of lies" (John 8:44). Where the individual human being is the highest and most perfect thing in nature, and carries his dignity within himself, the killing of unborn children is implicitly permitted if they stand in the way of their mother's right to self-determination or are of no benefit to society or the protection of the planet. Totalitarian states have no scruples about ordering the murder of prisoners to make money out of their organs.

Umberto Eco tried to offer humanists a purely natural ethics within the framework of identifying the cosmic Substance with an a-personally conceived God-principle. If a selfless commitment to good or to those who suffer innocently—even to the extent of giving up one's own life—fills the consciousness with happiness at having been of service to the harmony of the universe, this is scarcely going to satisfy either faith or reason. Instead of a survival with the physical substance of his person, what Eco hopes for is a survival of its unrepeatable qualities as "purely immaterial algorithms." The following sentence of Eco's impresses with its semantic subtlety without being able to disguise the superstition informing a reason uprooted from the ground of being:

> Who knows if death, rather than being an implosion, may be an explosion—the impression, from somewhere between the vortices of the universe, of the software (what others might call soul) created by our living, made up of memories and regrets, and thus our implacable suffering, or sense of peace for a duty fulfilled, and love.[203]

It is quite reasonable for man, with his instinct for self-preservation, to desire to secure his existence in the world; it is equally justifiable for him to

---

[201] Markus von Hänsel-Hohenhausen, *Hitler und die Aufklärung* (Frankfurt a.M., 2013), 103–4; Alexander Kissler, *Der aufgeklärte Gott. Wie die Religion zur Vernunft kam* (Munich, 2008).

[202] Cf. Joseph Ratzinger and Paolo Flores d'Arcais, *Gibt es Gott? Wahrheit, Glaube, Atheismus* (Berlin, 2006).

[203] Umberto Eco, "Wenn der andere ins Spiel kommt, beginnt die Ethik," 82–93, at 91.

recognize in his consciousness that the annihilation of his existence in the world altogether contradicts the meaning of being, revealed in his reason as the origin of his question about his origin and goal. But man is an "I" in relation to a "Thou" and, above all else, in relation to the Mystery which he does not have at his command but which reveals itself freely to him.

Israel's faith in God does not emerge from colored projections on a white surface that flash up in the eyes of the beholder. The Unknown One beyond the world reveals himself only through his self-being, through which he brings about our liberation from enslavement to the powers of this world and all-destroying death: "I am who I am" (Exod 3:14), he replies to Moses when he asks him his name. Beyond the historical liberation from Egypt, God reveals himself to us forever as the origin and guarantor of freedom: "I am the LORD your God, who brought you out of the land of Egypt, out of the house of slavery" (Exod 20:2); our old self has been crucified with Christ "so that the body of sin might be destroyed, and we might no longer be enslaved to sin. . . . But if we have died with Christ, we believe that we will also live with him" (Rom 6:6–8); "creation itself will be set free from its bondage to decay and will obtain the freedom of the glory of the children of God" (Rom 8:21).

Only if we take our bearings from God's liberating action can we preserve our freedom in a world that is drawn towards total control, as if some earthly power could eternally guarantee assured happiness to those who are totally supervised (*betreut*, as in sheltered or assisted living) and deprived of their freedom. It is impossible to build a solid house on the shifting sands of transience.

It is not a world government that will save the world with the totalitarian removal of people's rights to make their own decisions. Those who believe in God know that "the ultimate vocation of man is in fact one, and divine."[204] The mystery of humanity is so profound that it can only show itself to us in the light of God's revelation:

> Through Christ and in Christ, the riddles of sorrow and death grow meaningful. Apart from his Gospel, they overwhelm us. Christ has risen, destroying death by his death; he has lavished life upon us so that, as sons in the Son, we can cry out in the Spirit; Abba, Father.[205]

In Christ, the God-man, the opposition has become obsolete between the transcendent and the immanent development of the world, as well as between man's supernatural perfection and natural development.

---

[204] Vatican II, *Gaudium et Spes*, §22.
[205] Vatican II, *Gaudium et Spes*, §22.

Withdrawal from the world and idolatry of the world contradict the Christian life, which in Christ combines a universal orientation towards God with a concrete responsibility for the world.

Taking its orientation from the God-man mystery of Christ, the Second Vatican Council says of the autonomy of earthly realities:

> Now many of our contemporaries seem to fear that a closer bond between human activity and religion will work against the independence of men, of societies, or of the sciences.
>
> If by the autonomy of earthly affairs we mean that created things and societies themselves enjoy their own laws and values which must be gradually deciphered, put to use, and regulated by men, then it is entirely right to demand that autonomy. Such is not merely required by modern man, but harmonizes also with the will of the Creator. For by the very circumstance of their having been created, all things are endowed with their own stability, truth, goodness, proper laws and order. Man must respect these as he isolates them by the appropriate methods of the individual sciences or arts. . . .
>
> But if the expression, the independence of temporal affairs, is taken to mean that created things do not depend on God, and that man can use them without any reference to their Creator, anyone who acknowledges God will see how false such a meaning is. For without the Creator the creature would disappear.[206]

St. Augustine begins his *Confessions* by praising God for creating us human beings and drawing us to himself, even though we seem so tiny in the cosmos and dissolve in the history of the world like a drop of water in the ocean:

> Great art thou, O Lord, and greatly to be praised; great is thy power, and thy wisdom infinite. And thee would man praise; man, but a particle of thy creation; man, that bears about him his mortality, the witness of his sin, the witness that thou resistest the proud: yet would man praise thee; he, but a particle of thy creation. Thou awakest us to delight in thy praise; for thou madest us for thyself, and our heart is restless, until it repose in thee [Tu excitas, ut laudare te delectat, quia fecisti nos ad te et inquietum est cor nostrum, donec requiescat in te].[207]

---

[206] Vatican II, *Gaudium et Spes*, §36.
[207] St. Augustine, *Confessions* I.I.I.

Principles of being Catholic

1.   The Catholic believes—in contrast to mere opinions about the "unknown God" (Acts 17:23)—in the Triune *God* "with divine and Catholic faith,"[208] i.e., with revealed faith presented by the Church as a confession of faith.

     In the course of the history of the world and salvation, God, who said to Moses, "I am who I am" (Exod 3:14), revealed to the people of God and to the Church of Christ his own being and self-being in the Incarnation of his *Word*, and in the eschatological outpouring of his *Holy Spirit* as "grace and truth" (John 1:17), so that all "who believed in his name . . . [should] become children of God" (John 1:12).

2.   The Catholic is convinced that every human being, by means of his natural reason, can conclude with complete certainty—from the contingency of the world—the unconditionality of the existence of God, who makes himself known to him as the origin and goal of his existence, helping answer man's question as to the meaning of being and of his search for truth.

3.   The Catholic believes that the supernatural revelation of God in Jesus Christ—combined with the natural knowledge of God and the principles of being and knowledge that are evident to reason—remains present through the Holy Spirit in both the diachronic and the synchronic faith consciousness of the Catholic Church, the sense of faith shared by the whole people of God. For God himself speaks to us in his word through the teaching of the apostles in Sacred Scripture. And he himself communicates his truth and his grace in the living Tradition of the Church (preaching, catechesis, liturgy, the unanimous witness of the Fathers and Doctors of the Church). And God himself irreversibly interprets his word, spoken uniquely and for ever for our salvation, which was made flesh in Jesus Christ, in the ultimate binding decisions (the articles of the Creed, the dogmatic definitions) of the Church's Magisterium (the universal episcopate with the pope at its head).

4.   As a result of the Incarnation, the Catholic stands in an "I-Thou" relationship to God his Father (in the image and likeness of God), to the Son of God as his Redeemer and brother (child

---

[208] DH 3011; 3018.

of God), and to the Holy Spirit as his friend (sanctifying grace; deification).[209] God has revealed his name as the One Who Is, and as the triune love of Father and Son in the Holy Spirit. He has called us by name and given us the name of a son and daughter of God. Before God, we are persons, not specimens of a species or comrades in a collective.

5. Personal relationship and communication take place in the three divine virtues of faith (*fides*), hope (*spes*), and love (*caritas*).[210] Connected to these are the four cardinal virtues of prudence (*prudentia*), justice (*iustitia*), fortitude (*fortitudo*), and temperance (*temperantia*), which can be acquired through human effort.[211] These divine virtues are infused into the soul by God, and turn into a God-man synergy effect when grace joins with free will in a public act of confession in and with the whole Church.

   5.1 In faith, the Catholic—theocentrically—recognizes God as the Eternal Truth, freely and intentionally incorporating it into his spiritual self-realization.

   5.2 In hope, the Catholic—Christocentrically—intends God as the goal of his life's journey in following Christ to the Cross and Resurrection.

   5.3 In love, the Catholic internalizes—pneumatologically—that he is unconditionally wanted by the Triune God and grasps intellectually, and affectively, that this is the true ground of his existence as eternally predestined to inalienable salvation.

6. The Catholic takes the ecclesial and sacramental mediation of salvation as also being an element of the Christ event. For it follows from the Incarnation, and is the continuation of the mission of the Son and the making present (historical-immanent mediation) of his truth and grace in the Holy Spirit, who "from above" transcendentally mediates the saving work of Christ. This gives rise to the Christian responsibility for the world and commitment to world peace, social justice, human freedom, and dignity against the arbitrariness of the powerful.[212]

---

[209] Gerhard Ludwig Müller, *Vom Vater gesandt. Impulse einer inkarnatorischen Christologie für Gottesfrage und Menschenbild* (Regensburg, 2005).

[210] Josef Pieper, *Lieben-hoffen-glauben* (Munich, 1986).

[211] Josef Pieper, *Das Viergespann* (Munich, 1964).

[212] Gustavo Gutiérrez and Gerhard L. Müller, *An der Seite der Armen* (Augsburg, 2004); Gerhard Cardinal Müller, *Povera per i poveri. La missione della Chiesa* (Città del Vaticano, 2014).

7. The Catholic believes that the individual body of Jesus during his historical lifetime is now—after he has taken his seat post-Resurrection at the right hand of God in heaven—represented symbolically and really on earth by his ecclesial body, and that he is "truly, really, and substantially" present particularly in his sacramental Body,[213] which is what makes the Eucharist the inner constitutive principle of the Church and, at the same time, makes the Church the outward ground and visible subject of the celebration of the sacraments.[214] On account of the link between human corporeality, salvation in the incarnate Son of God, the embodiment of grace in the sacraments, and the hope of the resurrection of the flesh, a Catholic axiom is "*Caro cardo salutis.*"[215]

8. And since the identity of the Creator of the world and the Redeemer of mankind rules out any form of dualistic thinking in the understanding of God and the conception of man and the world (mild Platonism, Gnosticism, Manichaeism), as well as any monistic worldviews (rationalism, idealism, materialism, empiricism, positivism), Catholic thinking—which is to be deduced from the existence of the world and the word of revelation—must run as follows: "Since therefore grace does not destroy nature but perfects it, natural reason should minister to faith as the natural bent of the will ministers to charity [Cum enim gratia non tollat naturam, sed perficiat, oportet quod naturalis ratio subserviat fidei, sicut et naturalis inclinatio voluntatis obsequitur caritati]."[216]

9. The Catholic believes in the personal account that everyone must give before God's judgment seat for his or her deeds and omissions in this earthly life because it belongs to human dignity to be master of one's intellectual decisions and moral actions and, consequently, to expect from one's Creator and Redeemer the reward for one's good and evil deeds.

10. The Catholic acknowledges the Petrine principle of the Church.[217] By this is meant the hierarchical-sacramental constitution of the

---

[213] Henri de Lubac, *Corpus Mysticum. L'Eucharistie et l'Eglise au Moyen Age*, 1949; Eng. *Corpus Mysticum: The Eucharist and the Church in the Middle Ages* (Notre Dame, IN: University of Notre Dame Press, 2007), DI I 1051.

[214] Vatican II, *Lumen Gentium*, §11.

[215] Tertullian, *De resurrectione mortuorum* 8.3.

[216] St. Thomas Aquinas, *ST* I, q. 1, a. 8, ad 2.

[217] Gerhard Kardinal Müller, *Der Papst. Sendung und Auftrag* (Freiburg, 2017); Eng.: *The Pope: His Mission and His Task* (Washington, DC: The Catholic University of America Press, 2021).

pilgrim Church (*ecclesia peregrinans, militans*) encapsulated in Simon Peter. If Christ wished the Church to perdure until the end of history, then he also wished the authority he gave Peter at the beginning for the work of the Church to continue in his successors on his cathedra in Rome.[218]

11. The relationship between the Church as a (invisible, hidden) community of grace and as a socially constituted (visible, manifest) community of confession and worship cannot be grasped in the Platonic scheme of archetype and (shadowy) form. Rather, the Church is the corporeally real presence of Christ's grace in the world, which, as a sign of it, effectively mediates to us a community of life with God. Hence there is no private relationship with Jesus, the head of the Church, that bypasses his concrete presence in his ecclesial and sacramental Body.

12. The Catholic believes in God, hopes in him, and loves him in the same frame of mind, both virginal and maternal, in which Mary, "the mother of the Lord" (Luke 1:43), conceived and gave birth to her human Son, Jesus, who is the Son in the Triune God in all eternity, as the Messianic Son of God come in human flesh (Rom 8:3; Gal 4:4; Phil 2:7). Through the working of the Holy Spirit, she received and bore him in her womb and heart (Luke 1:31); but she also did not abandon him, staying with him right up to the revelation of his divine glory in his death on the Cross (John 17:1; 19:26). That is why she is the Mother of faith and Mother of the whole Church, which sees in her the archetype of her own virginal, bride-like relationship with God and maternal relationship with us. Strengthened by her example, we understand the mystical motif of the "birth of God in the soul"[219] in accordance with the epigram of Angelus Silesius (1624–1677): "Wird Christus tausendmal zu Bethlehem geboren und nicht in dir, du bliebest ewiglich verloren [If Christ were born a thousand times in Bethlehem and not in you, you would remain eternally lost]."[220]

---

[218] St. Thomas Aquinas, *SCG* IV, ch. 76.

[219] Hugo Rahner, *Die Lehre der Kirchenväter von der Geburt Christi aus dem Herzen der Kirche und der Gläubigen*; Rahner, *Symbole der Kirche. Die Ekklesiologie der Väter* (Salzburg, 1964), 13–87.

[220] Angelus Silesius, *Cherubinischer Wandersmann* I, 61.

The Marian principle[221] does mean merely recognizing the Marian dogmas and venerating Mary as both Virgin and Mother of God (Luke 1:48); it also means that the believer places boundless trust in God, who makes everything work out for the best for those who love him: "For those whom he foreknew he also predestined to be conformed to the image of his Son, in order that he might be the firstborn within a large family" (Rom 8:29). This is why, after the Lord's Prayer, Catholics pray the Ave Maria, which is composed of the words of the Angel Gabriel to Mary and the greeting of St. Elizabeth, the mother of St. John the Baptist, when Mary entered the house of Zechariah:

> Hail, Mary, full of grace,
> the Lord is with thee.
> Blessed art thou amongst women
> and blessed is the fruit of thy womb, Jesus.
> Holy Mary, Mother of God,
> pray for us sinners,
> now and at the hour of our death.
> Amen.

---

[221] Gerhard Ludwig Müller, *Die Frau im Heilsplan Gottes* (= *Mariologische Studien* 15) (Regensburg, 2002).

Chapter 4

"CATHOLIC": THE ATTRIBUTE OF
THE ONE CHURCH OF CHRIST
THAT LINKS ALL CHRISTIANS

"Catholic": a religiously narrowed term among Christians?

It is only since the sixteenth century that the average understanding of the term "catholic" has been narrowed to mean those doctrines and rites of the Church linked to the pope which differ from those of other Christian communions that emerged from the Reformation (the so-called controversial doctrines). "Christian" has since been the name given to the doctrines common to Catholics and Protestants, as distinguished from the separating confessions (*Augsburg Confession*; doctrinal decrees of the Council of Trent), whereas this adjective originally referred to the profession of faith of the newly baptized in Christ as the Messiah. Denominationalism (*Konfessionalismus*) has brought with it a shift in original Christian concepts, which not only need to be critically examined but even to be restored to their original and fuller meaning.

The German term "*christliche Konfessionen*" (Christian denominations) is derived from the confessional writings that the followers of Luther, Zwingli, and Calvin drew up to distinguish themselves from the hitherto existing Church, which, of course, they held responsible as the "Popish church" for the historical degeneration of the Catholic Church. Admittedly, they themselves came from the Catholic Church and did not want to abolish it, only to renew it according to the spirit of Christ, i.e., to re-form it. As theologians, they knew perfectly well that you cannot found a new Church because the Church was founded once only and is continually being built up by Christ in the Holy Spirit through word and sacrament. The most famous confession for Lutheranism is the *Confessio Augustana* (Augsburg Confession), which is a compilation of the essentials of Luther's Reformation theology put together by Philipp Melanchthon at the Diet of Augsburg (1530), and in which he, at the same time, kept the doors open for a future overcoming of the differences. Among the Calvinist-style "confessional writings and church ordinances of the church reformed according to God's Word," the *Heidelberg Catechism* (1563) is particularly well-known.

This kind of "confession" which establishes a church community is something alien to the Catholic understanding. Nor can one cite the Tridentine Profession of Faith[1] as a counter-argument, since it is merely an extension of the Symbols of the early Church to which the controversial themes have been added. Nevertheless, the pragmatic linguistic usage has prevailed according to which the terms "*Konfession*" or "denomination" are applied to Catholicism socially and by the state and civil authorities. Theologically speaking, the Catholic Church does not see herself as one denomination alongside others but rather as the one, holy, apostolic Church of Christ, to which the attribute "catholic" appertains in the original sense as infallibly defined by the Church Fathers and the Magisterium.

However, the relationship between the Christian communities is not only historically defined by their demarcation from each other in the past but is also characterized in the present day by their similar declarations against the encroachments of totalitarian systems or contemporary trends, which are an expression of their shared Christian conviction.

For example, a stand was taken[2] against National Socialism in Germany and its hostility towards both faith and humanity both by the German Protestant church in the "Theological Declaration of Barmen" (1934) and by Pope Pius XI, in collaboration with German bishops, in his 1937 encyclical *Mit Brennender Sorge* (With Burning Concern). The Bilateral Working Group of the German Bishops' Conference and the United Evangelical Lutheran Church of Germany presented a common confession of the Christian faith in our time in a document with the significant title *Gott und die Würde des Menschen* (God and the Dignity of Man).[3] Hence the term "confession" has the chance today to go beyond its historical meaning of designating what delimits and instead to *confess* what convictions and attitudes Christians hold in common in relation to the secular or non-Christian world. Cardinal Walter Kasper has gathered together from the many ecumenical-dialogue documents what he calls the

---

[1] DH 1862–1870.

[2] Konrad Löw, *Die Schuld. Christen und Juden im Urteil der Nationalsozialisten und der Gegenwart*, Gräfelfing, 2002.

[3] (Paderborn, 2017); Eng.: (Leipzig, 2020), https://www.eva-leipzig.de/product_info.php?info=p4910_God-and-the-Dignity-of-Humans.html.

"basic aspects of Christian faith in ecumenical dialogue" and offered a clear overview of them entitled *Harvesting the Fruits*.[4] The basis from which he proceeds here is the common belief in the Trinitarian God and salvation in Christ. The state of ecumenical dialogue is also shown by the title *Vom Konflikt zur Gemeinschaft* (From Conflict to Communion),[5] published by the Lutheran / Roman Catholic Commission for Unity to mark the commemoration in 2017 of the Reformation.

In translating the term "catholic Church" with the (seemingly) dissociated phrase "Christian church," Martin Luther (1483–1546) set the course for what has remained common-language usage to the present day. However, anyone who studies his *Small Catechism* (1529) in a spiritually profitable way will, even as a Catholic, discover to his surprise and delight that 90 percent of the statements in it accord with his Catholic faith. However, it has to be held against the well-meaning but misleading translation of "catholic" as "Christian" that the content of this attribute of the Church, which has evolved, makes it no longer permissible to render it purely etymologically with "universal," as this obscures the factual meaning that the term "catholic" has meanwhile accrued. Even in ancient times, Latin-speaking Christians did not translate the Greek word *katholikos* into the language of the Church as "universal" but rather adopted it as a foreign word, as a technical term for the attribute of the Church *catholica*, and passed this on to the later vernacular languages. The rendering of "catholic" as "Christian" makes little sense since it adds no further explanation to "Church." For the "Church of Christ" is—rendered literally—already the community belonging to Christ, the Lord (*Kyrios*). In all languages, one should stick to the Greek original instead of a vague translation, because the meaning of "catholic" includes not only the worldwide spread of the Church but also her orthodoxy and sacramental form.

When in particular the churches of the Eastern Orthodox tradition and the communities stemming from the Reformation also profess the holy and catholic Church together with the Catholic Church that sees in the pope the "perpetual and visible principle and foundation of unity,"[6] there is no question of their dissolving into the Roman Catholic Church through a simple conversion; rather, it signifies that all Christians want to do justice to the content of what "catholic" means in their common Creed.

---

4   Walter Kasper, *Harvesting the Fruits: Aspects of Christian Faith in Ecumenical Dialogue* (New York: Continuum, 2009); dt.: *Die Früchte ernten. Grundlagen christlichen Glaubens im ökumenischen Dialog* (Paderborn, 2011).

5   (Paderborn, 2013).

6   Second Vatican Council, *Lumen Gentium* (1964), §23; cf. §18.

In his *Confessio Orthodoxa*, the Metropolitan of Kiev Peter Mogila (1596–1646) was the first to present the Orthodox faith, i.e., catholic in the classical sense of the early councils, in a scientific-scholastic manner in that he brings out what unites it with the Catholic-Western Church and what distinguishes it, entitling it the *Orthodox Confession of the Catholic and Apostolic Eastern Church.*[7]

In the early days of the indulgence controversy, which, contrary to the will of all concerned, resulted in the schism of Western Christendom, Martin Luther, with his opposition to turning people's worries about the salvation of their souls into a business, was arguably more "catholic" than the leading curials and Albrecht of Brandenburg—the latter, as Archbishop of Mainz, Magdeburg, and administrator of Halberstadt at the same time, opposed the prohibition of the accumulation of offices—who used the "indulgence" to pursue their power (*Hohenzollern*) and Church (curial) policy without any regard for the credibility of the Church.

During the Day of Pardon Mass celebrated by Pope St. John Paul II in the Holy Year of the Incarnation 2000, the Roman Church, through the mouth of a cardinal, made a "confession of sins which have harmed the unity of the body of Christ": "Let us pray that our recognition of the sins which have rent the unity of the body of Christ and wounded fraternal charity will facilitate the way to reconciliation and communion among all Christians." And after a few moments' silence, the Pope continued the prayer:

> Merciful Father, on the night before his Passion your Son prayed for the unity of those who believe in him: in disobedience to his will, however, believers have opposed one another, becoming divided, and have mutually condemned one another and fought against one another. We urgently implore your forgiveness and we beseech the gift of a repentant heart, so that all Christians, reconciled with you and with one another will be able, in one body and in one spirit, to experience anew the joy of full communion. We ask this through Christ our Lord.[8]

In a time of uncertainty, Catholics, as well as all people of goodwill who are searching for God's truth in their lives, are faced with questions to which

---

7   Cf. Peter Hauptmann and Petrus Mogilas: *Klassiker der Theologie I*, ed. H. Fries and G. Kretschmar (Munich, 1981), 378–91, at 383–88.

8   Internationale Theologische Kommission, *Erinnern und Versöhnen. Die Kirche und die Verfehlungen in ihre Vergangenheit*, ed. Gerhard L. Müller (Freiburg, 2000); Eng.: *Memory and Reconciliation: The Church and the Faults of the Past*, https://www.vatican.va/roman_curia /congregations/cfaith/cti_documents/rc_con_cfaith_doc_20000307_memory-reconc -itc_en.html.

they seek to find an answer in "sincere dialogue"[9] with their bishops, the "proclaimers of truth and apostles of freedom."[10] These questions concern the global crisis of humanity, in which the Church offers her assistance and, at a deeper level, the ability of every human being to recognize his or her *high calling* to a community of life with God:

> Inspired by no earthly ambition, the Church seeks but a solitary goal: to carry forward the work of Christ under the lead of the befriending Spirit. And Christ entered this world to give witness to the truth, to rescue and not to sit in judgment, to serve and not to be served.[11]

"Catholic": an attribute of Christ's Church that can only be grasped in faith

If you look backwards from the Catholic-Reformation controversy that started on October 31, 1517, and examine the first and fundamental phase of the history of the Church and theology, you will find that the controversial doctrines—which Catholics and Protestants have had from the sixteenth to the twentieth centuries and regarded as being typically and distinctively Catholic—are largely absent from the definition of what "catholic" means. The controversial issues are, in fact, mainly related to the doctrine of the Church and the sacraments. The Reformers explicitly claim catholicity for themselves as the criterion of right faith. At the end of the first part of the *Confessio Augustana* [Augsburg Confession] (1530), which deals with the common basic doctrines of Christianity, the Protestant theologians, under the leadership of Philipp Melanchthon (1497–1560), argue that their teachings accord in every way with the Holy Scriptures and do not deviate from the teachings of "the Church Catholic, or even the Roman Church," or from the consensus of the Church Fathers. The dissent extends, they claim, only to a few abuses, and to purely human doctrines wrongly declared necessary for salvation, which, though are perhaps time-honored, are simply not contained in divine Revelation: hence it is wrong to call them (the Protestants) heretics.[12]

---

9   Second Vatican Council, *Gaudium et Spes* (1965), §43; *Unitatis Redintegratio*, §§9, 11.
10   St. Irenaeus, *Adversus haereses* 3.15.3.
11   Vatican II, *Gaudium et Spes*, §3.
12   Wilhelm Maurer, *Historischer Kommentar zur Confessio Augustana*, 2 vols. (Gütersloh, 1976 and 1978); Erwin Iserloh, ed., *Confessio Augustana und Confutatio. Der Augsburger Reichstag 1530 und die Einheit der Kirche* (Münster i.W., 1980); Harding Meyer and Heinz Schütte, *Confessio Augustana. Gemeinsame Untersuchung lutherischer und katholischer Theologen* (Paderborn, 1980); Otto H. Pesch, ed., *"Das Augsburger Bekenntnis" von 1530 damals und heute* (Mainz, 1980); Karl

However, they understood abuses in a fundamentally different way from the late medieval demand for reform of the Church in head and members (eformation in capite et membris). St. Catherine of Siena (1347–1380), who has meanwhile been elevated to the rank of Doctor of the Church, was a prominent preacher of repentance against internal abuses in the Church and the Curia, and many a bishop and pope took her warnings to heart.[13]

For Luther and Calvin's criticism goes beyond the moral failure of individuals, the secularization of the Church, and the politicization of the papacy and the bishops (as secular princes and court bishops). The Reformers were convinced that the grievances were rooted in the false teaching of the pope's followers, the Papists, about justification through works, and thus a kind of self-redemption through human activity, rather than through the justifying grace of Christ alone.

The Church—gathered around the pope and the bishops—did not deny the need to put an end to abuses and for an inner renewal of the Church and all Christians through grace, faith, hope, and love. But the Catholic Church stood by her conviction that there are also revealed truths about the Church and the sacraments which, beyond patristics, have since developed in the Church's faith consciousness—in the sense of a legitimate and necessary development of dogma in the context of a fundamental hermeneutics of the Catholic faith[14]—and must be held by Christians with a divine and Catholic faith for the sake of their salvation. The Council of Trent (1545–1563) explicitly addresses the binding doctrines of the faith that Protestants have partially or completely denied or misunderstood. These are the teachings on original sin and, in the Council's most detailed document, the justification of the sinner; also, on the sacraments in general and specifically the seven sacraments of Baptism, Confirmation, the Eucharist (as a Sacrifice and transubstantiation), Penance, Anointing of the Sick, the sacrament of Holy Orders—and thus the Church's constitution—and Matrimony. Finally, there are decrees on Purgatory, the saints, the veneration of relics, and on indulgences, the last of which, due to the shameful money business they were used for, had acted as a catalyst for the schism in Western Christianity that has now gone on for five hundred years.

Lehmann and Edmund Schlink, eds., *Evangelium-Sakramente-Amt der Einheit der Kirche. Die ökumenische Tragweite der Confessio Augustana* (Freiburg, 1982); Lat. And Eng.: https://www.ccel.org/ccel/schaff/creeds3.iii.ii.html.

[13] St. Caterina von Siena, *An die Männer der Kirche. Sämtliche Briefe* (Kleinhain).

[14] Johannes Feiner and Magnus Löhrer, eds., *Mysterium salutis. Grundriss Heilsgeschichtlicher Dogmatik I* (Einsiedeln, 1965); Gerhard Cardinal Müller, *Katholische Dogmatik. Für Studium und Praxis der Theologie* (Freiburg i.Br., 2016), 2–101.

The Reformers refer—for example in the Lutheran *Book of Concord* (1580)—not only to Holy Scripture as the first and unsurpassable norm for every Catholic doctrine and every theological conception (norma normans non normata) but also to the three early creeds of the Church (the Apostles' Creed, the Nicaea-Constantinopolitan Creed, and the symbol of the faith *Quicumque*) and hence to the dogma of Trinitarian theology and Christology. Connected to this are the decisions on the doctrine of the sacraments, the doctrine of grace, the formation of the canon, the inspiration and inerrancy of Sacred Scripture, and the condemnations issued against Marcion, the Gnostics, the Manichaeans, the Arians, the Nestorians, the Monophysites, the Donatists, the Pelagians, etc. This means that the Reformers also align themselves with the substance of Apostolic Tradition and its official ecclesial reception, and accept these fundamental principles of the catholicity of the Church.[15]

However, doubt is cast in principle on the formal criterion of catholicity, i.e., the authority of the Church's living Magisterium. They consider a fundamental opposition between scriptural and ecclesial teaching to be possible and to have, in fact, occurred since the end of the patristic period. Hence the pope is for the Reformers no longer, like Peter, the first witness of the word of God and the guarantor of its faithful and full proclamation, but rather is the corrupter of Scripture and the enemy of the salvation of souls: in other words, the end-times Antichrist. However, during his visit to Rome in 1966, the greatest Protestant theologian of the twentieth century, Karl Barth, in order to underline how fundamentally things had changed, stated, "The Pope is not the Antichrist!"[16]

Historically and systematically, Melanchthon deconstructed the papal primacy "of divine right" (*de iure divino*) in his treatise *De potestate et primatu Papae* (1537) (*Von der Gewalt und Obrigkeit [Jurisdiktion] des Papstes* [1541]; On the Power and Primacy of the Pope) and reduced it to a historically evolved leadership role according to human law (de iure mere ecclesiastico).

In the *Smalcald Articles* (1537), which were drawn up to overcome doctrinal differences at a council convened by the pope, Luther denies that the "Papists" are a Church. For the Church is not the authority it claims be under that name but what even a child of seven knows: "the holy believers and lambs who hear the voice of their Shepherd" are the Church of which we say in the

---

[15]   Wolfhart Pannenberg and Theodor Schneider, eds., *Verbindliches Zeugnis I. Kanon-Schrift-Tradition* (Freiburg, 1992); Dorothea Sattler and Gunther Wenz, *Das kirchliche Amt in apostolischer Nachfolge* (Freiburg, 2008).

[16]   Karl Barth, *Ad Limina Apostolorum* (Zürich, 1967), 18.

Creed, "I believe in one holy [catholic or] Christian Church [Credo sanctam ecclesiam catholicam sive christianam]."[17]

In his interpretation of the third article of the Apostles' Creed in the *Large Catechism* (1529), Luther had already reproached the Papists with having completely separated the Church from the Holy Spirit and his work of awakening and sanctifying faith in Christ through preaching, thus bringing it down to an external institution of salvation. It was, he claimed, no longer sanctification through justifying faith that constituted the essence of the Church, inasmuch as its ministry of communicating salvation in sermon and sacrament had degenerated into a function of its earthly claim to power. The priests had selfishly manipulated and controlled people's fear about salvation. In German, so as not to confuse "Kirche" (Church) with the building made of stone, it is best to say "eine christliche Gemeinde oder Sammlung" (a Christian congregation or assembly), or, best of all, "*eine heilige Christenheit*" (holy Christendom). The communion (*Gemeinschaft*) of saints ought to be rendered as a congregation (*Gemeinde*) of saints, a holy congregation "under one head, even Christ, called together by the Holy Ghost in one faith, one mind, and understanding [in the Latin version: eodem sensu et sententia] with manifold gifts, yet agreeing in love, without sects or schisms."[18] The Holy Spirit remains with her until the Last Day. But the Holy Spirit works in the Christian Church (in unitate ecclesiae catholicae) with the offices of the Church through the Gospel in its preaching and sacrament.[19] Though the Church is "properly (*proprie*) the congregation of saints and true believers,"[20] it is taught "that one holy Church is to continue forever (*perpetuo mansura sit*)."[21] For the true unity of the Church, it is sufficient, according to Ephesians 4:4–5—one body, one Spirit, one Lord, one faith, one baptism—to agree concerning the doctrine of the Gospel and the administration of the sacraments.

Of course, Catholic theology, too, endorses the adjunct here that ceremonies instituted by men, or specific theories of individual theologians, are not necessary for the unity of the Church. St. Thomas Aquinas already established that the saints, like us today, are permitted to have different opinions

---

[17] BSLK 460. Martin Luther, *The Smalcald Articles* 3, trans. F. Bente and W. H. T. Dau, in *Triglot Concordia: The Symbolical Books of the Evangelical Lutheran Church* (St. Louis: Concordia Publishing, 1921), 12, https://www.gutenberg.org/files/273/273-h/273-h.htm#link2H_4_0007.

[18] Martin Luther, "The Apostles' Creed," in *The Large Catechism*, art. 3, no. 54.

[19] BSLK 655–658.

[20] *Confessio Augustana*, a. 8, https://www.ccel.org/ccel/schaff/creeds3.iii.ii.html.

[21] *Confessio Augustana*, a. 7.

in everything that does not necessarily belong to the revealed faith.[22] In the Encyclical on the Study of Holy Scripture, *Providentissimus Deus* (1893), Pope Leo XIII explained this hermeneutical principle to mean that those views of the Church Fathers and modern exegetes on natural philosophy and science, which are conditioned by the times, do not belong to the truth of the faith.[23]

However, in the age of the Reformation, the question arose whether the office of bishop did not in fact belong from Apostolic Tradition to the essential constitution of the Church. After all, according to article seven of the *Confessio Augustana*, the office of bishop by divine right includes the ministry of word and sacrament, the judgment of false doctrines, and the duty to exclude heretics from the Church. And so pastors, too, owe them obedience in accordance with Christ's words to the apostles, "Whoever listens to you listens to me" (Luke 10:16). Only where they teach contrary to the Gospel, and establish laws contrary to it in the Church, is it God's command that they should not be obeyed. Luther merely leaves the questions unanswered of *how* this is determined in the case of conflict, and *to whom* the ultimate authority then belongs.

Seen in a clear light, the difference in the definition of the nature of the Church—based on the early Christian creeds—is not as irreconcilable as it would appear at first sight. For it is clear that the Church is essentially a community of life of the members of the body of Christ with their head. The Holy Spirit brings about the justification and sanctification of the sinner through the Gospel by means of sermon and sacraments (the latter including, to the Catholic way of thinking, alongside Baptism, the Eucharist, and Penance, as well as Confirmation, Anointing of the Sick, Holy Orders, and Matrimony). But the Church's social constitution in the apostolic authority of her ministers (deacon, priest, bishop, and the Bishop of Rome as the visible principle of unity), who are sacramentally appointed by the Holy Spirit, does not exist for its own sake, let alone for the sake of secular goals alien to the Church. Sacred authority is conferred by Christ in the Holy Spirit on the bishops/priests (Acts 20:28) so as to enable them to effectively communicate the word of God in the mission and with the authority of Christ—not as a subjective interpretation but as God's promise of salvation—and, in the sacramental signs, to mediate the sanctifying grace of Christ to the believer receiving them. Moreover, they exercise Christ's pastoral ministry in his name and hopefully also in a spirit of personal devotion, not like hired hands who do not care for the sheep (cf. John 10:13).

---

[22] St. Thomas Aquinas, *Super IV Sent. II*, dist. 2, q. 1, a. 3, in *Opera omnia 1*, ed. R. Busa, (1980), 130.

[23] DH 3289.

There is a consensus within the Reformation movement that the primacy of the Roman Pontiff, as the Successor of Peter, does not belong to the essential nature (*Wesen*) of the Church and, consequently, did not develop with and out of its essential nature either. Rather, it is merely an accidental addition, which can or must be shed again. It could be compared to the growing limbs of an organism, which belong essentially to it at every stage of growth, whereas the clothes that it has outgrown must be discarded and replaced by more suitable ones. Since, according to this view, the organizational form of the visible Church does not belong to its inner essence as a community of those who are truly justified in faith, the medieval papal system of Church governance can also be replaced by a regional church (*Landeskirche*) or "state church" model, as was the case in Lutheran countries until well into the twentieth century. Outside the Holy Roman Empire, the external church constitution in Calvinism developed in most cases in the direction of independent synods, i.e., as assemblies of lay people without consecrated bishops.

In summary, it can be said that the Reformers hold fast to catholicity as the predicate and criterion of the true Church. However, the predicate "catholic" as a designation for the Church begins to be officially rendered in German as "*allgemein*" (general/universal) or "*christlich*" (Christian), with equivalent renderings in other modern languages. Indeed, they claim catholicity for themselves, contrasting it to the "false Church" of the Roman pope, the members of which they deny to be Catholic so as to discredit them as Papists.

The Church of the "Old Faith," i.e., around the pope and the bishops, naturally held fast to the predicate "Catholic" as a self-designation of her historical continuity and confessional identity.

In contrast to this, the followers of Luther or Calvin neither could nor wanted to call themselves the "Lutheran" or "Calvinist" church. They understood themselves as "the Catholic Church of the *Augsburg Confession* reformed according to God's Word" (or according to a Calvin-inspired confession).[24] The terms "Protestants" or "Protestantism" (since the Diet of Speyer in 1529) aim, in more technical than theological language, to provide a collective term for all the ecclesial communities that emerged from the Reformation. Moreover, the common term "*evangelisch*" (evangelical/Protestant) as opposed to "*katholisch*" (Catholic) does not actually mean much when combined with "church." For the Protestant ecclesial communities today want to be "catholic" according to the words of the common (inter-Christian) creed; and the Catholics gathered

---

[24] Wilhelm Niesel, ed., *Bekenntnisschriften und Kirchenordnungen der nach Gottes Wort reformierten Kirche* (Munich, 1938).

around the pope do not want to conform in their faith to anything other than the Gospel (*Evangelium*) of Christ.[25]

The German terms "*katholisch*" and "*evangelisch*" (*Evangelium* = Gospel) used for Catholics and Protestants thus designate precisely what unites all Christians, and not what divides them. The same goes for the term "orthodox," which, in the meaning of correct opinion (ortho-doxy), must be the measure of every Christian communion. So the questions remain of whether we are expressing the same thing in terms of content when we use these terms and whether we are exploring the fullness of their content more deeply in our ecumenical dialogue.

In terms of content, "catholic" in its original meaning remains the measure for the understanding of "Church" in the separated Christian communities too. It is a matter of orthodoxy, based on the Bible and the early Church councils. The organizational separation since 1526, and the formation of the Lutheran and Calvinist confessions in the course of the sixteenth century, in the long run dissipated the awareness of belonging to the one Catholic Church.

Paradoxically, however, the deeper awareness that there can only be one Church remained, including in the bitter dispute over who represented the true Church. This was expressed in the never-ending attempts to restore the visible communion of all Christians in faith, liturgy, and life in the one Church.[26] In the nineteenth and twentieth centuries, the longing for the unity of all his followers, according to the will of Christ, was realized in the ecumenical movement in all Christian communities.

At the Council of Trent (1545–1563), the Church, united with the pope— as the ultimate criterion of her visible unity—definitively recognized the unity of all Christians in the Trinitarian-incarnational mystery of our redemption and justification, in the way that she affirmed and purposefully presented her own teaching on the ecclesial-sacramental making present of Christ's unique and final work of salvation, as compared to what were—from the Catholic point of view—the errors of the Reformers.

An unintended side effect of this was that the opposition between Christians was restricted to their opposing communions. The common ground of belonging to the one, holy, catholic, and apostolic Church turned into a battlefield of verbal and physical assaults on the conscience and self-respect of Christian brothers and sisters. Instead of using this as the starting point for overcoming the misunderstandings and unchristian animosities—culminating in wars of religion

---

[25] Ernst Öffner, *Evangelisch ist auch katholisch. Ein protestantischer Blick auf Kirche und Gesellschaft* (Munich, 2009).

[26] Paul Eisenkopf, *Leibniz und die Einigung der Christenheit. Überlegungen zur Reunion der evangelischen und der katholischen Kirche* (Paderborn, 1975); Ernst Christoph Suttner, *Quellen zur Geschichte der Kirchenunionen des 16. Bis 18. Jahrhunderts* (Freiburg, 2010).

in England, the Spanish Netherlands, France, and Germany—the opposing camps sought to discover behind the controversial doctrines, as a kind of idealistic abstraction, a *"Wesen"* (essence/nature/spirit) of Protestantism[27] or Catholicism[28] from which the controversial doctrines could then be deduced. They failed to realize that this turned the mystery of faith into a speculative system, or even falsified it into an ideology, so that it was possible for someone to be a cultural Protestant or a cultural Catholic without faith in God and Jesus Christ, without prayer and participation in Church life. (There certainly is a *"Wesen"* of Christianity, but it does not arise from the concept that the finite intellect makes of it, thus taking logical possession of it, but rather from the ever-greater mystery of God, which only allows itself to be known by means of the *analogia entis* [analogy of being] of reason, and according to the *analogia fidei* [analogy of faith] of reason enlightened by faith, without being taken possession of by them.)

But this is not a matter of a cultureless or anti-cultural Christianity, which would be a contradiction in terms, but rather a reduction of Christianity to an inner-worldly humanism, while denying the supernatural nature of divine Revelation and thus the origin of all humanity in the Incarnation of God in Jesus Christ.

In his work *Der deutsche Roman des 18. Jahrhunderts in seinem Verhältniss zum Christenthum* (1851), the German novel of the eighteenth century in its relationship to Christianity, Joseph von Eichendorff (1788–1857) impressively analyzes the history of the reinterpretation of Christianity since the Reformation as a "natural religion" via a "moral religion," and "religion of reason" to the universal "religion of humanity," which was inevitably bound to end (*verenden*, perish/die) in anti-Christianity.[29] For how could love not turn into hatred when it catches itself in the act of deceiving itself about the truth?[30]

The catholic faith of the *Augsburg Confession* was then stylized, under the influence of the Enlightenment and liberalism, into the religion of Protestant (evangelical) freedom.[31] The enlightened and mature Christian now determines autonomously what he or she believes. And no one notices that faith comes

---

[27] Karl Heim, *Das Wesen des evangelischen Christentums*, Leipzig, 1925; Emanuel Hirsch, *Das Wesen des reformatorischen Christentums* (Berlin, 1963); Eng.: *The Nature of Protestantism* (Minneapolis, MN: Fortress Press, 1963).

[28] Karl Adam, *Das Wesen des Katholizismus* (1957); Eng.: *The Spirit of Catholicism* (Garden City, NY: Doubleday Image, 1954).

[29] Joseph von Eichendorff, *Werke III. Schriften zur Literatur* (Munich, 1976), 171–379.

[30] Karl-Heinz Menke, *Macht die Wahrheit frei oder die Freiheit wahr? Eine Streitschrift* (Regensburg, 2017).

[31] Cf. Ernst Walter Zeeden, *Martin Luther im Urteil des deutschen Luthertums* (Freiburg. i.Br., 1952), 141–394.

from listening to the word of God, and that the conscience does not legislate for itself but "remains captive in God's word," as Luther declares before the Diet of Worms.[32] On the other hand, "Catholics who have arrived in the modern age" think that they should clear themselves of the accusation of uncritical belief in authority by "criticizing" the Church's teaching authority. They fervently hope that free-thinkers, and those who think for themselves, will pat them patronizingly on the back and certify that they have finally understood Kant, or are saying what people say in the twentieth century, what everyone in the media, is saying.

Beyond a hollow Enlightenment pathos and the ideological seducibility of modern man, it is clear that talk of free thinking is tautologous. Thinking is by its very nature free when it is directed towards the truth of existence and finds approval in the execution of reason as its bearer. It is precisely the negation of reason's capacity for truth that perverts tolerance and pluralism into the dictatorship of ideological conformism (*Einheitsdenken, pensée unique*). Where the transcendence of finite reason towards ever greater truth is denied, a conditional and limited idea of an individual or collective must put itself in the place of absoluteness: "You are nothing, your nation is everything"; "The Party is always right"; "But that's what everyone says."

But human reason is finite and already prone to error in its own object sphere, namely phenomena, and even more so in cognizing the essence of the things of the world. How much less can the finite spirit attain to the knowledge of God and his revelation if God does not reveal himself to it in his word and does not allow our receptive faculty to share in his reason through the infused light of faith by means of the human cognitive media associated with the divine Word and thus to begin to recognize his truth. These cognitive media are Sacred Scripture and the Apostolic Tradition, which contain and testify to the word of God in a human mode of speaking and presentation. But they, too, can only be properly interpreted if due attention is paid "to the customary and characteristic styles of feeling, speaking, and narrating which prevailed at the time of the sacred writer,"[33] and to an appropriate theological-historical hermeneutic.[34]

Revelation is, after all, not petrified in the letter of Scripture and preserved like a fossil under the dust of the past but rather present in the Church's living faith consciousness. The teaching office of the bishops and the pope participates in keeping faith consciousness up-to-date. And under the influence

[32] Bernd Moeller, *Luther in der Neuzeit* (Gütersloh, 1983); Harm Klueting, *Luther und die Neuzeit* (Darmstadt, 2011).

[33] Vatican II, *Dei Verbum*, §12.

[34] Louis Bouyer, *Das Handwerk des Theologen* (Einsiedeln, 1980).

of the Holy Spirit, who awakens our faith when we listen to the word of God in the Church's proclamation, the Magisterium offers a final, formal criterion of the truth of the eschatological and irreversible presence of God in his Word made flesh, Jesus Christ. So the Magisterium does not state with the external authority of the better-educated, or of a judge what it sees fit, according to its own taste, to tell the "immature laity" what they must believe and do in order to become worthy of God's grace and truth. The pope and the bishops cannot and must not impose their private judgment on the rest of the Church in religious and certainly not in profane matters. Their authority lies in the mandate to present the faith of the Church as revealed to all her members, including themselves.[35]

Every Catholic believes directly upon the authority of God, who communicates himself to him as the truth and the life, revealing himself in his word in Jesus Christ and in the Holy Spirit and bearing witness to himself in the testimony of the apostles by means of Sacred Scripture and the living Tradition of the Church herself. The teaching office of the bishops, in the apostolic succession to the apostles, serves only the word of God,

> teaching only what has been handed on, listening to it devoutly, guarding it scrupulously and explaining it faithfully in accord with a divine commission and with the help of the Holy Spirit, [because] it draws from this one deposit of faith everything which it presents for belief as divinely revealed.[36]

The starting point must be the common supernatural belief in God, who sent his Son into the world "in the likeness of sinful flesh" (Rom 8:3) and poured out the Holy Spirit into our hearts. All this is absorbed with heart and mind in the confession of faith. And it is only on this basis that divergent doctrines can be examined using scientific methods. This shows that it is not possible to express the events and consequences of the sixteenth-century controversy which led to the establishment of a churchdom alongside the hitherto existing Catholic Church in the classical categories of heresy and schism. And it did, of course, take people a long time to adjust to the completely changed situation.

From his own personal struggle to find a gracious God, Luther recognized the Pauline doctrine of the justification of the sinner solely through faith in Christ, without any human action, as the key to the whole relationship with God. The fact that man is redeemed by Christ alone, and justified by his grace alone,

---

[35] First Vatican Council, *Pastor Aeternus* (1870): DH 3070–3071; Vatican II, *Lumen Gentium*, §25.
[36] Vatican II, *Dei Verbum*, §10.

is so clearly attested in Scripture and so clearly confirmed by the Magisterium in the dispute with the Pelagian program of self-salvation that it is not clear without looking at Luther's view of original sin what the contradiction actually is between his Reformer's view and that of Catholic doctrine. It was only because the Reformers saw original sin not only in the loss of original grace but also in the total depravity of human nature that they considered they had secured the completely unmerited nature of grace against the claims of human cooperation and reward for merits.

The Council of Trent countered this, saying it is precisely out of the all-efficiency (*Allwirksamkeit*) of grace at the absolute beginning of the new relationship with God (*initium fidei*) that the cooperation of will that it sustains also elevates man and makes him a partner with God, which is in accordance with God's plan of salvation. The participation of the redeemed creature in the historical execution of God's eternal plan of salvation does not tarnish God's glory but just makes it fully manifest in nature, history, and the Church. The theocentricity and Christocentricity of Christian existence is fully in line with the Catholic faith, as it was shaped at the time of the Church Fathers and has since been known and lived for two thousand years down to the present day.

However, the focus on the inner certainty of personal justification in faith as an act of consciousness[37] could also lead to the exclusion of Catholic beliefs, lifestyles, and forms of piety that were interpreted as justification through works (*Werkgerechtigkeit*) and thus aroused opposition (the Mass as a Sacrifice, monastic vows, veneration of the saints). This is not about the abuses that occur among people even in the Church, which must always be combated.

Luther saw certain (unauthorized) Catholic practices as the logical consequence of a Church dogmatics that drew the truths of salvation not solely from the word of God in Scripture but also from human traditions—which thus contaminated them: the way lascivious pardoners selling indulgences handled people's need for salvation; the excessive Mass stipends; the buying of offices by spiritually unsuitable candidates; the perversion of episcopal and papal authority in claims to political and financial power; and the popular piety that has degenerated into foolish superstition.

Making Sacred Scripture alone count in salvation-relevant doctrines became for Luther a scalpel with which to excise the corrupt parts on the body of the Church and thus to regain the purity of her doctrine. The essential Catholic doctrines attested from Scripture and early Church Tradition

---

37   Paul Hacker, *Das Ich im Glauben bei Marin Luther. Der Ursprung der anthropozentrischen Religion* (Bonn, 2002).

are still shared by all Christians today. Significant differences arise where the hermeneutical scriptural principle "sola scriptura" is critically applied to the Church's sacramental making-present of salvation.

In two decrees, the Council of Trent (1546) pointed out the classical Catholic hermeneutics of all its doctrines on faith and morals against the Reformation challenge and, in so doing, formulated the epistemological principles of Catholic theology.[38] Vatican II set out the doctrine of divine Revelation and its transmission in the Church in more detail in the Dogmatic Constitution on Divine Revelation *Dei Verbum*.[39] It is the shared conviction that God's Revelation is the Gospel of Christ, which was promised by the prophets and proclaimed by Jesus himself and subsequently his apostles, and is therefore to be preached to all creatures as the source of all saving truth and norms of conduct for a Christian way of life.[40] This truth is, however, contained in written Tradition, i.e., those inspired by the Holy Spirit in the writing of Sacred Scripture, as well as in the unwritten Tradition of the Church. This formulation does not mean that they were not written down later but that not everything that was handed down by the apostles was written down by them and the evangelists; instead, some of it entered into the living consciousness of faith. The idea that divine Revelation is greater than Scripture results from the fact that the word of God cannot be articulated with a one-to-one correspondence in human language, meaning that the letter by itself kills, whereas in the Spirit the transcendence and the superabundance of its meaning becomes accessible and comes alive in the faith community of God's Church.

The Council of Trent makes the magisterial decision, in the authority of the Holy Spirit, as to exactly which books of the Old and New Testaments belong to the canon. The reason for their inclusion is not, however, the Church's authority as such but rather that these Scriptures have God as their author, were written in the Holy Spirit, and have been made known by him to the Church as inspired since the first Traditions of the Fathers, received from the apostles.[41]

The truth of divine Revelation, and its mediation in Sacred Scripture and the Apostolic Tradition of the Church, is thus the foundation of the profession of faith of the Catholic Church and the yardstick used "in strengthening its teachings and renewing morals in the Church."[42] Against the confusion of the times, the Council proclaims

---

[38] DH 1508.

[39] Vatican II, *Dei Verbum*, §§1–10.

[40] DH 1501.

[41] DH 1501.

[42] DH 1505.

that no one, relying on his own prudence, may twist Holy Scripture in matters of faith and practice [in rebus fidei et morum] ... according to his own mind, contrary to the meaning that Holy Mother the Church has held and holds—since it belongs to her to judge the true meaning and interpretation of Holy Scripture—and that no one may dare to interpret the Scripture in a way contrary to the unanimous consensus of the Fathers.[43]

If today, even in retrospect, we recognize a much broader basis of common ground in the central truths of the faith than did our forebears back then who were in conflict mode, we still cannot ignore the historical fact that Christian confessional communities stood against one another, each claiming that it alone was the true Church of Christ.

Since the Church, including her four attributes, is the subject of revealed faith, it is impossible to "prove" empirically in which visible ecclesial association identity with the Church founded by Christ and manifested in historical continuity is actually given. From a liberal point of view, which sees the contents of faith as a subjective reflection of the non-communicable and unknowable truth of God, the ecumenical question would be easy to solve: all Christian communions possess a partial truth, and when these truths are put together, they point to a unity in an immaterial greater whole. But this model fascinates only those who have already relinquished the claim of divine Revelation that God's truth enlightens every human being, that "the household of God, which is the church of the living God, [is] the pillar and bulwark of the truth" (1 Tim 3:15), and that Jesus wants the visible unity of his disciples so that the world might recognize that he was sent by the Father and might believe for its salvation (cf. John 17:20–23).

From their conviction that the true nature of the Church and its identification with a confessional community could be deduced from Holy Scripture, Protestant theology developed the theory of the pure primitive Church which, after a phase of apostasy under the pope, was restored in the sixteenth century by the Reformers from its historical deformations back to its pure primitive state.

On the other hand, the theory of early Catholicism,[44] which claims that Catholic elements—Church as the sacramental institution of salvation; the

---

[43]   DH 1507.

[44]   Cf. on this the discussion of the theory from Rudolph Sohm to Adolf von Harnack and Ernst Troeltsch in Karl-Heinz Menke, *Sakramentalität. Wesen und Wunde des Katholizismus* (Regensburg, 2012), 34–47; Gunther Wenz, *Der Kulturprotestant. Adolf von Harnack als Christentumstheoretiker und Kontroverstheologe* (Munich, 2001), 64–72; Chihon Josef Hwang, *Katholisch-theologisches Schrifttum im Spiegel der Kritik der Theologischen Literaturzeitung in der Zeit der Redaktion Adolf von Harnacks (1881–1910)* (Frankfurt a.M., 2002).

principle of Tradition; a hierarchical constitution instead of the mediation of grace in the word through faith; the reification of grace in the sacraments—had already been superimposed on the Church of the Gospel from the earliest times, is merely a revamping of the Great Apostacy theory. Since the time of Matthias Flacius Illyricus (1520–1575), this theory has held that after the pure original Church—and, at the latest, after the Council of Chalcedon or Gregory the Great; and in other versions already in late apostolic times—there was a progressive demolition of the nature of the Church, which was only reversed through Luther's discovery of the pure gospel.

However, the apostasy hypothesis does not take into account the conditions under which divine Revelation is transmitted in the medium of the history of the Church, which is both its addressee and the subject receiving it.

From the Catholic side, Cardinal Caesar Baronius (1538–1607) responded to Flacius's *Magdeburg Centuries* with his *Annales Ecclesiastici* (Ecclesiastical Annals). This has meant that for many centuries, and even to this day, the study of Church and dogmatic history has been read through the systematic-theological lens of confessional hermeneutics.

The institutionally identical community which believes itself—through all the changes—to have been and remained since apostolic times substantially the Church of Christ, which is called "catholic" in the common Creed, differs from all the others in recognizing in the Bishop of Rome the Successor of Peter, on whom Christ wanted to build his Church. With most churches and ecclesial communities that are not in full communion with her, the Catholic Church is united in a common belief in God and the central mysteries of salvation, as well as in the belief that God wishes the ecclesial community of all Christians to be the bearer that passes on the faith. A close study of the ecclesiology of Vatican II shows that the Catholic Church does not, puffed up with self-confidence, identify herself with the Church of Christ and just drop a few crumbs from the table to the rest in the shape of catholic elements.

The view that sees the Church of Christ as being the visible one led by the bishops presupposes a concept of "Church" which the Catholic Church shares only with the Orthodox Churches and which distinguishes her from the communities stemming from the Reformation. The Church is the unity of the invisible community of grace with its visible form, which is derived from the mystery of the divine-human unity of Christ; this unity requires not only a general but also a concrete historical visibility and is, as such, an object of Catholic belief. To speak here of revealed faith necessary for salvation signifies that this is not a purely human conviction, in the way that people are convinced their own father and mother are, subjectively irrefutably, the best parents in the world.

Vatican II fully addresses the theologically justified criticism raised by the Reformation that, in the Catholic Church of the time, at least de facto, the visible side of the Church—right down to her worldly entanglements—had diminished the invisible side which constituted her essence. However, the Council does not go to the opposite extreme of secularizing the visible form of the Church into a purely external, organizational one. If, as the *Confessio Augustana* claims,[45] the holy Church is the assembly of all believers with the power of the keys to open the kingdom of heaven, then the visible assembly cannot be just a profane appendage to the essence of the Church. Even less do the human words of the sermon, which awaken faith and the symbolic elements of the sacraments, bear any resemblance whatsoever to the inconsequential packaging in which the gifts that alone are important to me are wrapped.

It is therefore misleading, as happened in the past, to contrast a Protestant church of the word with a Catholic Church of the sacraments, or an invisible Church with a visible Church, as if these were mutually exclusive. What matters is the inner connection between the essential elements:

> Christ, the one Mediator, established and continually sustains here on earth His holy Church, the community of faith, hope, and charity, as an entity with visible delineation through which He communicated truth and grace to all. But, the society structured with hierarchical organs and the Mystical Body of Christ are not to be considered as two realities, nor are the visible assembly and the spiritual community, nor the earthly Church and the Church enriched with heavenly things; rather they form one complex reality which coalesces from a divine and a human element.
>
> For this reason, by no weak analogy, it is compared to the mystery of the Incarnate Word. As the assumed nature inseparably united to Him serves the divine Word as a living organ of salvation, so, in a similar way, does the visible social structure of the Church serve the Spirit of Christ, who vivifies it, in the building up of the body (cf. Eph 4:16).
>
> This is the one Church of Christ which in the Creed is professed as one, holy, catholic, and apostolic, which our Savior, after His Resurrection, commissioned Peter to shepherd (John 21:17), and him and the other apostles to extend and direct with authority (cf. Matt 28:18–20), which He erected for all ages as "the pillar and mainstay of the truth" (1 Tim 3:15). This Church constituted and organized in the world as a society subsists in the Catholic Church, which is governed by the Successor

---

45   *Confessio Augustana*, aa. 7; 8; 14.

of Peter and by the Bishops in communion with him, although many elements of sanctification and of truth are found outside of her visible structure. These elements, as gifts belonging to the Church of Christ, are forces impelling toward catholic unity.

Just as Christ carried out the work of redemption in poverty and persecution, so the Church is called to follow the same route, that she might communicate the fruits of salvation to men.[46]

In order to rule out any ecclesiological relativism as a consequence of rela-tivizing Christ's being the sole mediator of salvation, as asserted in the theory of "Religious Pluralism," in the year 2000 the Congregation for the Doctrine of the Faith published the document *Dominus Iesus*, which offers an authentic elucidation on the part of the Magisterium of Vatican II's famous formulation in the Dogmatic Constitution on the Church—"ecclesia Christi subsistit in ecclesia catholica [the Church of Christ subsists in the Catholic Church]":[47]

> The Lord Jesus, the only Savior, did not only establish a simple community of disciples, but constituted the Church as a *salvific mystery*: he himself is in the Church and the Church is in him (cf. John 15:1ff.; Gal 3:28; Eph 4:15–16; Acts 9:5). Therefore, the fullness of Christ's salvific mystery belongs also to the Church, inseparably united to her Lord. Indeed, Jesus Christ continues his presence and his work of salvation in the Church and by means of the Church (cf. Col 1:24–27), which is his body (cf. 1 Cor 12:12–13, 27; Col 1:18). And thus, just as the head and members of a living body, though not identical, are inseparable, so too Christ and the Church can neither be confused nor separated, and constitute a single "whole Christ." This same inseparability is also expressed in the New Testament by the analogy of the Church as the *Bride* of Christ (cf. 2 Cor 11:2; Eph 5:25–9; Rev 21:2, 9).
>
> Therefore, in connection with the unicity and universality of the salvific mediation of Jesus Christ, the unicity of the Church founded by him must be *firmly believed* as a truth of Catholic faith. Just as there is one Christ, so there exists a single body of Christ, a single Bride of Christ: "a single Catholic and apostolic Church." Furthermore, the promises of the Lord that he would not abandon his Church (cf.

---

[46] Vatican II, *Lumen Gentium*, §8.

[47] Vatican II, *Lumen Gentium*, §8. Alexandra von Teuffenbach, *Die Bedeutung des subsistit in (LG, §8). Zum Selbstverständnis der katholischen Kirche* (Munich, 2002).

Matt 16:18; 28:20), and that he would guide her by his Spirit (cf. John 16:13) mean, according to [the] Catholic Faith, that the unicity and the unity of the Church—like everything that belongs to the Church's integrity—will never be lacking.

The Catholic faithful *are required to profess* that there is an historical continuity—rooted in the apostolic succession—between the Church founded by Christ and the Catholic Church: "This is the single Church of Christ . . . which our Savior, after his Resurrection, entrusted to Peter's pastoral care (cf. John 21:17), commissioning him and the other apostles to extend and rule her (cf. Matt 28:18–20), erected for all ages as 'the pillar and mainstay of the truth' (1 Tim 3:15). This Church, constituted and organized as a society in the present world, subsists in [*subsistit in*] the Catholic Church, governed by the Successor of Peter and by the Bishops in communion with him" [LG, §8]. With the expression *subsistit in*, the Second Vatican Council sought to harmonize two doctrinal statements: on the one hand, that the Church of Christ, despite the divisions which exist among Christians, continues to exist fully only in the Catholic Church, and, on the other hand, that "outside of her structure many elements can be found of sanctification and truth," that is, in those Churches and ecclesial communities which are not yet in full communion with the Catholic Church. But with respect to these, it needs to be stated that "they derive their efficacy from the very fullness of grace and truth entrusted to the Catholic Church."

Therefore, there exists a single Church of Christ, which subsists in the Catholic Church, governed by the Successor of Peter and by the Bishops in communion with him. The Churches which, while not existing in perfect communion with the Catholic Church, remain united to her by means of the closest bonds, that is, by apostolic succession and a valid Eucharist, are true particular Churches. Therefore, the Church of Christ is present and operative also in these Churches, even though they lack full communion with the Catholic Church, since they do not accept the Catholic doctrine of the primacy, which, according to the will of God, the Bishop of Rome objectively has and exercises over the entire Church.

On the other hand, the ecclesial communities which have not preserved the valid episcopate and the genuine and integral substance of the Eucharistic mystery, are not Churches in the proper sense; however, those who are baptized in these communities are, by Baptism, incorporated in Christ and thus are in a certain communion, albeit imperfect, with the Church. Baptism in fact tends per se toward the full development of life in Christ, through the integral profession of faith, the Eucharist, and full communion in the Church.

"The Christian faithful are therefore not permitted to imagine that the Church of Christ is nothing more than a collection—divided, yet in some way one—of Churches and ecclesial communities; nor are they free to hold that today the Church of Christ nowhere really exists, and must be considered only as a goal which all Churches and ecclesial communities must strive to reach." In fact, "the elements of this already-given Church exist, joined together in their fullness in the Catholic Church and, without this fullness, in the other communities." "Therefore, these separated Churches and communities as such, though we believe they suffer from defects, have by no means been deprived of significance and importance in the mystery of salvation. For the spirit of Christ has not refrained from using them as means of salvation which derive their efficacy from the very fullness of grace and truth entrusted to the Catholic Church."

The lack of unity among Christians is certainly a *wound* for the Church; not in the sense that she is deprived of her unity, but "in that it hinders the complete fulfillment of her universality in history." [48]

The ecumenical search for Catholic unity

Most Christian communities are based on the Catholic Creed, the *symbolum fidei catholicae*. It goes back to the Ecumenical Councils of Nicaea (AD 325) and Constantinople I (AD 381). [49] The Creed is divided into three parts: the first two articles refer to God the Father and the Son: "We believe in one God, the Father Almighty. . . . And in one Lord Jesus Christ, the only begotten Son of God." In the third article, "the pilgrim Church," which Christ in the Holy Spirit

---

[48] Congregation for the Doctrine of the Faith (CDF), *Dominus Iesus* (2000), §§16–17, emphasis original.

[49] Karl Lehmann and Wolfhart Pannenberg, eds., *Glaubensgemeinschaft und Kirchengemeinschaft. Das Modell des Konzils von Konstantinopel (381)* (Freiburg i.Br., 1982); Reinhart Staats, *Das Glaubensbekenntnis von Nizäa-Konstantinopel. Historische und theologische Grundlagen* (Darmstadt, 1996); Adolf-Martin Ritter, *Das Konzil von Konstantinopel und sein Symbol. Studien zur Geschichte und Theologie des II. Ökumenischen Konzils* (Göttingen, 1965); John N. D. Kelly, *Early Christian Creeds*, 3rd ed. (London: Longmans, 1972); Hans Steubing, ed., *Bekenntnisses der Kirche. Bekenntnistexte aus zwanzig Jahrhunderten* (Wuppertal, 1970).

has made "the universal sacrament of salvation," confesses:[50] "And [we believe] in the Holy Spirit. . . . And in one, holy, catholic, and apostolic Church." [51]

There is less disagreement over the meaning of the predicate "catholic"[52] than over the question of which visible Church or ecclesial community is fully entitled to bear it.[53] What is meant by this attribute is not just the world-wide mission and the spatio-temporal dissemination of the Christian faith by the Church of Christ but also the passing on of divine Revelation in all the fullness of its truth and of eternal salvation to every human being. "The Church is not called catholic and universal because it embraces all individual groups of people, but because it is open to all individuals from every group [non propter singula generum, sed propter genera singulorum]."[54] The Risen Lord gives the disciples, and in them the Church, the universal commission to offer the forgiveness of sins and God's saving grace to all people "to the ends of the earth" (Acts 1:8), i.e., globally: "Go into *all* the world and proclaim the good news to the *whole* creation. The one who believes and is baptized will be saved" (Mark 16:15–16, emphasis added; cf. Matt 28:19–20; Luke 24:47; Acts 1:8; Rom 1:8; Eph 3:10).

States with imperialist ambitions, globally operating corporations that offer their products to any customer willing to pay, and the World Wide Web, which creates the impression of cosmic intercommunication—all these are also global players.

But the Catholic Church has no other interest than "[s]alvation and glory and power to our God" (Rev 19:1), which is to come to all people "from Jesus Christ, the faithful witness, the firstborn of the dead, and the ruler of the kings of the earth" (Rev 1:5), "the Almighty" (*ho Pantokrātōr*, ruler of the universe) (Rev 1:8). His Church must have a global presence because in Jesus Christ, her head, she is the efficient sign of the real union of God with all mankind. For all who "believe in the name of his Son Jesus . . . abide in him, and he abides in them" (1 John 3:23–24).

Jesus said quite explicitly that a person's "life does not consist in the abundance of possessions" (Luke 12:16) without any thought to the fact that power, prestige, and money are just transitory values and mere commodities. For the only thing that counts is to be "rich towards God" (Luke 12:21). In the shadow of death, God will say even-handedly to every poor wretch and every

---

[50] Vatican II, *Lumen Gentium*, §48.
[51] DH 150.
[52] Wolfgang Beinert, *Um das dritte Kirchenattribut. Die Katholizität der Kirche im Verständnis der evangelisch-lutherischen und römisch-katholischen Theologie der Gegenwart*, 2 vols., Essen, 1964.
[53] Wolfgang W. Müller, ed., *Katholizität. Eine ökumenische Chance* (Zürich, 2006).
[54] St. Thomas Aquinas, *In Boetii de Trinitate*, lect. 1, q. 1, a. 3.

rich wastrel, to every philistine and every playboy, to every disenfranchised slave and every egomaniacal potentate who has greedily or complacently placed all his hope in the specious riches of the world: "You fool! This very night your life is being demanded of you" (Luke 12:20). The imperishable meaning of existence is only revealed in the supra-empirical origin and goal of every human being, endowed with intellect (*Geist*) and freedom, when God inescapably confronts every creature as its Creator and Redeemer, Judge and Perfecter. For "'I am the Alpha and the Omega,' says the Lord God, who is and who was and who is to come" (Rev 1:8).

The Church is not a human institution that rises and falls again in the changing course of history. She belongs to when "[t]he time is fulfilled, and the kingdom of God has come near" (Mark 1:15, emphasis added), which is realized definitively in history and eschatologically with the Gospel of God's reign in the Person of Jesus Christ, in the mysteries of his earthly life,[55] his death on the Cross, and his Resurrection from the dead. For God has made known to us his "plan for *the fullness of time*, to gather up all things in him [Christ]. . . . And he has put all things under his feet and has made him the head over all things for the church, which is his body, the fullness of him who fills all in all" (Eph 1:10, 22–23, emphasis added). Everyone should see

> the plan of the mystery hidden for ages in God . . . that through the church the wisdom of God in its rich variety might now be made known . . . in accordance with the eternal purpose that he has carried out in Christ Jesus our Lord, in whom we have access to God in boldness and confidence through faith in him. (Eph 3:9–12)

The Church adheres to the "teaching of the apostles" (Acts 2:42) and "the sound words of our Lord Jesus Christ and the teaching that is in accordance with godliness" (1 Tim 6:3)—the *sana doctrina*. In this way she maintains her orthodoxy, i.e., the true worship of God that gives thanks for his blessings, and active love of neighbor (orthopraxy). It is integral to the Church's mission to protect the faithful from false teachers (heretics), who "have swerved from the faith" (1 Tim 6:21, ESV) and thus endanger salvation.

Since the Pietist theologian Gottfried Arnold (1666–1714)—in his *Unparteyische Kirchen- und Ketzerhistorie* (Impartial History of the Church and Heresy) (1699)—interpreted Church history according to the schema of progressive decay until it rose again in the "Reformation" of the sixteenth century,

---

[55] Cf. Leo Scheffczyk, ed., *Die Mysterien des Lebens Jesu und die christliche Existenz*, Aschaffenburg, 1984; Joseph Ratzinger, *Jesus von Nazareth. Beiträge zur Christologie* = JRGS 6, ed. G. L. Müller (Freiburg i.Br., 2013).

the heretics were upgraded to the genuine believers who opposed the decline of the Gospel in the official Church. Sebastian Franck (1499–1542) rounds off the hermeneutics of suspicion against the reliability of Church Tradition. According to him, Church history, too, is written by the victors (the orthodox), even though it was made by the losers, the unconventional thinkers who were lambasted as heretics.[56] But if the Catholic confession is the realization of the teaching of Jesus and the apostles in the faith consciousness of the Church, then heresy cannot be the product of the unconventional thinking that arises in a free discourse on finite things. Premised on historical fact and the definitive truth of God's self-revelation in his Word, his Son, Jesus Christ, heresy is "the offense of error differing from Catholic truth [crimen erroris a veritate catholicae distinguitur]."[57]

Martin Luther, with whose Ninety-Five Theses or *Disputation on the Power and Efficacy of Indulgences* of October 31, 1517, the schism of Western Christianity in doctrine and ecclesial-sacramental life began,[58] had no desire to separate himself from the Catholic Church. He had been baptized and confirmed in the Catholic Church and eventually brought to Confession and First Holy Communion. He grew into it from childhood with a youthful, fresh spirit, and he became a convinced Catholic as a student of theology. He felt called to a life as a religious according to the evangelical counsels of poverty, obedience, and celibate chastity. He received the sacrament of priestly ordination and was appointed to a chair of Sacred Scripture as a doctor of theology to instruct young students in the sacred science. Nothing was further from his mind than to found a new Church bearing his name. For, as a theologian, he knew only too well how absurd it was to call the Church of Christ after the name of one of the members of his body and not after her head.[59]

Talking about the "Church of the Pope" or the "Papists" resulted from the absurdities of inter-Christian polemics, which resound like a shrill insult in the ears of a Catholic who is convinced in conscience of the truth of his faith. For it is, after all, a common Christian, and thus Catholic, basic conviction that the head of the Church, from whom all grace flows down to the members of the body and infuses them with divine life, is Christ alone. The respective

---

56 Sebastian Franck, *Paradoxa ducenta octoginta* (1534), 14.

57 St. Augustine, *Contra Cresconium* 2.14.

58 Louis Bouyer, *Parole, Église et Sacrements dans le protestantisme et le catholicisme* (Paris, 1960); Eng.: *The Word, Church, and Sacraments in Protestantism and Catholicism* (San Francisco: Ignatius Press, 2004); Gerhard Ludwig Müller, *Mit der Kirche denken. Bausteine und Skizzen zu einer Theologie der Gegenwart* (Würzburg, 2007).

59 Cf. on this the road from the Fathers of the Church to the Catholic Church, as in the case of St. John Henry Cardinal Newman: Louis Bouyer, *Du protestantisme à l'église* (Paris, 1954).

pope is called the visible head of the Church only inasmuch as his service to unity refers to the Church as a visible entity.[60]

Two hundred and fifty years before Luther, St. Thomas Aquinas, the *Doctor communis* of Catholic theology, had already differentiated the terminology:

> The head influences the other members in two ways. First, by a certain intrinsic influence, inasmuch as motive and sensitive force flow from the head to the other members; secondly, by a certain exterior guidance. . . . Now the *interior influx of grace* is from no one save Christ,—*nisi solo Christo*—whose manhood, through its union with the Godhead, has the power of justifying; but the influence over the members of the Church, as regards their *exterior* guidance, can belong to others; and in this way others may be called heads of the Church. . . . First, inasmuch as Christ is the head of all who pertain to the Church in every place and time and state; but all other men are called heads with reference to certain special places, as bishops of their churches. Or with reference to a determined time as the Pope is the head of the whole Church, viz. during the time of his pontificate. . . . Secondly, because Christ is the head of the Church by his own power and authority; while others are called heads, as taking Christ's place [inquantum vicem gerunt Christi], according to 2 Corinthians 2:10, "For what I have pardoned, if I have pardoned anything, for your sakes I have done it in the person of Christ [*in persona Christi*]," and 2 Corinthians 5:20, "For Christ therefore we are ambassadors, God, as it were, exhorting by us."[61]

But since Luther now derives the certainty of faith from the inner consciousness enlightened by the Holy Spirit, which he finds externally confirmed in the word of God in Holy Scripture, an unbridgeable gulf gradually opens up for him between the teaching of Scripture and the teaching of the Church: because Holy Scripture is God's word, it alone has authority in the Church, which can never be relativized or surpassed by the purely human authority of the pope and the bishops (in an ecumenical council). Consequently, however, the obedience to Church authorities required as relevant for salvation goes against Luther's principle that certainty of salvation can

---

[60] Cf. Martin Grabmann, *Die Lehre des heiligen Thomas von Aquin von der Kirche als Gotteswerk. Ihre Stellung im thomistischen System und in der Geschichte der mittelalterlichen Theologie* (Regensburg, 1903), 194–266; Heinrich Berresheim, *Christus als Haupt der Kirche nach dem heiligen Bonaventura* (1939) (Münster i.W., 1983).

[61] St. Thomas Aquinas, *ST* III, q. 8, a. 6, emphasis added.

only find support in the absoluteness of God and cannot be built on the fickleness of creatures.[62]

He had thus come to the conclusion that the true Church of Christ, as an interior community of grace, had been corrupted by the false (institutional) Church of the pope and his followers. The Church as an exterior community of sacraments and law had interposed itself like a mediating authority between God and the Christian who grasped salvation in the certainty of faith. The personal relationship to Jesus in the believing heart had, he claimed, been replaced by the profession of factually correct statements of truth about God, Christ, and grace. And for the merit of formal orthodoxy, the Christian was then rewarded for lip service with salvation. Thus, for Luther, an irreconcilable contradiction arose between the Church as mediator of salvation and the immediacy of faith in God.[63]

What lies at the heart of his desire to reform is not the moral transgressions and breaches of official duty, or the all-too-human behavior of both ecclesiastical superiors and leading laymen. For these phenomena have not disappeared even in the Church that was reformed according to his principles, as Luther himself was forced to note bitterly. His criticism is rather of an "ecclesial system" that seemed to base the forgiveness of sin and the justification of the sinner not on "faith alone through grace alone," but also on human works and pious religious exercises. The sacraments are for him just signs of the promised grace, not the instruments that automatically convey grace when they are used, which is how he (mis)interpreted the doctrine of the objective efficacy of the sacraments, which *ex opere operato* convey grace independently of the subjective holiness of the recipient or the holiness of their ministers.

Nevertheless, the break with the constituted Catholic Church is not absolute as far as the central truths of the Trinity, Incarnation, and the Redemption are concerned.[64] At the same time, Luther makes the resumption of full communion conditional on the pope and bishops converting to the Gospel, albeit in a way that he regards as obvious.[65]

---

[62] Adolf Stakemeier, *Das Konzil von Trient über die Heilsgewissheit*, Heidelberg, 1947; Stephanus Pfürtner, *Luther und Thomas im Gespräch. Unser heil zwischen Gewissheit und Gefährdung*, Heidelberg, 1961; Otto Hermann Pesch, *Die Theologie der Rechtfertigung bei Martin Luther und Thomas von Aquin. Versuch eines systematisch-theologischen Dialogs* (Mainz, 1985).

[63] Nevertheless, Luther cannot be co-opted in support of an interpretation of Christianity without dogmas and sacraments. Cf. Felix Körnera, Wolfgang Thönissen, eds., *Vermitteltes Heil and Martin Luther und die Sakramente* (Paderborn, 2018).

[64] An ecclesiology grounded in the mystery of the Trinity and the Incarnation is regarded by Protestant (*evangelisch*) theology as an excellent basis for ecumenical dialogue as it is presented by Wolfhart Pannenberg, *Systematische Theologie III* (Göttingen, 1993), 265–472.

[65] Cf. Wolfgang Thönissen, *Dogma und Symbol. Eine ökumenische Hermeneutik* (Freiburg, 2008).

The difference in doctrine and liturgy cannot be deduced simply from the usual designations. For the "Catholic Church" is also wholly committed to the Gospel of Christ, just as the "Protestant/Reformation Churches" want to be catholic by preaching the Gospel in a catholic-universal way—namely, in *all* its fullness to the *whole* of humanity.[66]

The great opportunity to begin the ecumenical dialogue with the central truths of divine Revelation is taken into account by the Second Vatican Council:

> The way and method in which the Catholic Faith is expressed should never become an obstacle to dialogue with our brethren. . . . At the same time, the Catholic Faith must be explained more profoundly and precisely, in such a way and in such terms as our separated brethren can also really understand. . . . When comparing doctrines with one another, they should remember that in Catholic doctrine there exists a "hierarchy" of truths, since they vary in their relation to the fundamental Christian faith.[67]

Of course, the hierarchy of truths must not be conceived of as a mechanical ordering of the mysteries of the faith according to the criteria of greater and lesser importance, or as a dividing of one revelation into fundamental articles and secondary dogmas. Because of the analogy of knowledge springing from natural reason and that based on divine Revelation, an inner analogical-organic connection exists between all truths (*nexus mysteriorum*) which make known to us the one and true God, so that we may attain eternal salvation (cum fine hominis ultimo) through faith, hope, and love.[68]

In his treatise *Von den Konziliis und Kirchen* (On the Councils and the Church) (1539), Luther describes the history of Catholic orthodoxy with the Church's great decisions on belief in the Triune God and in the God-man mystery of Jesus Christ, the universal and only Savior of the world, beginning with the Councils of Nicaea (AD 325) and Constantinople I (AD 381), to the Council of Ephesus (AD 431) and the great Council of Chalcedon (AD 451).

He believes that it was precisely through his reforming work that the true catholic Church re-emerged. For, in his view, it had degenerated through the claims to power of the medieval papacy into a mercantile system of administering grace. Despite being well aware of the problem of how to translate the Greek-origin expressions "church" and "catholic" accurately into German, as far

---

[66] Cf. Ernst Öffner, *Evangelisch ist auch katholisch. Ein protestantischer Blick auf Kirche und Gesellschaft*, Münchenm, ³2009.

[67] Vatican II, *Unitatis Redingratio*, §11.

[68] DH 3016.

as content is concerned, Luther nevertheless sticks clearly to the traditional concept and content of "catholic." *The people of God who believe in Christ are the "sancta et catholica ecclesia* [holy and catholic Church]."[69]

> *Ecclesia*, however, ought to mean the holy Christian people, not only of the time of the apostles, who are long since dead, but clear to the end of the world, so that there is always living on earth a Christian, holy people in which Christ lives, works, and reigns *per redemptionem*, through grace and forgiveness of sins, the Holy Ghost per vivificationem et sanctificationem, through the daily purging out of sins and renewal of life.[70]

The pope and his bishops, on the other hand, who consider themselves alone and without the people to be "the" Church, are for Luther not the true Catholic Church. And he sees the *Ecclesia Romana* (Church of Rome) only as the assembly of the faithful of the Diocese of Rome, in whose name the pope has no right to claim supremacy over the other local Catholic churches.

If we now make a leap of five hundred years across the Christian confessional divides into our own time, it is still possible to discover considerable agreement on the question of *what* the Church is: (1) in her origin in Christ; (2) in her universal mission; and (3) in the definition of her essential characteristics and external marks. In accordance with the promise that Christ would remain with her until the end of the world, the Church, too, continues indestructibly as the holy, New Covenant people of God gathered in Christ.

The five marks listed by Luther are based on the entire Catholic Tradition and are to be found substantially—although sometimes formulated differently— in the Dogmatic Constitution on the Church of the Second Vatican Council:

> 1. God's word; 2. Baptism; 3. the Sacrament of the Altar; 4. the power of the keys; and 5. the apostolic ministry, which "it consecrates or calls ministers, or has offices which they occupy. For we must have bishops, pastors, or preachers, to give, administer, and use, publicly and privately, the four things, or precious possessions that have been mentioned for the sake of and in the name of the Church, or rather because of their institution by Christ."[71]

---

[69] WA 50, 625; Luther, *On the Councils and the Churches*, 213, https://wolfmueller.co/wp-content /uploads/2018/10/Work-on-Councils_100618.pdf.

[70] WA 50, 625; Luther, *On the Councils and the Churches*, 213, emphasis added.

[71] WA 50, 632–633; Luther, *On the Councils and the Churches*, 228.

Nevertheless, as a result of the tragic division of Western Christendom, there has been a confessional narrowing of the term "catholic," albeit more in general usage than in exact theological terminology. A considerable tension has arisen with respect to its original meaning in our common Creed, since the communities that emerged from the Reformation have called themselves after their Lutheran, Zwinglian, Calvinist, or Free Church confessions, and some of them, in the English-speaking world of Lutherans in particular, have rendered the adjective "Catholic" as "Christian."

The Church that has remained in communion with the pope and the bishops, on the other hand, has from the start seen herself as maintaining continuity with the Catholic Church. She therefore saw no need to change her name. She calls herself, in a theologically accurate way, "Catholic" and not "Roman Catholic" (except in pragmatic usage). For the reference to St. Peter's Roman Church is implied in the predicate "catholic" and not assigned to it as an additional limiting predicate. In relation to the churches and ecclesial communities that have consciously separated from her, such as the Old Catholics, Anglicans, etc., she is not limited but instead fully catholic, because the Roman Church is the *ecclesia principalis* (principal church) within the *communio ecclesiarum* (community of churches).[72] For according to St. Cyprian of Carthage, Rome is the location of the chair of Peter and the principal Church from which priestly unity—here: "episcopal," in that the bishop is the first of the priests—is derived: "Petri Cathedra atque ecclesia principalis, unde unitas sacerdotalis exorta est."[73]

A different relationship exists with the Orthodox and pre-Chalcedonian (Oriental) Churches of the East, since the loosening of unity took place historically more by accident. The present relationship is no longer determined by mutual excommunication, since Pope Paul VI and the Ecumenical Patriarch Athenagoras I consigned the—in themselves absurd—excommunications of 1054 to oblivion (December 7, 1965).[74]

---

72 Henri de Lubac, *Catholicisme. Les aspects sociaux du dogme* (1938); Eng.: *Catholicism: Christ and the Common Destiny of Man* (Tunbridge Wells, England: Burns and Oates, 1950); Hans Urs von Balthasar, *Katholisch. Aspekte des Mysteriums* (= *Kriterien 36*) (Einsiedeln, 1975).

73 St. Cyprian, *Epistula* 55.8; cf. *Epistula* 59.14; 68; *De unitate Ecclesiae* 4.

74 Cf. As an overview Johannes Oeldemann, *Die Kirchen des christlichen Ostens. Orthodoxie, orientalische und mit Rom unierte Ostkirchen*, 2008 (Lit.); Ferdinand R. Gahbauer, *Byzantinische Dogmengeschichte. Vom Ausgang des Ikonoklasmus bis zum Untergang Konstantinopels (1453)* (Heiligenkreuz, 2010); Ilarion Alfeyev, *La Chiesa orthodossa*, 2 vols. (Bologna, 2013, 2014); on Catholicism in the Orthodox Church, cf. vol. 2, 436–448; Dimitru Staniloe, *Orthodoxe Dogmatik* (Gütersloh, 1985); *Ökumenischer Patriarch Bartholomaios I. Begegnung mit dem Mysterium. Das orthodoxe Christentum heute verstehen* (Paderborn, 2019).

The task of the ecumenical movement cannot be to construct out of the different Christian communions a Church unified in a human manner, which others could deconstruct again. Their unity will be brought about by the Holy Spirit in the image of the Son's unity with the Father. We still have to ask the Holy Spirit to show us the way in which unity in Christ can be lived again visibly in the communion of the "holy Catholic Church."

The questions arise as to what exactly we mean by "catholic," how we can live catholicity in the one Church in such a way as to preserve the legitimate patrimony of all, and how, in the larger whole, the hitherto separate communities can grow more deeply together, "until all of us come to the unity of the faith and of the knowledge of the Son of God, to maturity, to the measure of the full stature of Christ" (Eph 4:13).

Of course, as a theologian, I do not start the following reflections on the catholicity of faith and the Church from the inflated standpoint of neutral theorizing. For God's Church is founded by and in Christ. She does not emerge from the theoretical construct[75] of an ecclesiology, which can, after all, be no more than a limited intellectual reconstruction of God's logic, which he has revealed to us in the mystery of his Church. Personal faith as participation in the faith consciousness of the whole Church precedes theological reflection and can never be rationalistically reduced to a human thought structure, or even deduced from it.

As a Catholic, bishop, and cardinal of the Roman Church, I believe, live, and feel with the Catholic Church, which recognizes in the Bishop of Rome the Successor of Peter, whom Christ placed "over the other apostles, and instituted in him a permanent and visible source and foundation of unity of faith and communion."[76] With my former Munich colleague Wolfhart Pannenberg (1928–2014), however, I am convinced that the concept of being Catholic best expresses, in a theologically appropriate way, what unites Christians and what presses for the visible unity of the Church.

Pannenberg rightly criticized that the "Ökumenische Arbeitsgemeinschaft für Liturgische Texte in Deutschland" (Ecumenical Working Group for Liturgical Texts in Germany)[77] did not have the courage to translate "ecclesia catholica" as "katholische Kirche," unlike the "catholic Church" adopted by most of the mainstream Christian communions for the English translation:

---

75   Peter L. Berger and Thomas Luckmann, *The Social Construction of Reality: A Treatise in the Sociology of Knowledge* (New York: Doubleday, 1966).

76   Vatican II, *Lumen Gentium*, §§18, 23.

77   In Gottesdienst (11 und 12 / 1971), 26.

It must be regretted that in the [German] Protestant confessional writings of the sixteenth century this predicate of the Church was displaced in the translations of the Apostolic and Nicene Creeds and replaced by the term *"christliche Kirch."* It is in this form that the Creeds are still recited at many services even today.[78]

Certainly, this calls for an explanation. But it would also have been an opportunity to clarify the attributes of the Church in the common Creed in an ecumenical context.

Without playing down the remaining differences in important questions of faith—which, however, do not concern the central mysteries (Trinity, Incarnation, justification/redemption) but mainly the ecclesial-sacramental mediation of salvation—the ecumenical movement does not aim at a unity yet to be created by simply negating the faith of one's own confession but rather at a communion of all Christians in the one, holy, catholic, and apostolic Church. During his visit to Rome, the great Protestant theologian Karl Barth put it this way: conversions "can have significance only if they are in the form of conscientiously necessary 'conversion'—not to another church, but to Jesus Christ, the Lord of the one, holy, catholic, and apostolic church."[79]

What is "Catholic" is not the elements that are left over as a relic of specifically Roman doctrines and pious practices—e.g., the seven sacraments, including the Sacrifice of the Mass/Eucharist and the sacramental priesthood, as well as papal primacy, veneration of Mary and the saints, monastic vows, popular piety, etc.—when what is common to all Christians is stripped away; rather, it is an expression of what is Christian in the *entire* faith and in the community of the one and holy Church of God.

In visible unity, no one has to betray his identity at the expense of what his conscience tells him to be the truth (*Wahrheitsgewissen*), but all may hope for an increase in their fellowship with Christ, the head, and the members of his body, which is the Church. This is why the Second Vatican Council also emphasizes the significance and importance of the "Churches and ecclesial communities" still separated from the Roman Catholic Church: "For the Spirit of Christ has not refrained from using them as means of salvation [uti

---

[78] Wolfhard Pannenberg, *Das Glaubensbekenntnis, ausgelegt und verantwortet vor den Fragen der Gegenwart* (Gütersloh, 1982), 154. In English, "catholic" is now almost universally used, one exception being in conservative Lutheran versions, but frequently the word is not capitalized in Protestant usage.

[79] Karl Barth, *Ad Limina Apostolorum* (Zürich, 1967), 18.

tamquam salutis mediis] which derive their efficacy from the very fullness of grace and truth entrusted to the Church."[80]

This is not to be interpreted as a naïve self-reference on the part of an absolutized particular standpoint. The concrete Catholic Church, with the pope as the visible principle of her unity, is certainly convinced in faith that in her the catholicity of the Church is institutionally *fully* realized, at least in her doctrine, in the sacramental mediation of salvation, and in the apostolic constitution. But *the whole* of catholicity in its fullness of life is not realized within her visible boundaries alone. And the efficacy of the fullness of grace and truth entrusted to the Catholic Church is not, of course, derived from the pope and the bishops, any more than it is from Protestant pastors, but from Christ alone, who speaks to us in the Holy Spirit through the proclamation of his holy, universal Church and imparts his grace in her sacramental celebrations. For, as was already stated by St. Thomas Aquinas three centuries before the drama of the sixteenth century, it is, strictly speaking, the task of the ministers of the Church "not to give grace, but to give the sacraments of grace."[81] Thus the efficacy and truth of the means of salvation in the "Churches and ecclesial communities separated from the Roman Apostolic See"[82] does not derive from the constituted form of the Roman Catholic Church but rather from the invisible head of the Catholic Church, to which we all belong through Baptism even though at the visible level, i.e., the unity of all her members in the one body, full communion does not yet exist, in order that, in Jesus's words to the Father, "the world may know that you have sent me" (John 17:23).

The difference lies rather in the relationship between the invisible and the visible Church, i.e., the inner community of grace and the ecclesial-sacramental mediation of it. But here, too, the contrast regarding what the "Church in the proper sense"[83] is remains no more than a relative one. In the view of Johann Adam Möhler (1796–1838), a pioneering nineteenth-century Catholic and irenically minded ecumenist, "Luther's notion of the Church is . . . not false, though it is one-sided." He sums up this insight as follows:

> Luther, moreover, has rightly seen the necessity of admitting that a revelation, emanating immediately from God, requireth a divinely instituted Church, and the Christian Faith a far higher than a mere human guarantee. But his fault was that he did not seriously weigh

---

[80]   Vatican II, *Unitatis Redintegratio*, §3; cf. *Lumen Gentium*, §8.

[81]   St. Thomas Aquinas, *ST* suppl., q. 36, a. 3; cf. q. 37, a. 4, ad 2.

[82]   Vatican II, *Unitatis Redintegratio*, §13.

[83]   Cf. *Confessio Augustana*, a. 8, and CDF, *Dominus Iesus*, §17.

what was signified by the words, [i.e., that] the immediate revelation in Christ is external; for, otherwise, he would have understood that a divinely instituted Church is necessarily visible, founded as it is by the Word of God become visible, and that the warranty of faith must needs be external. . . . Thus far, certainly, the invisible is to be ranked before the visible Church; and the latter is eternally renovated out of the former. But, this kingdom of God begins, grows, and ripens within us, after it has first externally encountered us, and made the first steps to receive us into its bosom.[84]

"Catholic" is therefore not a section of Christianity in the form of special communal traditions but rather its original, evolved *fullness*. Thus, St. Pacian of Barcelona († AD 390) could say:

Christian is my name, but Catholic my surname
[Christianus mihi nomen est, catholicus vero cognomen].[85]

To be formally and really "Catholic" is certainly a gift (*Gabe*) but no less a task (*Aufgabe*). A Christian can also founder on it if the credibility of the Church is obscured by a narrow-mindedness of the intellect, a lukewarm moral will, and sinning against love.

---

[84] Johann Adam Möhler, *Symbolik oder Darstellung der dogmatischen Gegensätze der Katholiken und Protestanten nach ihren öffentlichen Bekenntnisschriften*, ed. J. R. Geiselmann, Cologne and Olten, 1958, 489 (§49); Eng.: *Symbolism: Or, Exposition of the Doctrinal Differences between Catholics and Protestants as Evidenced by Their Symbolical Writings*, 6th ed. (London: Gibbings, 1906), 334–35.

[85] St. Pacian of Barcelona, *Epistula* 1.7.

Chapter 5

QUO VADIS, ECCLESIA CATHOLICA?

The biblical context of the proverbial question "Quo vadis?," which expresses concern for the future of an undertaking, is Jesus's journey to his Passion and death on the Cross. But it also points ahead to the post-Easter conferral of the universal pastoral office for the whole Church on Simon Peter, who it was that asked Jesus, "Lord, where are you going? [*Domine, quo vadis?*]." And Jesus answered him, "'Where I am going, you cannot follow me now; but you will follow afterwards" (John 13:36). And when he appears to them post-Easter at the Sea of Tiberias, the Risen Lord takes up this intimation again, promising martyrdom to the chief shepherd of the Church: "But when you grow old, you will stretch out your hands, and someone else will fasten a belt around you and take you where you do not wish to go" (John 21:18).

There is the legend that Peter encountered Jesus as he was fleeing from Rome to escape martyrdom. Once again he asks, "Where are you going, Lord?" and this time Jesus answers him, "I am going to Rome to be crucified again." And that is the essential point of this story. Renewal of the Church does not come through fleeing from the Cross and persecution, or through a cozy conformity to the spirit of this world, but only through following the crucified and risen Christ. Now and in the future, the path of the Church leads only from truth to life (cf. John 14:6): "Jesus Christ is the same yesterday and today and for ever" (Heb 13:8).

Catholic reform; or, how does the Church get back into shape?

Do not be conformed to this world, but be transformed by the renewing of your minds, so that you may discern what is the will of God
[Nolite conformari huic saeculo, sed reformamini in novitate sensus
vestry]. (Rom 12:2)

As is clear in the Latin translation of the Vulgate, St. Paul sets conformity to the world against reform of the Church out of the unsurpassable
newness of Christ.

Likewise, in the highly dramatic crisis of the Church in the second century,
Irenaeus of Lyons (ca. AD 135–200), the "father of Catholic dogmatics," asserted
the definitive newness of Jesus Christ against the speculative innovations of
the Gnostics.[1] It is not through better structures that the true world revolution
of God's Incarnation brings forth the new man. Rather, Christ in his divine
Person is God's innovative investment in our world that brings mankind the
highest return: *adoption in the Son's place.* The sons and daughters of God are
therefore also "heirs of God and joint heirs with Christ" (Rom 8:17).

It is not man of the old creation who creates a new world for himself;
there is "a new creation" (Gal 6:15), and in Christ man overcomes the old world
of selfishness, brutality, sin, and death. When Paul warns against conformity
to the world, he is not referring to the world as God's creation assigned to
humanity as a "common home,"[2] or the "the garden of Eden to till it and keep
[*ut operaretur terram*]" (Gen 2:17) in which God put humankind (*adam*). Paul
is referring to the old eon. This is the world under the crushing power of evil
and enmity towards God (cf. Rom 1:30).

Those who are led by the Spirit of God leave behind the "works of the flesh,"
which are "fornication, impurity, licentiousness, idolatry, sorcery, enmities, strife,
jealousy, anger, quarrels, dissensions, factions, envy, drunkenness, carousing, and
things like these" (Gal 5:19). Those who do such things forfeit their inheritance:
the kingdom of God. By contrast, "the fruit of the Spirit is love, joy, peace,
patience, kindness, generosity, faithfulness, gentleness, and self-control. . . . If
we live by the Spirit, let us also be guided by the Spirit" (Gal 5:22–25). When
the apostle calls for reform, he means that we should become like Christ and be
conformed to him in thinking and speaking, in our actions and suffering. We
should take his spirit of humility and dedication as our example. For everyone
who believes in God in Christ, a comprehensive personal orientation towards

---

[1]   St. Irenaeus, *Adversus haereses* 4.34.1.

[2]   Pope Francis, *Laudato Si'* (2015), §§17–19; cf. on this Gerhard L. Müller, "What Is the Meaning
of God as the Creator of the World?," in *Sustainable Development in the Context of Laudato Si'*,
ed. Jan Szyszko (Warsaw, 2016), 39–53.

God is inseparable from responsibility for our own person, our fellow human beings, the environment, and the resources of the earth.[3]

The Church received from her divine founder the mission to proclaim to mankind—at all times and in all circumstances—the good news (Gospel) of their dignity and freedom, which are anchored in the transcendence of God. She is not committed to what is culturally or lifeworldly old or new. The Church looks to the supernatural as the elevation of the natural, to the eternal in time, to God in Jesus of Nazareth, his Son and our Savior.

After three hundred years of persecution and contempt, Christianity became the determining spiritual and moral power in the Roman Empire and its successor states. When Columbus crossed the horizon of old Europe in the morning hours of October 12, 1492, this globalized human consciousness, bringing with it, despite the crisis of divisions within the Western Church, the spread of the Christian faith to every country in the world. But with the rise of the new scientific method[4] also came a mechanistic worldview with which only the deistic-pantheistic understanding of God seemed compatible. Whereas in the entire Jewish and Christian Tradition the *"person* of a rational nature"[5] was always regarded as the highest and most perfect thing in the whole of reality and as the highest realization of being,[6] the personhood of God now appeared as an anthropomorphic, even infantile, analogy that fell far short of the supra-personal and impersonal inexhaustibility of nature and its identity with the infinite God-substance. In the face of developments in natural and historical science, and in view of the new image of man and society, the Church's doctrine, based as it is on supernatural Revelation, seemed less and less communicable. After the phenomenology of Immanuel Kant, it was felt that the dogmatic doctrines of the faith had to be transformed into the concept of a moral and humanitarian religion.[7]

---

3   Karl Lehmann, *Glauben bezeugen, Gesellschaft gestalten* (Freiburg, 1993); Lehmann, *Frei vor Gott. Glauben in öffentlicher Verantwortung* (Freiburg, 2003).

4   Francis Bacon, *Novum organon* (1620) (= PhB 400) (Hamburg, 1990); Eng.: *The New Organon: Or True Directions Concerning the Interpretation of Nature* (Oxford: Clarendon Press, 2009), https://www.google.co.uk/books/edition/Novum_organum/tH4_AAAAYAAJ?hl=en.

5   Boethius, *De duabus naturis*, ch. 3, emphasis added (PL 64 :1343): "persona est naturae rationalis individua substantia."

6   St. Thomas Aquinas, *ST* I, q. 29, a. 3: "person significat id quod est perfectissimum in tota natura, scilicet subsistens in rationali natura."

7   Immanuel Kant, *Die Religion innerhalb der Grenzender bloßen Vernunft B* (1794): *Werke in Zehn Bänden 7*, ed. W. Weischedel (Darmstadt, 1968), 649–879. Cf. On this the analysis of the de-Christianizing of the sense of culture offered at almost the same time by Joseph von Eichendorff, *Der Deutsche Roman des achtzehnten Jahrhunderts in seinem Verhältnis zum Christentum*: id. *Werke III* (Munich, 1976), 171–378.

Two opposing theoretical and practical reactions to the new situation tended to emerge, first in academic theology and then, from the nineteenth century onwards, in the wider Church community. Should you encapsulate yourself in a past Christian cultural world, or sell yourself to the "modern age" and carry on living off your pension until your foreseeable death? The two schools of thought accuse their respective opposites of either abandoning the substance of the faith or failing to connect with modernity. It seems that, in the conflict between identity and relevance, the helmsman of the barque of Peter is left with the sole option of being devoured by Scylla or swallowed by Charybdis. Should one position oneself on one side, or with faith and reason critically and constructively venture a new synthesis that both preserves the substance of the faith and reflects and sets an example of lived faith—in such a way that the world comes to a new understanding of the liberating potential of the Gospel and embraces it?

For since the Enlightenment and the French Revolution, history has oscillated restlessly between attempts to reverse the development of society in a restorative manner (to paradise lost), or to accelerate it in a progressive manner (to paradise on earth). But the "Enlightenment" has long since ceased to bask in the rays of the rising morning sun. In the twentieth century, the fatal consequences of "humanism without God"[8] brought humanity face to face with the possibility of its own self-destruction.[9] In view of the ambivalence of every scientific and technological development, as well as the "dialectic of enlightenment"[10] between freedom and totalitarianism, it is impossible for the Church to swing back and forth with the pendulum. Supranaturalism and rationalism, integralism and modernism, conservative and liberal theology, "Christians for Socialism," "German Christians," "Catholicism from below," and traditionalism, pre-conciliar and post-conciliar Catholicism—all these are gymnastics performed with greater or lesser success on the swinging pendulum. But the only progress they bring is down the road to irrelevance when the clock stops ticking. It is not a matter of signing up for this or that ship but rather—to pursue the

---

[8]   Henri de Lubac, *Le Drame de l'Humanisme athée* (Paris, 1983); Eng.: *The Drama of Atheist Humanism* (San Francisco: Ignatius Press, 1995); translation of the 1983 edition, including chapters omitted from the 1949 translation.

[9]   Alberto Castaldini, *Il Dio nascosto e la possibilità di Auschwitz. Prospettive filosofiche e teologiche sull'Olocausto* (Cluj-Napoca, Romania, 2016); Aleksandr Solzhenitsyn, *The Gulag Archipelago*, trans. Thomas P. Whitney (New York: Harper and Row, 1817), https://archive.org/details /TheGulagArchipelago-Threevolumes/The-Gulag-Archipelago__vol1__I-II__Solzhenitsyn /page/n13/mode/2up.

[10] Max Horkheimer and Theodor W. Adorno, *Dialektik der Aufklärung. Philosophische Fragmente* (Frankfurt a.M., 1968).

image—of outwitting the song of the sirens like "Odysseus lashed to the mast,"[11] and of setting the compass of the "little barque of Peter"[12] securely to Christ.

Before we set off on the epochal journey into a globalized and digitalized world, we Christians do not have the option of apocalyptically conjuring up the end of the world,[13] or dreaming utopian dreams of the year AD 2540, when through indoctrination, genetic manipulation, and social scoring we shall finally arrive in Aldous Huxley's grotesque *Brave New World*,[14] or in George Orwell's *Nineteen Eighty-Four*, or on his *Animal Farm*.[15]

For the myth of the twenty-first century,[16] like the Gnostic myth of yore, boils down to the self-deification of man, whose descent into every kind of deviltry is not long in coming. The beguiling slogan *"Homo homini Deus"*[17] promises a paradise of self-determined man, which, however, after passing through a hell full of "greed and lust," beckons only as a mirage.

Christianity, however, is not a myth from the past that needs to be refurbished and made fit for use today as a "civic religion"[18] for society, or as a religious aid organization in the service of the United Nations, or ready to become superfluous in a "religion without God."[19] What the Church should concern herself with is the Gospel as "the power of God for salvation to everyone who has faith" (Rom 1:16) and the knowledge of God and Christ for eternal life (cf. John 17:3), not melting glaciers, global warming, or the European migration pact. And someone called to be the Vicar of Christ does not need to offer his services as a chaplain to the Council for Inclusive Capitalism in a partnership with the Vatican.[20]

---

[11] Hugo Rahner, *Odysseus am Mastbaum: id., Griechische Mythen in christlicher Deutung*, Basel, 1984, 281–328; Eng.: *Greek Myths and Christian Mystery* (Cheshire, CT: Biblio-Moser, 1963); Rahner, *Flumina de ventre Christi: id., Symbole der Kirche. Die Ekklesiologie der Väter* (Salzburg, 1964), 177–564, at 239–271.

[12] Hugo Rahner, *Das Schifflein des Petrus. Zur Symbolgeschichte des römischen Primats*, 473–503.

[13] Ewald Weber, *Welt am Abgrund. Wie Co$_2$ unser Leben verändert* (Darmstadt, 2018).

[14] Aldous Huxley, *Brave New World* (London: Chatto and Windus, 1932).

[15] George Orwell, *Nineteen Eighty-Four* (London: Secker and Warburg, 1949); Orwell, *Animal Farm: A Fairy Story* (London: Secker and Warburg, 1945).

[16] Yuval Noah Harari, *Twenty-One Lessons for the Twenty-First Century* (London: Jonathan Cape, 2018).

[17] Yuval Noah Harari, *Homo Deus: A Brief History of Tomorrow* (London: Harvill Secker, 2016); Ludwig Feuerbach, *Das Wesen des Christentums* (1841), intro. Ludwig Feuerbach, *Werke in sechs Bänden*, vol. 5 (1976), 30, etc.; so already in the projection theory of the Polish atheist Kazimierz Łyszczyński, *De non existentia Dei* (1674).

[18] Jean-Jacques Rousseau, *The Social Contract*, bk. 4, 8.

[19] Ronald Dworkin, *Religion without God* (Cambridge, MA: Harvard University Press, 2013).

[20] Hannah Brockhaus, "Council for Inclusive Capitalism Launches Partnership with Vatican," *Catholic News Agency*, December 9, 2020, https://www.catholicnewsagency.com/news/46848

What the Christian faith sets against the myth of the twenty-first century is not another myth, whether old or new, but solely God's truth, which makes those who know it free (John 8:32).

In view of the unimagined possibilities of the steep ascent and precipitous fall of the high-altitude hike of our species, the Catholic Church currently sees her historical task as being to develop discernment criteria according to the principle to "test everything; hold fast to what is good" (1 Thess 5:21).

The Church, as the body of Christ, is the world's "universal sacrament of salvation."[21] She believes: "Christ, who died and was raised up for all, can through his Spirit offer man the light and the strength to measure up to his supreme destiny."[22]

In overcoming both metaphysical and moral relativism, the Church points to God's truth as the meaning of being, and to the good as the goal of man.[23] Against the placelessness of modern man, she sets the orientation towards revealed faith.[24] Her teaching is not a fluid context of meaning consisting of narrative and poetic explorations of the meaning of the world but rather an affirmative dogmatic promise made by God: "But when the goodness and loving-kindness of God our Savior appeared, he saved us . . . through the water of rebirth and renewal by the Holy Spirit" (Tit 3:4–5). With respect to dialectical theology, which considers any analogous knowledge of God to be impossible, and also against its counterpart in liberal theology, which considers dogma, the sacraments, and canon law (the *ius divinum*) to be the epitome of pre-modern Catholic Christianity, the Protestant theologian Erik Peterson (1890–1960), even before his conversion to the Catholic faith, stated:

> Now, it is not as if theology had to side with the realist epistemologists in the philosophers' dispute between idealist and realist epistemologists for the purposes of human dogmatizing; rather, it must be in such a way that the realistic character of theological knowledge is connected with the real character of Revelation. Only on the premise that God became man and thereby enabled us to participate in *scientia divina* [divine knowledge], only on this premise does it make sense to speak of a real, if merely analogical, knowledge of God in theology.[25]

/council-for-inclusive-capitalism-launches-partnership-with-vatican; Wikipedia, "Inclusive Capitalism."

[21] Second Vatican Council, *Lumen Gentium* (1964), §48.

[22] Second Vatican Council, *Gaudium et Spes* (1965), §10.

[23] Karl Lehmann, *Zuversicht aus dem Glauben* (Freiburg, 2006).

[24] Karl Lehmann, *Es ist Zeit an Gott zu denken. Ein Gespräch mit Jürgen Hoeren* (Freiburg, 2000).

[25] Erik Peterson, *Was ist Theologie* (1926), Eng.: *Theological Tractates* (Redwood City, CA: Stanford University Press, 2011); Peterson, *Theologische Traktate* (1951), 9–43, at 16 (= *Ausgewählte*

There could be no repositioning of the Church, and no criterion distinguishing between "true and false reform"[26] of the Church, if that meant leaving her foundation hanging in the balance: "God has spoken in his Son. That is what the dogma says and by which alone theology lives."[27]

The Church is not an old building whose structure could be made safe by a modern architect: gutted, completely rebuilt, and then given over to a new function.[28] Book titles such as *Reform: Dieselbe Kirche anders denken* (Reform: Thinking the Same Church Differently) are misleading, because the Church is the subject of revealed faith and not a thought product conceived in the mind of a theologian which saw the light of day on his desk.

Theology serves only the understanding of the word of God, not its correction by man according to rationalistic criteria, or the adaptation of sexual ethics to hedonistic criteria in a neo-Marxist-materialistic view of man. From the self-revelation of the Triune God, who imparts salvation to us through faith, "the Church has been seen as [according to St. Cyprian of Carthage] 'a people made one with the unity of the Father, the Son, and the Holy Spirit.'"[29] The Church is the pilgrim people of God the Father, the body of Christ, and the temple of the Holy Spirit. She is not "suffering from the frustration and the final threat of exodus on the part of those who want to reconcile the Church with the world and the times,"[30] because here the subject and object of reform are confused. Quite the other way round: the task is to reconcile the world through Christ with God (2 Cor 5:18). God constitutes and forms his Church through the human nature of Christ, which he assumed when the Word (Logos) became flesh for the salvation of the world. Reform does not happen by returning to a previous outer form of the Church but by conforming it to her inner form, i.e., the being and nature of Christ. The Church of Christ is, then, in the right shape when she is there as a "Church for others,"[31] for the world for which God, out of love, gave his only Son (cf. John 3:16). The Church will not become more attractive through an improved corporate design if she

---

Schriften 1), ed. Barbara Nichtweiss (Würzburg, 1994).

26 Yves Congar, *Vraie et Fausse Réforme dans L'Église* (Paris, 1951).

27 Congar, *Vraie et Fausse Réforme dans L'Église*, 34.

28 George Weigel, *Die Erneuerung der Kirche. Tiefgreifende Reform im 21. Jahrhundert* (Illertissen, 2015); Weigel, *The Irony of Modern Catholic History: How the Church Rediscovered Itself and Challenged the Modern World to Reform* (New York: Basic Books, 2019); Michael Bollig, ed., *Christsein in einer Kirche der Zukunft* (Würzburg, 2012).

29 Vatican II, *Lumen Gentium*, §4.

30 Otto Friedrich, *Liberale Kritik am nachsynodalen Schreiben "Querida Amazonia" von Papst Franziskus: Vision 2* (2000), 5.

31 Dietrich Bonhoeffer, *Widerstand und Ergebung. Briefe und Aufzeichnungen aus der Haft* (= DBW 8) (Munich, 1998), 560.

does not open the way to belief in Jesus Christ, the only mediator of salvation, through her own intellectual and spiritual credibility.[32]

In view of the epochal challenge facing the Church for the immanent and transcendent future, the term "reform of the Church" cannot be reduced to attempts to secularize her by adapting to the behavior of the statistical majority of people in matters of sexuality and marriage, at the same time rigorously leaving aside any orientation towards God, towards the God-man Jesus Christ, and the Church as the sacrament of salvation. Historically, what was meant by the reform of the Church in her head and members was always an inner renewal in Christ, which then manifested itself in a true following of Christ and finally also convinced the lukewarm and the distant.[33] Think of the monastic reforms from Cluny to Ss. Catherine of Siena, Teresa of Avila, and John of the Cross, or the Gregorian Reform and its struggle for the freedom of the Church in feudal times.

The delay in the renewal of the Church in Christ is what led—in the sixteenth century—to the schism in Western Christendom. The only reason why this process, which was later to go down in Church history as "the Reformation," did not lead to the marginalization of the Catholic Church was that in the saints, the great theologians, and zealous pastors she developed intellectual and spiritual forces that brought her a new blossoming. With the Council of Trent, this "Catholic Reform,"[34] which had already taken hold in Spain and Italy before the German Protestant Reformation, spread to the other countries that had remained Catholic. Vatican II gathered all the reform movements around the Bible, the liturgy, the renewed study of patristics, scholasticism and modern theology, Catholic Action, social criticism, and social ethics, and made it possible for them to be communicated with the scientific-technical spirit of modernity.

The reason for the exponentially worsening crisis of the Catholic Church since then was not the Council's teaching but rather its political interpretation and ideological appropriation. Just as the Council of Trent carried Catholic reform into the nineteenth century, Vatican II, with its central statements on divine Revelation, faith, Jesus Christ, and the Church in the world today, can serve as the broad outline guiding a Catholic reform for the twenty-first century.

---

[32] Karl Lehmann and Rudolf Schnackenburg, *Brauchen wir noch Zeugen? Die heutige Situation in der Kirche und die Antwort des Neuen Testaments* (Freiburg, 1992); Louis Bouyer, *The Decomposition of Catholicism* (Chicago: Franciscan Herald Press, 1969).

[33] Rudolf Voderholzer, *Zur Erneuerung der Kirche. Geistliche Impulse zu aktuellen Herausforderungen* (Regensburg, 2020).

[34] Hubert Jedin, *Katholische Reformation oder Gegenreformation? Ein Versuch zur Klärung der Begriffe nebst einer Jubiläumsbetrachtung über das Trienter Konzil* (Lucerne, 1946); Hubert, *Katholische Reform und Gegenreformation:* HKG IV (Freiburg, 1967), 449–604.

The only and the true reformer of the Church is God, for she is his. We are merely the inhabitants of his house but also co-responsible citizens in the city of God. So, as Paul said, what is needed is for us to be renewed in Christ. But, with all the confusion and polarization, the Church can give the impression of flabby secularization, making it possible to write of the "decomposition of Catholicism."[35]

In origin, essence, and mission, the Church is the body of Christ. But the members and also the Church as a socio-political power—which outsiders and uneducated Catholics notoriously confuse with the Church as the people of God, body of Christ, and temple of the Holy Spirit—can individually and collectively sin or historically fail. Every Catholic is free to evaluate the success or failure of Vatican diplomacy vis-à-vis the Nazi Third Reich or the "Ostpolitik" of Cardinal Secretary of State Agostino Casaroli. Likewise, every Catholic today is free to assess the policy on China or papal statements on climate change according to professional criteria, without this calling into question the dogmatically binding nature of the authority of the Roman Church and the pope. Only blatant theological ignorance, heretically distorting the doctrine of the Roman primacy, can demand absolute obedience to the pope even in matters that have nothing to do with teaching on faith and morals. The German bishops had already spoken out in 1875 against such an arbitrary claim to papal authority, in a way that suited one's own particular shade of ideology, when they rejected Otto von Bismarck's misinterpretation of Vatican I and were confirmed in so doing by Pope Pius IX.[36]

What is needed here is to acquire suitable criteria from the standpoint of faith, i.e., the knowledge of the nature of the Church in the light of divine Revelation:

> While Christ, holy, innocent, and undefiled (Heb 7:26), knew nothing of sin (2 Cor 5:21), but came to expiate only the sins of the people (cf. Heb 2:17), the Church, embracing in her bosom sinners, at the same time holy and always in need of being purified, always follows the way of penance and renewal.
>
> The Church, "like a stranger in a foreign land, presses forward amid the persecutions of the world and the consolations of God, announcing the Cross and death of the Lord until he comes" (cf. 1 Cor 11:26). By the power of the Risen Lord, she is given strength that she might, in patience and in love, overcome her sorrows and her

---

[35] Louis Bouyer, *La Décompostion du Catholicisme* (Paris, 1968); Eng.: *The Decomposition of Catholicism*. Cardinal Paul Poupard, *La Décroyance. Entretiens avec Véronique Dufief* (Dijon, 2011).

[36] DH 3112–3117.

challenges, both within herself and from without, and that she might reveal to the world, faithfully though darkly, the mystery of its Lord until, in the end, it will be manifested in full light.[37]

It is not the Church that is the subject of our reform programs. For as God's work it is perfect and "never to be reformed [nunquam Ecclesia reformabitur]," as Pascal says, citing the famous Church writer Tertullian (ca. AD 150–220).[38]

Because of the different concept of "the Church," the axiom "*ecclesia semper reformanda* [the Church must always be reformed]"[39] cannot be applied in its original Reformation sense, because it does not accord with the Catholic view of the essential indestructibility of the Church, the infallibility of her doctrine, and the objective efficacy of the sacraments. Here, looking at the members of the Church and the behavior of popes, bishops, their curiae, and heads of departments in matters of ecclesial and personnel policy, with its mixture of old nepotism and new favoritism, the fitting expression would instead be: "*ecclesia semper purificanda* [the Church must always be purified]." Paul did not ask Christians to tinker around with the Church, the body of Christ, or to supply the temple of the Holy Spirit with new interior and exterior architecture. This is the Spirit who descended on the Church on the day of Pentecost and to whom the Church prays, "When you send forth your Spirit, they [all creation] are created; and you renew the face of the ground" (Ps 104:30). The Lord is the physician (Exod 15:26; Matt 9:12) and we are his patients. Reform means being renewed and transformed by Christ according to his likeness [*meta-morphein*] (Rom 12:2).

A second "Reformation" from Germany?

Men must be changed by religion, not religion by men. . . . When was the impudence with which one speaks, disputes, and writes against piety more commonplace and self-assured? When was there in all circles of the population not only greater neglect, but even contempt for sacred things, the sacraments, ecclesiastical authority, and God's

---

[37] Vatican II, *Lumen Gentium*, §8.

[38] Pascal, *Pensées*, frag. 889.

[39] Theodor Mahlmann, „*Ecclesia semper reformanda*," *Eine historische Aufarbeitung. Hermeneutica Sacra. Studien zur Auslegung der Heiligen Schrift im 16. und 17. Jahrhundert*, ed. T. Johansson (Berlin, 2019), 382–441.

commandments? When were our religion and our Faith more openly made the target of ridicule even among the common people? When was there a more pernicious division of the Church?[40]

This is not taken from the opening speech inaugurating the "Synodal Way" in Frankfurt 2020 but from the opening oration given by Cardinal Aegidius of Viterbo (1439–1532) at the Fifth Lateran Council in Rome on May 3, 1512.

This council was unable to prevent the imminent schism of the Western Church but, in fact, merely promoted it through its abstruse denial of reality. It had become bogged down in questions of structure, instead of asking about the meaning of the Gospel for the life of the Church and the individual Christian. And now a reform of the universal Church in her head and members is once again supposed to emanate from Germany.

With the suggestive tautology of the "*Synodaler Weg*" (Synodal Way/ Path), the Conference of German Bishops (*Deutsche Bischofskonferenz* [DBK]), together with the Central Committee of German Catholics (*Zentralkommittee der deutschen Katholiken* [ZdK]), a political lay organization, wants to counter the Church's loss of credibility as a result of the scandalous child abuse by a number of clergy—between 1945 and 2020—with a politicization of the Gospel and a self-secularization of the Church. However, instead of counteracting the breach of trust with renewed obedience to God's commandments, they want to adapt God's commandments and the Church's teachings to suit the spirit of the age. The individual's personal sin is no longer located in an evil will nor theologically interpreted with the drama of original sin (*peccatum originale* or *peccatum hereditarium*). Instead, in the German media, the perpetrators are declared to be the victims of God's unfulfillable commandments as they are expressed in the "Church system" (*System Kirche*), which is then absurdly compared with the final phase of the Communist Honecker regime in the German Democratic Republic (East Germany) and thus denounced as a kind of dictatorship. For fear of exposing themselves to the accusation of a "cover-up," which was blind to their own shortcomings, the bishops left the verdict on the priestly lifestyle to experts who are remote from the faith and, being located within the German context—a "space of resonance" (*Resonanzraum*) shaped by culture-war prejudices and the assumptions of religious criticism—automatically alienate theological concepts such as grace and sin, vocation and priesthood, celibacy and evangelical counsels, Catholic and Church. In the vulgar materialist view of man as an instinct-driven being, the free adoption of a celibate lifestyle can, so the argument goes, only lead to

---

[40] Gian Domenico, Mansi 32, 669–676.

unexpressed and thus pent-up sexual lust, which is then released in uncontrollable violence against the weakest. Believing in science and intimidated by the mainstream media, the bishops do not seek to overcome the crisis through a recentering on the omnipotence of grace and appealing to the responsibility of free will, or in the discipline and spirituality of the clerical office.

But the only way of escaping the secularization trap is for believers to renew their relationship with God in faith, hope, and love. True reform is only in Christ: "Do not be conformed to this world, but be transformed by the renewing of your minds, so that you may discern what is the will of God— what is good and acceptable and perfect" (Rom 12:2).

The "false reform" of the Church in the sense of secularization is, on the other hand, linked to the following conditions: the abolition of priestly celibacy; the ordination of women to the priesthood; the replacement of sexual morality with the pleasure principle; the destruction of marriage, which as a heterosexual variant of homosexual relationships is robbed of its essence; and the replacement of the authority of the shepherds appointed by Christ with functionaries empowered by the "people." It is not because it is in the Person of Christ, the head of the Church,[41] that the priest proclaims the word of God, mediates grace sacramentally, and as a good shepherd lays down his life for Christ's flock that a sense of clerical power develops which is discharged on the weakest as a sexual crime. Quite the contrary, it is the traitor to the priesthood, who has degenerated into a functionary and hireling, who allows himself to lose control and commit such monstrous deeds.

Tampering with the ordained ministry instituted by Christ, without calling the guilty personally to account, is a kind of collective punishment making the many good priests guilty by association and is also an irresponsible cause of uncertainty and confusion to young men wanting to follow the call of Christ. With these old chestnuts of Liberalism, all the "Synodal Way" offers is bad therapy applied to the wrong object and employing inappropriate remedies. Such therapy is no more effective than if the dentist used radiotherapy on his patient's foot as a cure for pneumonia.

The disastrous decision to push through this agenda at all costs, even if it contradicts Catholic teaching, amounts both formally and in content to setting oneself up against the constitution of the Catholic Church and establishing a German-Catholic Church. Such a monstrosity is separated in doctrine, life, and constitution from the Catholic Church founded by Christ.[42] Because of the discrepancy between goodwill and theological expertise, it is impossible

---

[41] Vatican II, *Lumen Gentium*, §29; *Presbyterorum Ordinis*, §2.

[42] Vatican II, *Lumen Gentium*, §8; *Dei Verbum*, §10.

to say for certain whether this point is clear to all involved. At the tumultuous Second Council of Ephesus (AD 449), which was to go down infamously in Church history as the "Robber Council," the violent majority at the Synod, led by the power-conscious Patriarch Dioscorus of Alexandria, wanted to impose the Monophysitism of Eutyches by force using cunning and trickery. But the deacon Hilarius, as the legate of Pope Leo the Great, had the courage to stand up to them and shout out the famous word: "*Contradicitur* [contradicted]!"[43]

German bishops who have not stood up against this blatant breach of the Catholic Church's constitution with a "*contradicitur*" could, however, learn from their predecessors, who bravely defended the freedom of the Catholic Church against the rise of the modern total state in the nineteenth century. The latter pointed out to the Prussian Protestant-minded Imperial Chancellor Bismarck (1815–1898), who notoriously failed to understand things Catholic, "The Pope cannot change the constitution given to the Church by her divine founder, as an earthly ruler can change the constitution of a state. In all essential points the constitution of the Church is based on divine directives, and therefore it is not subject to human arbitrariness."[44] Likewise, in his encyclical on the Church and the German Reich, *Mit Brennender Sorge* (1937), Pope Pius XI countered the German defiance of Rome,[45] making it quite clear that a national church separated from the *communio* and doctrine of the Roman Church is heading towards certain downfall:

> Faith in the Church cannot stand pure and true without the support of faith in the primacy of the Bishop of Rome. The same moment when Peter, in the presence of all the apostles and disciples, confesses his faith in Christ, Son of the Living God, the answer he received in reward for his faith and his confession was the word that built the Church, the only Church of Christ, on the rock of Peter. Thus was sealed the connection between the Faith in Christ, the Church, and the Primacy. True and lawful authority is invariably a bond of unity, a source of strength, a guarantee against division and ruin, a pledge for the future: and this is verified in the deepest and sublimest sense when that authority, as in the case of the Church, and the Church alone, is sealed by the promise and the guidance of the Holy Ghost and his irresistible support. Should men who are not even united by faith in Christ come and offer you the seduction of a national

---

[43] Pierre-Thomas Camelot, *Ephesus und Chalcedon* (Mainz, 1964), 121.

[44] DH 3114.

[45] Hans Urs von Balthasar, *Der antirömische Affekt. Wie lässt sich das Papsttum in die Gesamtkirche integrieren* (Freiburg, 1974).

German Church, be convinced that it is nothing but a denial of the one Church of Christ and the evident betrayal of that universal evangelical mission for which a world Church alone is qualified and competent. The live history of other national churches, with their paralysis, their domestication, and subjection to worldly powers, is sufficient evidence of the sterility to which is condemned every branch that is severed from the trunk of the living Church. Whoever counters these erroneous developments with an uncompromising "No" from the very outset not only serves the purity of his faith in Christ, but also the welfare and the vitality of his own people.[46]

In contrast to the Protestant understanding of the Church, in which the Church does not have a sacramental-hierarchical structure by divine right,[47] the constitution of the visible Church is not subject to the whims of her members, allowing them to appeal to the sense of faith of the people of God and claim to have been inspired by the Holy Spirit. Synods or councils are full or partial assemblies of the episcopate under the direction of the pope, and they have a completely different meaning from "synods" in communities stemming from the Reformation. In the latter, the hierarchical constitution of the Church, based on the apostolic succession of the bishops, was deliberately replaced with a "synodal" constitution based on the universal priesthood of the faithful, which, in the opinion of the Reformers, rules out the sacramental ordination of bishops, presbyters, and deacons.

The Reformed congregations led the way in the sixteenth century, while the Lutherans only followed suit after the abolition of the monarchies in Germany in 1918 and the consequent end of the system of state churches (*Landeskirchen*) governed by the local ruler. In the Scandinavian countries, national Lutheran churches existed until recently, just as the Anglican-established Church still exists in England today. But the "synodal constitution" in the Reformation-based communities cannot be called democratic in a political sense, any more than the hierarchical constitution of the Catholic Church can be denounced as un-democratic. For here as there, the Church constitution is not derived from the will of the people as sovereign. Insofar as the Church is the people of God, God is recognized among all Christians in revealed faith as sovereign over the Church. For the God of the covenant and Lord of the law said to the Israelites, "I will take you as my people, and I will be your God" (Exod 6:7). It is the same

---

[46]   Pope Pius XI, *Mit Brennender Sorge* (1937), §22.
[47]   Cf. Vatican II, *Lumen Gentium*, §8.

God who, through the prophets, promises to restore the messianic people of God: "And you shall be my people, and I will be your God" (Jer 30:22).

Indeed, the totality of believers cannot err when they are in agreement with one another in their confession of the revealed faith (*infallibilitas in credendo*). It is simply a wicked and stupid caricature of the Catholic Church's constitution to describe it as a two-class society with the bishops, on the one hand, giving the orders and the laity, on the other, receiving them. For the special priesthood of the apostolic office and the common priesthood of the faithful are a sharing of all the baptized in the one high priesthood of Jesus Christ. In this way, all are called and enabled to participate, advising and shaping, in the whole life of the Church in *martyria*, *leiturgia*, and *diakonia* according to their calling.[48]

The sacred music of Palestrina and the writings of G. K. Chesterton, or even the dedicated care offered by an anonymous nurse—without encroaching here on the judgment of God, who alone knows man's inner being—play a more significant role in the Church than an expertly pursued career as a bishop. It is, after all, about preserving, in the power of the Holy Spirit, the faith received once and for all, not of weakening it in its substance or changing it according to the taste of the times:

> That discernment in matters of faith is aroused and sustained by the Spirit of truth. It is exercised under the guidance of the sacred teaching authority, in faithful and respectful obedience to which the people of God accepts that which is not just the word of men but truly the word of God. Through it, the people of God adheres unwaveringly to the Faith given once and for all to the saints, penetrates it more deeply with right thinking, and applies it more fully in its life.[49]

History teaches us the bitter lesson that, regionally, even the majority of bishops can fail, as in the Arian crisis in the East of the Roman Empire. Even one of the four great Western Church Fathers was obliged to note with horror, "The whole world groaned in astonishment to find itself Arian [Ingemuit totus orbis et Arianum se esse miratus est]."[50] Other examples are the flourishing Catholic Church in North Africa, which split into a majority of Donatist bishops and a minority of bishops who remained Catholic, and, in the sixteenth century, the cowardly apostasy of the English bishops during the reign of King Henry VIII. Only Cardinal John Fisher (1469–1535), the bishop of

---

[48] Vatican II, *Lumen Gentium*, §19.

[49] Vatican II, *Lumen Gentium*, §12.

[50] St. Jerome, *Altercatio Luciferiani* 19.

Rochester, refused to accept the Act of Supremacy (November 3, 1534) with which a megalomaniacal king elevated himself to "Supreme Head of the Church of England."[51] St. John Fisher, like St. Thomas More (1448–1535), paid with his life for his loyalty to the Catholic Church—with the pope as the Successor of St. Peter and the visible head of the Church—by being beheaded at Tower Hill in London. The consequence of the divisions in the episcopate was always a tremendous internal weakening of the Church, and often the complete disappearance of the Catholic Church in these regions.

The secularization of the Church, the relativization of her doctrine, the de-naturation (*Ent-wesentlichung*) of her liturgy into an aesthetic game of symbols (*Zeichenspiel*), and the de-moralization of the Christian ethos are the way that leads not into the future but into the abyss. Immorality among Christians is always rooted in apostasy from true faith, as is illustrated by St. Irenaeus of Lyons using the example of the Gnostics, who felt themselves to be above the simple Catholics who were faithful to the Magisterium:

> Wherefore also it comes to pass that the most perfect among them addict themselves without fear to all those kinds of forbidden deeds, of which the Scriptures assure us that they who do such things shall not inherit the kingdom of God.[52]

The Bishop of Lyons is referring to St. Paul, who in the Letter to the Galatians contrasts the "works of the flesh" with the "fruit of the Spirit":

> Now the works of the flesh are obvious: fornication, impurity, licentiousness, idolatry, sorcery, enmities, strife, jealousy, anger, quarrels, dissensions, factions, envy, drunkenness, carousing, and things like these. I am warning you, as I warned you before: those who do such things will not inherit the kingdom of God. (Gal 5:19–21)

In their enlightened sense of self, they considered themselves above the immature Church Christians: "they run us down (who from the fear of God guard against sinning even in thought or word) as utterly contemptible and ignorant persons, while they highly exalt themselves."[53]

In view of the world's traumatic experiences with German presumption in claiming superiority, it is a grotesque denial of reality when the German

---

[51] Vincent Nichols, *St. John Fisher: Bishop and Theologian in Reformation and Controversy* (Stoke-on-Trent, England: Alive, 2011).

[52] St. Irenaeus, *Adversus haereses* 1.6.3.

[53] St. Irenaeus, *Adversus haereses* 1.6.4.

"Synodal Way" now thinks it can revive the tired universal Church with its insights and bring it up to speed.

Even though the Catholic Church in an individual nation may at times, thanks to favorable circumstances, make a greater contribution to charity or theology than others, this is no cause for arrogance but rather reason to give thanks to God, who gave us this opportunity. However, Germanness (*Deutschtum*)—as a cultural factor in the Federal Republic of Germany, in Austria, in parts of Switzerland, and also abroad—is not part of the constitution of the Catholic Church by divine right. And, above all, it should not be climbed like a summit on which vanity lies basking for so long that it fails to notice the storm that is brewing. For the Catholic Church is not a world federation of national churches; she is the community of local churches with their bishops (*communio ecclesiarum*) which recognize the Bishop of Rome to be the Successor of Peter. The multiplicity of nations within the Church has the providential purpose of their mutually enrichment but also correcting each other. Despite being rightly proud of his English culture, in his autobiographical *Apologia pro vita sua* (1864), St. John Henry Cardinal Newman rejected any attempt to assert the prepotency of one nation in the Catholic Church: "I think it would be a very serious evil, which Divine Mercy avert! that the Church should be contracted in Europe within the range of particular nationalities."[54]

Only the Roman Church is mother and teacher of all the churches (mater et magistra omnium ecclesiarum), and this is not because of the greatness of ancient Roman culture and the genius of the Italians who designed, in all their celestial splendor, St. Peter's Basilica and the Sistine Chapel. Nor is this intended to raise unreasonable claims; it means simply that the Roman Church is to be an apostolic example to the other churches. In the famous *Consilium de emendanda Ecclesia* (March 9, 1537), which a commission including the famous Cardinals Contarini, Sadolet, and Pole submitted to Pope Paul III on Church reform,[55] the conclusion is drawn from Rome's task as mother and teacher of all churches that "therefore she should also be especially distinguished by her worship and her moral purity."[56] Rome not only has rights to assert with respect to the *communio ecclesiarum*; it must also serve the credibility of the universal Church through its outstanding ethos.

According to St. Irenaeus of Lyons, primacy among the apostolic churches belongs to the *Ecclesia Romana*, because of the greater authority that results

---

54 St. John Henry Newman, *Apologia pro vita sua* (London: Longmans, Green, 1890), ch. 5, p. 269.

55 Hubert Jedin, *Vorschläge und Entwürfe zur Kardinalsreform*: id., *Kirche des Glaubens-Kirche der Geschichte. Ausgewählte Aufsätze und Vorträge II* (Freiburg, 1966), 118, 147.

56 In Olivier de la Brosse et al., *Lateran V und Trient* (Mainz, 1978), 494.

from being "founded and organized at Rome by the two most glorious apostles, Peter and Paul."[57] Against the Gnostics' delusion of superiority, the martyr-bishop refers to the testimony of the apostolic churches, "which preached the faith to all men" (Rom 1:8). They are built on the word of God in Scripture and Tradition, and only they can derive the legitimacy of their bishops from the apostles. This can be impressively demonstrated

> by indicating that Tradition derived from the apostles, of the very great, the very ancient, and universally known Church founded and organized at Rome by the two most glorious apostles, Peter and Paul; as also [by pointing out] the Faith preached to men, which comes down to our time by means of the successions of the bishops. For it is a matter of necessity that every Church should agree with this Church, on account of its preeminent authority [ad hanc ecclesiam propter potentiorem principalitatem necesse est omnium convenire ecclesiam].[58]

The position of the Catholic, with respect to the Roman Pontiff, cannot depend on personal sympathy or the possibility of co-opting him in support of one's own ideology.[59] Before the Amazon Synod, "progressive" Catholics vied with one another in loyalty to the pope and outdid each other in an unseemly personality cult around Pope Francis at the expense of his predecessor. But since the expected result of married priests and female deacons was not delivered, the old anti-Roman reflexes started twitching again. The Central Committee of German Catholics (ZdK) reacted to the pope's post-synodal letter *Querida Amazonia* (Beloved Amazon) with primitive Febronianism, the German equivalent of Gallicanism:

> We very much regret that Pope Francis did not take a step forward in his letter. Rather, it strengthens the existing positions of the Roman Church both in terms of access to the priesthood and the participation of women in ministries and offices of the Church.[60]

---

57   St. Irenaeus, *Adversus haereses* 3.3.2; cf. Christian Gnilka, Stefan Heid, and Rainer Riesner, *Blutzeuge. Tod und Grab des Petrus in Rom* (Regensburg, 2010).

58   St. Irenaeus, *Adversus haereses* 3.3.2.

59   George Weigel, *The Next Pope: The Office of Peter and a Church in Mission* (San Francisco: Ignatius Press, 2020); Edward Pentin, *The Next Pope: The Leading Cardinal Candidates* (Manchester, NH: Sophia Institute Press, 2020).

60   Quoted from George Weigel, "*Wittenberg in Zeitlupe*," *Die Tagespost*, March 20, 2020, 11.

From the highest possible standpoint, i.e., where the world-spirit has already climbed to its loftiest height in Germany and needs only to move straight ahead, God's revelation is finally being supplied with an interpretation that is in line with progress, but its course is being slowed down by the Roman Church. The "backdown" of the man on whom left-wing liberalism had pinned such great hopes can only be explained, to its own clientele, as Pope Francis allowing himself to be intimidated by dense but devious conservative cardinals, who have not yet made it to the lofty heights of a German explanation of the world. While the German passion for boasting of their country's technical progress and moral superiority at the expense of its neighbors in the East and South was already unbearable when exhibited in a Prussian-Protestant context, the latest lesson for the universal Church, orchestrated in a national Catholic key, is no more than a provincial farce of the blandest mediocrity.[61]

Because intellectual hubris is always accompanied by a sense of higher moral right, any means is deemed justified if it leads to a good end. The chosen method of the protagonists, who allow themselves to be celebrated by anti-Catholic media as "reformers of the Church," is polarization. They hope to achieve victory for their party by driving their opponents out of the Church or marginalizing them as "conservative Catholics." The media are shamelessly exploited to serve the goal of ridding the Church of those who "put on the brakes." There is an unblinkered manipulation of public opinion and, in order to push through the synodal agenda, female politicians are enlisted who "genuinely sympathize" with the oppressed women in the Church and the priests deformed by celibacy. But media campaigns and political pressure split the Church. They promote inner resignation among faithful Catholics in their own communities, or open disobedience to the word of God and rebellion against the pope and against the bishops in communion with him.

These "reformers" do not take well to being contradicted, and react, as ever, to factual arguments with nothing more than personal defamation or the monotonous repetition of slogans on banners fluttering backwards and forwards in the breeze, as if casting to the winds the apostle's admonition to his successor: "Whoever teaches otherwise and does not agree with the sound words of our Lord Jesus Christ and the teaching that is in accordance with godliness, is conceited, understanding nothing, and has a morbid craving for controversy and for disputes about words" (1 Tim 6:3–4). Ideologues claim for themselves the right to brand their assumed opponents as arch-conservatives,

---

[61] Instructive on the stereotypes vis-à-vis Rome at home in the German-Catholic milieu are Klaus Bergholt, *Kriminell, korrupt, katholisch? Italiener im deutschen Vorurteil* (Stuttgart, 2018); and Lothar Rilinger, *Urbs Aeterna III. Begegnungen mit der deutschsprachigen Kultur in Rom* (Mainz, 2020).

because they imagine themselves to be on the higher plane of the objective progress of history. But as long as this is an unproven position on the shaky ground of the finite, which a created reason can never absolutize, every Catholic who adheres to the faith of the Catholic Church may claim for his consciousness the freedom of conscience not to "give his adherence to God revealing Himself [in Christ] unless, under the drawing of the Father, he offers to God the *reasonable and free* submission of faith."[62]

In his *Commonitorium*, Vincent of Lérins (AD 434) already diagnosed in "such that are not content with the rule of faith [*regula fidei*] delivered once for all, and received from the times of old . . . and are constantly longing to add, change, take away, in religion" a heretical addiction to innovation, "as though the doctrine, 'Let what has once for all been revealed suffice,' were not a heavenly, celeste dogma, but an earthly rule [*terrena institutione*]—a rule which could not be complied with except by continual emendation, nay, rather by continual fault-finding."[63]

Whether a teaching of the Church conforms with revelation is decided by the Magisterium (in its *infallibilitas in docendo* [infallibility in teaching]), not by the private theologian who, with his philosophical opinions and merely philological-historical interpretations of Scripture, in the ideal case commends himself to an enlightened and Church-critical following as a "victim of the official Church." Around the year AD 200, Tertullian, writing against the heresies that arose later in his *Prescription against Heretics*, conceded to the apostolic Church the exclusive right to possess the Apostolic Tradition, along with the competence to judge the meaning of the Sacred Scriptures: "To know nothing in opposition to the rule (of faith), is to know all things."[64]

A Catholic is one who recognizes the fundamental hermeneutics of the Church's faith, and so who does not use the pretext of a paradigm shift to tear down the cathedral and turn the stones of the building into a leisure center:

> Sacred Tradition and Sacred Scripture constitute the one sacred treasure of the word of God entrusted to the Church. In full adherence to this, the whole holy people, united with their pastors, remain constantly in the teaching and communion of the apostles, in the breaking of bread and prayer (see Acts 2:42),[65] so that in adhering to the Faith that has been handed down, putting it into practice and confessing it, a unique harmony exists between leaders and faithful.

[62] Second Vatican Council, *Dignitatis Humanae* (1965), §10.
[63] St. Vincent of Lérins, *Commonitorium* 21.2.
[64] Tertullian, *De praescriptione haereticorum* 14.5.
[65] Cf. Matthias Joseph Scheeben, *Über die Eucharistie und den Messkanon*, ed. Michael

But the task of authentically interpreting the word of God, whether written or handed on, has been entrusted exclusively to the living teaching office of the Church, whose authority is exercised in the name of Jesus Christ. This teaching office is not above the word of God, but serves it, teaching only what has been handed on, listening to it devoutly, guarding it scrupulously and explaining it faithfully in accord with a divine commission and with the help of the Holy Spirit, it draws from this one deposit of faith everything which it presents for belief as divinely revealed.

It is clear, therefore, that Sacred Tradition, Sacred Scripture, and the teaching authority of the Church, in accord with God's most wise design, are so linked and joined together that one cannot stand without the others, and that all together and each in its own way, under the action of the one Holy Spirit, contribute effectively to the salvation of souls.[66]

The barque of Peter on a wobbly course

A great gale arose, and the waves beat into the boat, so that the boat was already being swamped. . . . He [Jesus] woke up and rebuked the wind, and said to the sea, "Peace! Be still!". . . And they . . . said to one another, "Who then is this, that even the wind and the sea obey him?" (Mark 4:35–41)

The relativization of the identity of the Catholic Church and Christianity "in the Protestant Reformations"[67] of the early modern period was followed by the fundamental denial of the supernatural revelation of God in the Christ event that followed the rise of Enlightenment philosophy in Western Europe (from about 1650). The Catholic Church's reaction was not just one of out-and-out rejection. Within the Church, opposing ideologically narrower positions were taken with respect to the new general intellectual-philosophical

Stickel-broek (Regensburg, 2011); Hans Lietzmann, *Die Entstehung der christlichen Liturgie nach den ältesten Quellen* (Berlin, 1926, repr. Darmstadt, 1962); Hermann Volk, *Sonntäglicher Gottesdienst* (Münster, 1956); Ferdinand Hahn, *Der urchristliche Gottesdienst* (= SBSt 41) (Stuttgart, 1970); Herbert Klos, *Die Sakramente im Johannesevangelium. Vorkommen und Bedeutung von Taufe, Eucharistie und Buße im vierten Evangelium* (= SBSt 46) (Stuttgart, 1970); Eero Huovinen, *Baptism, Church and Ecumenism: Collected Essays* (Helsinki: Luther-Agricola Society, 2009); George Augustin and Markus Schulze, *Glauben feiern. Liturgie im Leben der Christen*, FS A. Redtenbacher (Mainz, 2018).
[66] Vatican II, *Dei Verbum*, §10.
[67] Carlos Eire, *Reformations: The Early Modern World 1450–1650* (New Haven, CT: Yale University Press, 2016).

climate. The internal polarization, which continues to this day, began in France with the anti-clerical Civil Constitution of the Clergy (July 12, 1790), the purpose of which was to detach the Church from Rome and transform it into a national church. The clergy disintegrated into the factions of priests and bishops who took the oath or those who refused to take it. Throughout the nineteenth and twentieth centuries, the dichotomy between liberal and conservative-minded Catholics remained a constant. The total negation of the Enlightenment and political and social revolution, on the one hand, stands opposed to the willingness to compromise or capitulate completely. A tragic figure in this conflict was Jean-Baptiste Gobel (1727–1794), who, as Bishop of Paris, renounced the Catholic faith, participated in the cult of the goddess Reason at Notre Dame, and lost his head under the guillotine for atheism. This is the insane outcome when the Church establishment enters into an alliance with the mortal enemies of Christianity and itself engages in a culture war against the Church.

The appropriate Catholic response to the challenge of Enlightenment naturalism must be an innovative synthesis of belief in God, who is above the world yet present in it, and the new scientific worldview. The only way for the Church to meet the challenges facing her is by measuring human beings against God, not by subjecting faith to the always fallible knowledge that comes from finite reason. Otherwise, the revealed faith will be ground down between the rationalist and empiricist millstones of the deistically eroded idea of God and the mechanistically atrophied image of man. Christianity does not remain true to its original truth if it allows itself to be reduced to a religion of reason for the educated, or to a religion of humanity for the broad middle-class majority, or to the superfluous appendix of an eco-religion that sacrifices the existence of humanity on the altar of the goddess Gaia—with its twaddle about the *terra mater* (mother earth).

In recent Church history, the dichotomy has once again surfaced in the reception of the Second Vatican Council. Some want to go back to before the Council, which they consider to be a dangerous compromise with a contemporary world that is alienated from God. They link the Council symbolically to the changing forms of the liturgy and the historical con-ceptualizations of doctrine, without making any clear distinction between its substance and its outward presentation.

Others want to go beyond the teaching of the Council by invoking its spirit. These modernists are more dangerous, because they are prepared to relinquish the substance. They are in the comfortable position of being able to avail themselves of unlimited human and financial resources provided by the apparatus of the Church. They have the support of the secular media, which are keen to fuel intra-Church power struggles. But those in positions of responsibility in the Church ought to be able to see through these "mechanisms of scandalization."[68]

This latter group do not want to recognize the Dogmatic Constitution on Revelation and the Dogmatic Constitution on the Church as authentic interpretations of revealed truth. The actual intention of the Council Fathers—whose executors the progressives (e.g., of the School of Bologna) claim to be[69]—was, to their way of thinking, to strategically establish a world-savvy Church which wanted to free itself from Christianity in its dogmatic, sacramental, and ecclesial form.

One cannot help feeling that the comprehensive integration of even what is a diametrical contradiction of Christian truth—in the form of a secularized apocatastasis—will only have achieved its goal when the Antichrist has finally received an honorary doctorate from the Faculty of Theology at the University of Tübingen. And, as Vladimir Soloviev (1853–1900) resolved the apocalyptic scenario in his "A Short Tale of the Antichrist," we, too, hope for a loud and distinct "*Contradicitur!*" against the new Doctor of Theology: "Pope Peter II rose. His face flushed, his body trembling with indignation, he raised his staff in the direction of the Emperor. 'Our only Lord,' he cried, 'is Jesus Christ, the Son of the living God!'"[70]

This ideology is also what supplies the enormous amounts of energy expended on using the Synods on the Family (2015 and 2016) to overturn—in theory and practice—the dogma of the indissolubility of marriage, which is clearly grounded in the word of Christ. This tragi-comedy was staged again prior to, and alongside, the Amazon Synod (2019), in order to desacralize the priesthood, to agitate—contrary to the defined teaching of the Church—for women's access to sacramental ordination or, on the pretext of inculturation and with the veneration of neo-pagan idols, to undermine the theocentricity of the Catholic liturgy.

No one expects the answer to man's search for God's truth and the meaning of life from the secularized, yet fully bureaucratized, Church. And who would want to open his heart to a functionary who has ousted the good shepherd from the altar?

---

[68] Hans Mathias Kepplinger, *Die Mechanismen der Skandalisierung. Warum man den Medien gerade dann nicht vertrauen kann, wenn es darauf ankommt* (Reinbek bei Hamburg, 2018).

[69] Peter Seewald, *Benedikt XVI. Ein Leben* (Munich, 2020), 532.

[70] Wladimir Solowjew, *Deutsche Gesamtausgabe VIII*, ed. Ludolf Müller (Munich, 1980), 259–294, at 283–285; Eng.: Vladimir Soloviev, "A Short Tale of the Antichrist," in *War, Progress, and the End of History: Three Conversations, Including "A Short Tale of the Antichrist"* (Hudson, NY: Lindisfarne Press, 1990). See also https://www.goodcatholicbooks.org/antichrist.html.

Empfehlung	Some advice:
Sich nicht zu ducken:	Do not cower.
Das Schiff liefe nicht vorwärts,	The ship would not go forward,
Stünde nicht aufrecht im Wind	The sail would not stand upright
Das Segel	In the wind. [71]

Catholic in a time of creative minorities

In the famous dialogue between the then President of the Italian Senate, Marcello Pera, and Cardinal Joseph Ratzinger—shortly before his election as pope—on the state of the faith in a time of the rapid de-Christianization of Europe and the dictatorship of agnostic and anti-Church relativism, the concept of the"creative minority" was brought into play to define the position of the Church in the modern world.[72]

Although Christians in Europe are still the majority in terms of numbers, given the dominant immanentism they lack the intellectual and spiritual strength to testify to, and live out, man's transcendental relatedness to God, the reality of God's Incarnation in Christ, and his sacramental presence in the Church in such a way that the Christian faith does not seem to contemporaries like some relic of a lost past but becomes a plausible pointer to a future full of light on this side of death and beyond it.

Recently, there have been Church documents and programs with ideas for reforms that want to bring the Church closer to the people again, and which aim to make the Church more credible, but which deliberately avoid the name of God. The churches that have been sold off, but whose outer shell still bears witness to the lost faith in the living God, have been transformed inside into concert halls, discotheques, gourmet temples, museums, and ossuaries. It is the tell-tale sign that the mission of the Church has been inwardly abandoned when the ecclesial infrastructure is allowed to decay, churches are demolished, monasteries and seminaries are closed, the sponsorship of kindergartens, hospitals, ecclesiastical colleges, and theological faculties is dropped, or catechesis and preaching are turned into entertainment programs. And it is just sad and distressing when priests and religious enjoy indulging in a secular and bourgeois lifestyle and, on top of it, regard this as making them up-to-date. Those who abandon their identity can no longer hope to be relevant."[I]f salt

---

[71]   Günter Kunert,"Empfehlung," in Marcel Reich-Ranicki, ed., *Die besten deutschen Gedichte* (Berlin, 2013); Werner Brettschneider, *Die moderne deutsche Parabel. Entwicklung und Bedeutung* (Berlin, 1980), 34.

[72]   Joseph Ratzinger, *Eine nichtkonfessionelle christliche Religion? Reflexionen im Anschluss an den Vorschlag von Senatspräsident Pera*: JRGS 3, 747–777.

has lost its taste, . . . [i]t is no longer good for anything, but is thrown out and trampled under foot" (Matt 5:13).

The road to a new evangelization can only go via people who live in God's mystery and radiate God's joy.

True reform of the Church has often emanated from the monasteries and lay religious communities, in which the depth of their relationship with God, their radical discipleship of Christ, and the permeation of their souls with the love of the Holy Spirit brought about a renewal of the Church's spiritual strength. The monasticism that grew up around St. Benedict was such a "creative minority" at the time when antiquity was crumbling, and it became the seed from which a burgeoning of the Christian West was germinated. It is from its Christian roots, too, that today's world must also draw the strength to avert man's self-abolition and self-hatred in postmodern transhumanism.

In Christ—the Word of God made flesh—the Church is "a sign and instrument both of a very closely knit union with God and of the unity of the whole human race."[73] Therefore, we cannot come to the aid of the Church with worldly consulting agencies, or save her from bankruptcy as if she were a business enterprise by investing many millions of euros, or modernize her like a political party with a program tailored to appeal to young voters. No, what we should be doing is sending up a thousand prayers imploring the grace of conversion for ourselves and our neighbors.

For the Church of Christ does not comply with the demands of those who enroll as her members, but lives from God's promises. And here the witness, sacrifice, and credibility of the faithful and their shepherds are more important than anything that is done in the way of sales management and political electioneering. A Church that is ashamed of her eschatological alienness and prophetic offensiveness in the world, and secularizes herself by abandoning her theocentricity and Christocentricity, is not going to lead the lost sheep back to Christ's pasture.

For it is only from experiencing a community in faith, hope, and love that people will be won over to the Gospel of God's unconditional loving care for us and to the indestructible calling of every human being to eternal life.

People only come to Holy Mass on Sundays and holidays if they are baptized. And they are only baptized if they have accepted the faith of their own free will and in the love of their hearts. And they only accept the faith when they have been introduced with hearts and minds into the mystery of God's grace in mystagogy and catechesis. And they are only convinced of Christ when credible missionaries preach the Gospel of Jesus the Christ to them,

---

[73] Vatican II, *Lumen Gentium*, §1; see §14.

253

and when priests are ready to be "examples to the flock" (1 Pet 5:3) of Christ, "the shepherd and guardian of your souls" (1 Pet 2:25).

The central concerns of the Church are not climate change, environmental protection, migration policy, and positions of power for lay people. Nor is the Church an NGO that could adopt the agenda of ideologies hostile to the faith and collaborate with them in certain sub-sectors. And the ways to a new evangelization cannot be to relativize God's commandments, to abolish the indissolubility of sacramental marriage and eliminate its natural substance as the exclusive union of a man and a woman, and to extend the exceptions to the rule of priestly celibacy as if it were possible—out of pragmatic considerations—to regionally "relax" God's calling and the charism of celibacy for the sake of the kingdom of God.

Christianity is nothing other than "the good news [Gospel] of Jesus Christ, the Son of God" (Mark 1:1). Hence, it cannot be compared with the historical religions which, each in its own way, portray human existence in the metaphors and ciphers of their changing cultures in the light or darkness of a vague transcendence.

Rather, what the Church confesses springs from the self-revelation of the one, almighty Creator of all that finitely exists when he speaks to the prophets of Israel.

God is the radically transcendent one who revealed himself to Moses as the savior of his chosen people from slavery and as the guarantor of their freedom and human dignity. He does not approach us under the veil of necromancy and magic. When man asks for and seeks the truth, he answers: "I am who I am" (Exod 3:14). He is our Creator and Father, the God of Abraham, Isaac, and Jacob. And, at the climax of salvation history, Jesus makes known to his disciples the name of his Father and reveals to us the presence of God in the name of the Son from the Father in the Holy Spirit. With regard to God, we know where we come from, where we are going, and what is the indestructible meaning of our lives.[74] What Eugenio Scalfari, the doyen of journalistic atheism in Italy, failed to understand in his conversation with Pope Francis as a result of his materialistic and thus atheistic monism—which meant that he inevitably produced a distorted version of it—is that we Christians do not believe in a deified human being but rather in the one, sovereign, eternal, infinite God, who became man in his Word, the "Father's only Son" (John 1:14), and dwelt among us and will remain with us always as the risen Christ.

The development of the human spirit in culture and history, the technological mastery of the material foundations of our earthly existence, and the

---

[74] Vatican II, *Gaudium et Spes*, §10.

progress in science, medicine, and social organization are part of the unfolding of human nature. But they cannot catch up with or overtake the absolute newness of the grace that has come into the world in the God-man Jesus Christ.

In Christ, all human beings, irrespective of their age and the style of their epoch, their talents and education, are as individual persons immediate to God, without this deactivating the mediation that comes through the work of Christ in the sacraments and community of the Church. In the loving countenance of God, man comes face-to-face with the question of truth and is thus inevitably confronted with having to distinguish between what is morally good and what is evil and to be avoided.

Why is it that—according to Joseph Ratzinger—the creative minorities of convinced believers who follow Christ are so important for the Church—and for society with its tired, despondent, and disoriented Christian majorities?:

> That is why in the Church itself and for the Church, but above all beyond the Church and for society as a whole, convinced minorities are important—people who in their encounter with Christ have found the precious pearl (i.e., the kingdom of God) [cf. Matt 13:45] that gives value to the whole of life, so that the Christian imperatives no longer seem like lead weights paralyzing man, but like wings bearing him upwards.[75]

---

[75] Joseph Ratzinger, JRGS 3, 755.

EPILOGUE

The *hard core* of modern atheism is man's hatred of himself for being a creature of God, which he does not want to be, and, consequently, the proud refusal of the "superman" (*Übermensch*) to love himself, as well as his neighbor, because God is love (1 John 4:8, 12).

His *weak spot* is his longing, nevertheless, to be loved.

> All my hot tears in streamlets trickle
> Their course to thee!
> And all my final hearty fervor—
> Up-glow'th to THEE!
> Oh, come thou back,
> Mine unfamiliar God! my PAIN!
> My final bliss![1]

If a distressed agnostic were to ask me how to overcome his metaphysical doubts about the meaning of existence and his ambivalent sense of self-worth, as it wavers between superhuman fantasies and posthuman self-deprecation,[2] I would advise him to pray the Eighth Psalm:

---

[1] Friedrich Nietzsche, „Der Zauberer," *Also sprach Zarathustra* IV: *Sämtliche Werke 4*, ed. G. Colli and M. Montinari (Berlin, 1980), 316; Eng.: *Thus Spoke Zarathustra*, https://www.gutenberg.org/files/1998/1998-h/1998-h.htm#link2H_4_0073.

[2] Yuval Noah Harari, *Homo Deus: A Brief History of* Tomorrow (London: Harvill Secker, 2016).

[W]hat is man that you are mindful of him, and the son of man that you care for him? Yet you have made him a little lower than the heavenly beings and crowned him with glory and honour.... O Lord, our Lord, how majestic is your name in all the earth! (Ps 8:4–5, 9 ESV)

And if a pessimist asks me about the Catholic vaccine against world-weariness (*Weltschmerz*)³ and the "sickness unto death,"⁴ I respond with the words: *If God says yes to you, you no longer have the right to say no to yourself. "For the Son of God, Jesus Christ, . . . was not 'Yes and No'; but in him it is always 'Yes.' For in him every one of God's promises is a 'Yes'" (2 Cor 1:19–20).*

And when Jesus's disciples are asked today and tomorrow why they put their hope in God alone in life and in death, they will say: "So we have known and believe the love that God has for us. God is love, and those who abide in love abide in God, and God abides in them" (1 John 4:16).

---

3   Jean Paul, *Selina oder über die Unsterblichkeit* (Tübingen, 1827), I, 132.
4   Søren Kierkegaard, *Sygdommen til Døden*,1849. Eng:. *The Sickness unto Death* (Princeton, NJ: Princeton University Press, 1941).